The Complete Instant Pot Air Fryer

COOKBOOK

500 Quick & Easy Instant Pot
Recipes For Instant Pot Air Fryer Lid

Frankie Palmer

CONTENTS

BEEF, LAMB AND PORK RECIPES 56

SNACKS, APPETIZERS & SIDE DISHES 118

DESORTS 148

INTRODUCTION

Imagine: owning an air fryer and an instant pot without having to buy two different machines.

Sounds crazy, right? Well, you can have that with the Instant Pot Air Fryer Lid, a new addition to the instant pot line.

Air frying is a healthier way to fry your food and isn't as calorie-filled as other means. You can broil, bake, reheat, and even dehydrate your favorite foods right there in the instant pot.

This is perfect for when you want to make some wings, or fry up some fish, without needing to deep-fry or buy an air fryer. Just pop it into your instant pot and air fry away!

It's simple to use, and if you are trying out air frying but without buying another machine, it not only offers more options in the kitchen, but also, a whole new set of skills to work on. We'll go over how it works here.

How it Works

It's similar to the regular instant pot. Essentially, you need to finish cooking your food generally in the instant pot. You remove the lid and then put the air fryer lid on top of it, plugging it in.

From there, you set the cooking program at the top, from air fry to broil to other options. Change the time and temperature, and then press start.

You can also turn the food too halfway by lifting the lid to stop cooking and put the lid on top of the gray protective lid on the side with the logo on it, not the one that has lines on it. If you don't do this after about 10 seconds, it'll just continue cooking.

When done, this will then show a display that says "end cool," so you can take the lid off and remove that pad.

This lid works with pretty much all 6-quart IP models minus the Duo Evo Plus, Duo SV, Instant Pot Max, or the Smart Wi-Fi instant pot.

Benefits of Using the Air Fryer

- There are many benefits of this instant pot lid, and they include:
- Super easy air frying without another device.
- A safe storage cover that attaches to the lid firmly and easily.
- It fits a lot of food, perfect for wings!
- The air fryer will only work if the lid is properly on.
- The handle is always cool, so you don't have to worry about burning hands.

This is perfect if you want to fry up some wings or fish, or even if you just want to dehydrate some fruit as a snack!

Common Mistakes/Errors Using the Air Fryer

The biggest mistake is it's not something you can use alone. You HAVE to have an instant pot.

Another common mistake is filling it more than the max fill line. If you do, it won't cook your food right.

Another common issue is the cord. The cord is short, so you have to plug it near an outlet. NEVER use this with a lid with a power strip or extension cord.

Speaking of the plug, it's oddly-shaped, so if you're going to plug it in where your toaster is, that won't work. That combined with how short it is, does make a problem.

Finally, sometimes it's hard to turn the foods. It can be hard with foods near the bottom.

There also isn't an instruction manual, just a Getting Started user manual. You have to go to the website in order to find out how to use this.

Tips and Tricks

With the air fryer, how you cook the foods does determine how good it'll turn out. Air frying is best done with pressurized dishes, or any frozen foods added to it.

Broiling is best used for melting food on top of food, such as cheese over pasta.

Brownies and cakes are best made in the bake function of this too.

If you want to make fruit leather, or fruit chips such as apple chips, press the dehydrate button to do this. This does stay on the longest, but it's the coolest temperature setting.

With this, it's best if you avoid anything that has batter on top of it. If you do want to bread food, wash breadcrumbs and egg over it rather than other dipped foods.

If the air fryer food is not becoming crispy, you may need to toss the food in some oil. Preheat the air fryer to a high temperature, so the food has hot air blasted. You also may need to toss the foods when you're reminded.

Finally, always use recipes with this. While this doesn't come with recipes specifically for the instant pot, ideally, you can use many of the same air fryer recipes to cook this in your instant pot.

BREAKFAST

Effortless Creamy Potato & Spinach Frittata

Ready in about: 25 minutes | Serves: 4

Ingredients

2 cups spinach, chopped
6 eggs, lightly beaten
3 cups potato cubes, boiled

¼ cup heavy cream
1 cup grated mozzarella cheese
1 tbsp parsley, chopped

¼ tsp dried thyme
Salt and black pepper to taste

Directions

Arrange the potatoes on a greased baking pan. In a bowl, whisk the eggs, heavy cream, spinach, thyme, salt, and pepper and pour over the potatoes. Place the pan into the air fryer basket. Insert the basket into the IP and put the air fryer lid on top. Select Bake and set the temperature to 380 F and the cooking time to 16 minutes. Push Start. At the 10-minute mark, open the lid and, sprinkle the mozzarella cheese and parsley over the frittata and cook for the remaining 6 minutes. The frittata should be nice and golden. Serve sliced.

Banana & Hazelnut Cupcakes

Ready in about: 40 minutes | Serves: 6

Ingredients

2 eggs, lightly beaten
2 ripe bananas, mashed
½ cup melted butter
½ cup honey

1 tsp vanilla extract
2 cups flour
1 tsp baking powder
½ cup dark chocolate chips

½ tsp baking soda
1 tsp ground cinnamon
½ cup chopped hazelnuts

Directions

Spray 6-hole muffin with oil spray. In a bowl, whisk butter, honey, eggs, banana, and vanilla until well-combine. Sift in flour, baking powder, baking soda, and cinnamon without overmixing. Fold in the hazelnuts and chocolate. Pour the mixture into the muffin holes and place in the air fryer basket. Insert the basket into the IP and put the air fryer lid on top. Select Bake and set the temperature to 350 F and the time to 30 minutes. Push Start. Serve cooled.

Cinnamon Mango Bread

Ready in about: 60 minutes | Serves: 6

Ingredients

3 ripe mangoes, mashed
½ cup melted butter
1 egg, lightly beaten

½ cup brown sugar
1 tsp vanilla extract
1 tsp baking powder

½ tsp grated nutmeg
½ tsp ground cinnamon

Directions

Spray a loaf tin with cooking spray and line with baking paper. In a bowl, whisk melted butter, egg, sugar, vanilla, and mangoes. Sift in flour, baking powder, nutmeg, and cinnamon and stir without overmixing. Pour the batter into the tin and place the tin in the air fryer basket. Insert the basket into the IP and put the air fryer lid on top.

Select Bake and set the temperature to 325 F and the cooking time to 30 minutes. Push Start. When cooking is complete, poke a toothpick in the center to be sure it's done. Allow the bread to sit for 10 minutes. Use a knife to loosen the bread from the loaf, then set the bread on a wire rack to cool completely. Serve sliced.

Classic Caprese Sandwich

Ready in about: 20 minutes | Serves: 2

Ingredients

1 tomato, sliced

4 slices sourdough bread

2 tbsp mayonnaise

2 slices ham

2 lettuce leaves

Salt and black pepper to taste

Directions

On a clean board, lay the sourdough slices and spread with mayonnaise. Top 2 of the slices with ham, lettuce, tomato, and mozzarella. Top with the remaining two slices to form two sandwiches.

Spritz with cooking oil and transfer to the air fryer basket. Insert the basket into the IP and put the air fryer lid on top. Select Broil and set the temperature to 360 F and the cooking time to 14 minutes. Push Start. When done, remove the sandwiches. Serve.

English-Style Hash Browns

Ready in about: 25 minutes | Serves: 4

Ingredients

1 brown onion, chopped

4 russet potatoes, peeled, grated

3 garlic cloves, chopped

½ cup grated cheddar cheese

1 egg, lightly beaten

3 tbsp finely thyme sprigs

Salt and black pepper to taste

Directions

In a bowl, mix the potatoes, onion, garlic, cheese, egg, salt, black pepper, and thyme. Press the hash brown mixture into a greased baking pan. Place the pan into the air fryer basket. Insert the basket into the IP.

Put the air fryer lid on top. Select Bake and set the temperature to 400 F and the cooking time to 30 minutes. Push Start. When ready, the hash browns should be perfectly golden brown on top and crispy. Serve immediately.

Cheddar & Bacon Egg Muffins

Ready in about: 30 minutes | Serves:6

Ingredients

6 bacon rashers, cut into small pieces

1 brown onion, chopped

6 eggs, lightly beaten

½ cup grated cheddar cheese

2 tbsp chopped chives

Salt and black pepper to taste

Directions

Spray a 6-hole muffin pan with cooking spray. In a bowl, add eggs, bacon, chives, onion, cheese, salt, and pepper and stir to combine. Pour into muffin cups and place inside the air fryer basket. Insert the basket into the IP and put the air fryer lid on top. Select Bake and set the temperature to 350 F and the cooking time to 12 minutes. Push Start. Serve immediately.

Cheddar Egg Quiche with Veggies

Ready in about: 60 minutes | Serves: 4

Ingredients

2 medium tomatoes, diced

2 medium carrots, diced

6 eggs

1 cup whole milk

1 head broccoli, cut into florets

¼ cup feta cheese, crumbled

1 cup grated Cheddar cheese

1 tsp dried thyme

Salt and black pepper to taste

1 tsp chopped parsley

Directions

Pour 1 cup of water into your IP and insert a trivet. Throw the broccoli and carrots in a steamer basket and place the basket on the trivet. Seal the lid, select Stem, and cook for 3 minutes.

When ready, do a quick pressure release. Transfer the veggies to a greased baking pan. Crack the eggs in a bowl and add the parsley, salt, pepper, and thyme. Using a whisk, beat the eggs while adding the milk gradually until a pale mixture is attained.

Top the broccoli and carrots with tomatoes and feta and cheddar cheeses. Pour the egg mixture over the layering and top with the cheddar cheese. Place the baking pan inside the air fryer basket.

Insert the basket into the IP and put the air fryer lid on top. Select Bake and set the temperature to 350 F and the cooking time to 40 minutes. Push Start. The quiche should be puffy and brown. Poke the center to make sure it's thoroughly cooked. Serve hot or at room temperature.

Ham & Sausage-Hash Brown Casserole

Ready in about: 50 minutes | Serves: 4

Ingredients

6 ounces frozen hash browns, shredded

2 tbsp olive oil

½ pound turkey sausages

½ pound ham, sliced

2 garlic cloves, minced

8 ounces baby spinach

½ cup ricotta cheese

½ cup mozzarella cheese, grated

4 eggs

½ cup yogurt

½ cup milk

Salt and black pepper to taste

1 tsp smoked paprika

Directions

Heat the olive oil in your IP on Sauté. Add the turkey sausage and ham and stir-fry for about 8-10 minutes; set aside. Add the hash browns and garlic to the pot and cook for 4 minutes. Stir in the spinach for 3-4 minutes until it wilts completely. Transfer the sautéed mixture to a baking pan. Add the reserved sausage and ham.

In a bowl, thoroughly combine the cheese, eggs, yogurt, milk, salt, pepper, and paprika. Pour the cheese mixture over the hash browns in the pan. Place the baking pan in the air fryer basket.

Insert the basket into the IP and put the air fryer lid on top. Select Bake and set the temperature to 380 F and the cooking time to 30 minutes. Push Start. Allow to cool for a few minutes, then serve.

Easy Fried Pickles

Ready in about: 15 minutes | Serves: 2

Ingredients

1 egg, beaten

8 pickles, sliced into rounds

4 tbsp flour

1 tbsp olive oil

½ cup breadcrumbs

1 tsp paprika

Salt to taste

Directions

Combine the flour, paprika, and salt in a small bowl. In another bowl, combine the breadcrumbs and olive oil. Dredge in the flour first, dip them in the beaten egg, and then coat them with the crumbs.

Arrange on the greased air fryer basket. Insert the basket into the IP and put the air fryer lid on top. Select Air Fry and set the temperature to 350 F and the cooking time to 10 minutes. Push Start. At the 5-minute mark, flip the fritters and cook them for the remaining 5 minutes. The fried pickles should be golden and crispy.

Cherry & Almond Scones

Ready in about: 30 minutes | Serves: 4

Ingredients

½ cup sliced almonds
¾ cup chopped cherries, dried
2 cups flour

⅓ cup sugar
¼ cup cold butter, cut into cubes
½ cup + 2 tbsp milk

1 egg
2 tsp baking powder
1 tsp vanilla extract

Directions

Mix together the flour, sugar, baking powder, almonds, and dried cherries. Rub the butter into the dry ingredients with hands to form a sandy, crumbly texture. Whisk together the egg, ½ cup of the milk, and vanilla extract.

Pour into the dry ingredients and stir to combine. Sprinkle a working board with flour, lay the dough onto the board, and give it a few kneads. Shape into a rectangle, and using a round cookie cutter, stamp out scones.

Arrange the scones on a parchment-lined baking pan and place in the air fryer basket. Brush the scones with the remaining milk. Insert the basket into the IP and put the air fryer lid on top.

Select Bake and set the temperature to 380 F and the cooking time to 16 minutes. Push Start. The scones should be risen and golden. Serve cooled.

Creamy Coconut Potato Bake

Ready in about: 24 minutes | Serves: 3

Ingredients

½ cup coconut cream
1 tbsp olive oil

3 potatoes, sliced
2 eggs, beaten

2 oz cheddar cheese
1 tbsp all-purpose flour

Directions

Coat the potatoes with olive oil and spread them onto the air fryer basket. Insert the basket in your IP and put the air fryer lid on top. Select Air Fry and set the temperature to 350 F and the cooking time to 12 minutes. Push Start.

To prepare the sauce, mix the two beaten eggs, coconut cream, and flour until the cream mixture thickens. Remove the potatoes, line them in a ramekin and top with the cream mixture and cheese. Return to the IP and cook for 12 more minutes until the top is golden brown. Serve and enjoy!

Yummy Caramel French Toast

Ready in about: 15 minutes | Serves: 3

Ingredients

2 eggs
6 slices white bread
6 tbsp caramel

¼ cup heavy cream
⅓ cup sugar mixed with
1 tsp ground cinnamon

1 tsp vanilla extract

Directions

In a bowl, whisk eggs and cream. Dip each piece of bread into the egg and cream. Dip the bread into the sugar and cinnamon mixture until well-coated. On a clean board, lay the coated slices and spread three of the slices with about 2 tbsp of caramel each around the center.

Place the remaining three slices on top to form three sandwiches. Arrange the sandwiches on the greased air fryer basket. Insert the basket into the IP and put the air fryer lid on top. Select Air Fry and set the temperature to 380 F and the cooking time to 10 minutes. Push Start. At the 5-minute mark, turn the sandwiches and cook for the remaining 5 minutes. Serve immediately.

Veggie Chicken with Homemade Asian Sauce

Ready in about: 25 minutes | Serves: 4

Ingredients

4 boneless and skinless chicken breasts cut into cubes

2 carrots, sliced   1 yellow bell pepper, cut into strips   15 oz broccoli florets

1 red bell pepper, cut into strips   1 cup snow peas   1 scallion, sliced

Sauce

1 tsp sesame oil   3 tbsp soy sauce   1 tsp sriracha

1 tbsp rice wine vinegar   2 tbsp oyster sauce   2 garlic cloves, minced

1 tsp cornstarch   1 tbsp brown sugar   1 tbsp grated ginger

Directions

In a large bowl, combine the sauce ingredients. Add the chicken, bell peppers, and carrots; toss to coat. Place on a lined baking sheet. Place the baking sheet inside the air fryer basket. Insert the basket into the IP and put the air fryer lid on top. Select Bake and set the temperature to 370 F and the time to 18 minutes. Push Start. At the 12-minute mark, add snow peas and broccoli and cook for the remaining 6 minutes. Top with scallion.

Cinnamon Toast Sticks

Ready in about: 15 minutes | Serves: 3

Ingredients

1 ½ tbsp butter   ⅛ tsp cinnamon powder   Salt and black pepper to taste

5 slices bread   A pinch of nutmeg powder

3 eggs   A pinch of clove powder

Directions

In a bowl, add clove powder, eggs, nutmeg powder, and cinnamon powder. Beat well using a whisk. Season with salt and pepper. Use a bread knife to apply butter on both sides of the bread slices and cut them into 3 or 4 strips. Dip each strip in the egg mixture and arrange them in one layer in the greased air fryer basket.

Spritz with cooking spray. Insert the basket into the IP and put the air fryer lid on top. Select Air Fry and set the temperature to 350 F and the cooking time to 6 minutes. Push Start. At the 3-minute mark, flip the toasts and spray the other side with cooking spray and cook for the remaining 3 minutes. Check regularly to prevent them from burning. The toasts should be golden brow. Dust them with cinnamon and serve.

Homemade Mushroom & Kale Frittata

Ready in about: 10 minutes | Serves: 2

Ingredients

1 cup chopped mushrooms   2 tbsp heavy cream   Salt and black pepper to taste

3 oz feta cheese, crumbled   2 cups kale, chopped

4 eggs, lightly beaten   1 tbsp parsley, chopped

Directions

In a bowl, whisk the eggs and heavy cream until combined. Stir in kale, mushrooms, feta, parsley, salt, and pepper. Pour into a greased baking pan. Place the pan into the air fryer basket. Insert the basket into the IP.

Put the air fryer lid on top. Select Bake and set the temperature to 380 F and the cooking time to 16 minutes. Push Start. When done, the frittata should be fluffy and golden. Allow to cool off for 5 minutes. Serve sliced.

Gratin Dauphinois with Asiago Cheese

Ready in about: 45 minutes | Serves: 6

Ingredients

½ cup grated Asiago cheese
½ cup milk

5 large potatoes, peeled and sliced
½ cup sour cream

½ tsp nutmeg
Salt and black pepper to taste

Directions

Combine the sour cream, milk, pepper, salt, and nutmeg in a bowl. Add in the potato slices and stir to coat them well. Transfer the mixture to a baking dish. Place the baking pan inside the air fryer basket. Insert the basket into the IP and put the air fryer lid on top. Select Bake and set the temperature to 390 F and the time to 30 minutes. Push Start. At the 20-minute mark, sprinkle with the cheese and cook for the remaining 10 minutes.

Easy Cheesy Asparagus

Ready in about: 30 minutes | Serves: 6

Ingredients

2 eggs, beaten
1 lb asparagus spears

¼ cup flour
1 cup breadcrumbs

½ cup Parmesan cheese, grated
Salt and black pepper to taste

Directions

Combine the breadcrumbs and Parmesan cheese in a bowl. Season with salt and pepper. Line a baking sheet with parchment paper. Dip the spears into the flour first, then into the eggs, and finally coat with crumbs.

Arrange them on the fryer basket. Insert the basket into the IP and put the air fryer lid on top. Select Air Fry and set the temperature to 380 F and the cooking time to 8 minutes. Push Start. Serve with melted butter if desired.

Gingery Pancakes with Raspberries

Ready in about: 30 minutes | Serves: 3

Ingredients

1 ½ tsp stem ginger, chopped
1 cup flour
1 tsp baking powder

3 eggs, beaten
1 cup milk
2 tsp butter, melted

4 tbsp ginger syrup
1 cup fresh raspberries

Directions

In a food processor, place the ginger, flour, baking powder, eggs, milk, and butter and pulse until well combined. Working in batches, pour the batter into a greased baking pan. Place the baking pan inside the air fryer basket.

Insert the basket into the IP and put the air fryer lid on top. Select Air Fry and set the temperature to 350 F and the cooking time to 5 minutes. Push Start. The pancakes should be golden brown. Repeat with the remaining batter. Serve with ginger syrup and fresh raspberries.

Chorizo Frittata

Ready in about: 12 minutes | Serves: 2

Ingredients

½ chorizo, sliced
4 eggs
1 sweet potato, boiled and cubed

½ cup frozen corn
½ cup Romano cheese, grated
Salt and black pepper to taste

1 tbsp chopped parsley

Directions

Beat the eggs with salt and pepper in a bowl. Stir in the remaining ingredients. Pour the mixture into a greased baking pan. Place the baking pan inside the air fryer basket. Insert the basket into the IP and put the air fryer lid on top. Select Bake and set the temperature to 350 F and the cooking time to 12 minutes. Push Start. Serve.

Coconut Cornmeal Pudding

Ready in about: 60 minutes + cooling time| Serves: 6

Ingredients

3 ½ cups coconut milk	3 tbsp butter	¼ tsp salt
¼ cup brown sugar	½ tsp cardamon	1 ½ cups yellow cornmeal
½ tsp vanilla extract	½ tsp ground nutmeg	½ cup flour
½ tsp cinnamon	1 cup granulated sugar	½ cup raisins

Directions

In a small bowl, mix ½ cup of the coconut milk, brown sugar, vanilla, and cinnamon; set aside until ready to use. Melt the butter in your IP on Sauté. Add the remaining coconut milk, cardamom, nutmeg, granulated sugar, salt, cornmeal, flour, raisins, and ½ cup of water and bring to a simmer, whisking constantly, so there are no lumps. Remove to a lightly greased baking pan. Place the pan into the air fryer basket.

Insert the basket into the IP and put the air fryer lid on top. Select Bake and set the temperature to 350 F and the time to 45 minutes. Push Start. At the 15-minute mark, pour the pudding with the vanilla mixture and cook for the remaining 30 minutes. The pudding is done when a toothpick inserted comes out dry and clean.

Effortless Egg-in-a-Hole

Ready in about: 15 minutes | Serves: 2

Ingredients

1 tbsp butter	2 eggs
2 bread slices	Salt and black pepper to taste

Directions

Brush a baking pan with butter. Make a hole in the middle of the bread slices with a bread knife and arrange them on the pan. Break an egg into the center of each hole. Season with salt and pepper. Place the pan inside the air fryer basket. Insert the basket into the IP and put the air fryer lid on top. Select Bake and set the temperature to 350 F and the cooking time to 8 minutes. Push Start. The egg whites should be set, the yolks still runny. Serve.

Alfredo Cauliflower Florets

Ready in about: 20 minutes | Serves: 4

Ingredients

1 tbsp butter, melted	¼ cup alfredo sauce	1 tsp sea salt
4 cups cauliflower florets	1 cup breadcrumbs	

Directions

Whisk the alfredo sauce along with the butter. In a shallow bowl, combine the breadcrumbs with the sea salt. Dip each cauliflower floret into the alfredo mixture first, and then coat in the crumbs. Drop the prepared florets into the air fryer basket. Insert the basket into the IP and put the air fryer lid on top. Set the temperature to 350 F and the timer to 15 minutes. Shake the florets twice. Serve and enjoy!

Cheddar Cauli Tater Tots

Ready in about: 35 minutes | Serves: 10

Ingredients

1 egg, beaten
1 onion, diced
2 lb cauliflower florets, steamed
5 oz cheddar cheese

1 cup breadcrumbs
1 tsp chopped parsley
1 tsp chopped oregano
1 tsp chopped chives

1 tsp garlic powder
Salt and black pepper to taste

Directions

Mash the cauliflower in a large bowl. Add the onion, parsley, oregano, chives, garlic powder, salt, pepper, and cheddar cheese. Mix with your hands until fully combined and form 12 balls out of the mixture.

Dip the tater tots into the egg and then coat with breadcrumbs. Arrange them on the air fryer basket and fit in your IP. Place the air fryer lid on top. Select Air Fry and set the temperature to 350 F and the cooking time to 15 minutes. Push Start. At the 8-minute mark, flip the tater tots and cook for the remaining 7 minutes. Serve.

South American Empanadas

Ready in about: 20 minutes | Serves: 3

Ingredients

2 tsp olive oil
1 shallot, finely chopped

9 oz pizza dough
6 oz chorizo, cubed

2 tbsp of parsley
½ red bell pepper, cubed

Directions

Heat the olive oil in your IP on Sauté. Add the chorizo, the bell pepper, and shallot and fry for about 5 minutes. Remove and stir the parsley. Set the mixture aside. Using a pin, roll the dough to half-inch of thickness.

With a water glass or steel rings, cut the dough into rounds of 2 inches each. Scoop 1 spoon of the chorizo mixture on each of the rounds. Press all edges between the thumb and the index finger to create a scallop shape. Place the empanadas in a greased baking pan. Place the baking pan inside the air fryer basket. Insert the basket into the IP and put the air fryer lid on top. Select Bake and set the temperature to 350 F and the cooking time to 12 minutes. Push Start. The empanadas should be golden brown. Serve with your preferred sauce.

Pork & Turkey Calzone

Ready in about: 20 minutes | Serves: 4

Ingredients

1 Pizza dough
2 cups cooked and shredded turkey
1 egg, beaten
4 oz cheddar cheese, grated

1 oz mozzarella cheese
1 oz bacon, diced
1 tsp thyme
4 tbsp tomato paste

1 tsp basil
1 tsp oregano
Salt and black pepper to taste

Directions

Divide the pizza dough into 4 equal pieces, so you have the dough for 4 small pizza crusts. Combine the tomato paste, basil, oregano, and thyme in a bowl. Brush the mixture onto the crusts; just make sure not to go all the way and avoid brushing near the edges on one half of each crust. Place the turkey and season with salt and pepper. Top the meat with some bacon. Divide the cheddar and mozzarella cheeses between the pizza crusts, making sure that you layer only one half of the dough. Brush the edges of the crusts with the beaten egg.

Fold the crusts and seal with a fork. Place them on the air fryer basket. Insert the basket into the IP and put the air fryer lid on top. Select Bake and set the temperature to 350 F and the time to 10 minutes. Push Start.

Cheddar & Sausage Egg Bake

Ready in about: 20 minutes | Serves: 6

Ingredients

2 tbsp olive oil
6 eggs
1 red pepper, diced
1 green pepper, diced

1 yellow pepper, diced
1 sweet onion, diced
1 lb ground breakfast sausage
2 cups cheddar cheese, shredded

2 tbsp fresh parsley, chopped
Salt and black pepper to taste

Directions

Heat the olive oil in your IP on Sauté. Add the sausage and cook until brown, stirring occasionally, about 5 minutes. Transfer to a baking pan. Top with onion, red pepper, green pepper, and yellow pepper. Spread the cheese on top. In a bowl, beat the eggs with salt and black pepper. Pour the mixture over the sausage mixture.

Place the pan inside the air fryer basket. Insert the basket into the IP and put the air fryer lid on top. Select Bake and set the temperature to 350 F and the cooking time to 16 minutes. Push Start. Serve topped with parsley.

Artichoke & Bell Pepper Frittata

Ready in about: 25 minutes | Serves: 2

Ingredients

½ cup canned artichoke hearts, chopped
1 tbsp olive oil
1 green onion, sliced
1 bell pepper, thinly sliced

4 eggs
2 tbsp Parmesan cheese, grated
2 tbsp milk

2 tablespoons milk
Salt and black pepper to taste
1 tbsp fresh chives, chopped

Directions

Heat the oil in your IP on Sauté. Stir-fry green onion and bell pepper for 3-4 minutes. In a bowl, whisk the eggs, milk, salt, and pepper until combined. Stir in artichokes, sauteed vegetables, and chives. Pour into a greased baking pan. Place the pan into the air fryer basket. Insert the basket into the IP and put the air fryer lid on top.

Select Bake and set the temperature to 380 F and the cooking time to 16 minutes. Push Start. At the 10-minute mark, sprinkle the Parmesan cheese over the frittata and cook for the remaining 6 minutes. When done, the frittata should be lightly browned and puffed. Allow to cool for 5 minutes, then serve sliced.

Blondies with Walnuts

Ready in about: 35 minutes | Serves: 6

Ingredients

1 egg, beaten
6 oz white chocolate
1 cup white chocolate chips

6 oz butter
¾ cup white sugar
3 eggs

2 tsp vanilla extract
¾ cup flour
¼ cup cocoa powder

Directions

Melt the chocolate and butter in your microwave for 60-90 seconds. Remove and stir until you obtain a smooth mixture. Let cool slightly, then whisk in eggs and vanilla. Sift in the flour and cocoa and stir to mix well.

Sprinkle the walnuts over and fold in the white chocolate chips. Pour the batter into a parchment-lined baking pan and fit in the air fryer basket. Insert the basket into the IP and put the air fryer lid on top. Select Bake and set the temperature to 350 F and the cooking time to 20 minutes. Push Start. Poke the center with a knife to be sure it's thoroughly cooked. Allow to cool off for a few minutes, then slice into bars. Serve and enjoy!

Easy Cheese Rarebit

Ready in about: 15 minutes | Serves: 3

Ingredients

4 ½ oz cheddar cheese, grated
3 bread slices

1 tsp smoked paprika
2 eggs, beaten

1 tsp dijon mustard
Salt and black pepper to taste

Directions

In a bowl, mix the eggs, mustard, cheddar cheese, and paprika. Season with salt and pepper. Spread the mixture on the bread slices. Place them on the greased air fryer basket. Insert the basket into the IP and put the air fryer lid on top. Select Bake and set the temperature to 360 F and the cooking time to 12 minutes. Push Start. Serve.

Walnut Banana Muffins

Ready in about: 15 minutes | Serves: 4

Ingredients

¼ cup mashed banana
¼ cup powdered sugar
1 cup flour

1 tsp milk
1 tsp chopped walnuts
½ tsp baking powder

¼ cup oats
¼ cup butter, room temperature

Directions

Place the sugar, walnuts, banana, and butter in a bowl and mix to combine. In another bowl, combine the flour, baking powder, and oats. Mix the two mixtures and stir in the milk. Pour the batter into a greased muffin tin. Place the tin inside the air fryer basket. Insert the basket into the IP and put the air fryer lid on top. Select Bake and set the temperature to 320 F and the cooking time to 12 minutes. Push Start. Check with a toothpick; when the toothpick comes out clean, your muffins are done.

Swiss-Style Pinwheels

Ready in about: 25 minutes + chilling time | Serves: 6

Ingredients

8 ham slices
1 ½ cups Gruyere cheese, grated

1 sheet puff pastry
4 tsp Dijon mustard

Directions

Place the pastry on a lightly floured flat surface. Brush the mustard over and then arrange the ham slices; top with the cheese. Start at the shorter edge and roll up the pastry. Wrap it in a plastic foil and place in the freezer for 10 minutes until it becomes firm and comfortable to cut. Cut the pastry into 6 round slices with a sharp knife. Line a baking sheet with parchment paper and lay on the pinwheels, spritz them with cooking spray.

Place the sheet inside the air fryer basket. Insert the basket into the IP and put the air fryer lid on top. Select Bake and set the temperature to 370 F and the cooking time to 16 minutes. Push Start. Serve with pizza sauce.

British Bacon & Egg Melts

Ready in about: 25 minutes | Serves: 2

Ingredients

1 tbsp butter, softened
2 whole eggs

2 smoked bacon slices
2 bagels, halved

2 ounces cheddar cheese, grated

Directions

Pour 1 cup of water into your IP and insert a trivet. Place the eggs on the trivet and seal the lid. Select Manual and cook for 8 minutes on High. Once cooking is complete, do a quick pressure release. Place the eggs into an ice-cold water bath for a few minutes. When cooled, peel and chop them; set aside.

Spread butter on one side of the bagels. Add the eggs on top and season with salt and pepper. Place bacon and cheese on top. Arrange the bagels on the air fryer basket. Insert the basket into the IP and put the air fryer lid on top. Select Bake and set the temperature to 400 F and the cooking time to 4 minutes. Push Start. Serve warm.

Quick Cinnamon & Banana Bread

Ready in about: 60 minutes | Serves: 6

Ingredients

1 egg, lightly beaten
½ cup brown sugar
3 ripe bananas, mashed

½ cup melted butter
1 tsp vanilla extract
1 ½ cups plain flour

1 tsp baking powder
½ tsp grated nutmeg
½ tsp ground cinnamon

Directions

In a bowl, mix melted butter, egg, sugar, vanilla, and bananas. Sift in flour, baking powder, nutmeg, and cinnamon and stir without overmixing. Pour the batter into a parchment-lined loaf tin and place in the air fryer basket. Insert the basket into the IP and put the air fryer lid on top. Select Bake and set the temperature to 300 F and the cooking time to 35 minutes. Push Start. Let cool before slicing. Serve and enjoy!

Yogurty Mini Quiches

Ready in about: 30 minutes | Serves: 8

Ingredients

4 eggs, beaten
1 shortcrust pastry
3 oz chopped ham

½ cup grated cheese
3 tbsp Greek yogurt
¼ tsp garlic powder

Salt and black pepper to taste

Directions

Take 8 ramekins and sprinkle them with flour to avoid sticking. Cut the shortcrust pastry into 8 equal pieces to make mini quiches. Line the ramekins with the pastry. Combine all of the other ingredients in a bowl.

Divide the filling between the ramekins. Working in batches, place them in the air fryer basket. Insert the basket into the IP and put the air fryer lid on top. Select Bake and set the temperature to 330 F and the cooking time to 20 minutes. Push Start. The quiches should be puffy and brown. Let them sit for 10 minutes before serving.

Osaka Tofu Frittata

Ready in about: 20 minutes | Serves: 2

Ingredients

3 oz tofu, crumbled
3 whole eggs
1 tsp cilantro, chopped

1 tsp cumin
2 tbsp soy sauce
1 tbsp green onions, chopped

Sal and black pepper to taste
1 tsp olive oil

Directions

In a bowl, mix the eggs, soy sauce, cumin, pepper, olive oil, and salt. Add the tofu to a greased baking pan and pour the egg mixture on top. Place the pan in the air fryer basket and fit it in your IP. Set the air fryer lid on top. Cook for 10 minutes at 400 F until golden brown. Serve with a sprinkle of cilantro and green onion.

Italian-Style Prosciutto Cups

Ready in about: 20 minutes | Serves: 2

Ingredients

4 tomato slices
2 bread slices
2 prosciutto slices, chopped

2 eggs
¼ tsp balsamic vinegar
2 tbsp grated mozzarella

¼ tsp maple syrup
2 tbsp mayonnaise
Salt and black pepper to taste

Directions

Grease two large ramekins. Place one bread slice on the bottom of each ramekin. Arrange 2 tomato slices on top of each bread slice. Divide the mozzarella between the ramekins. Crack the eggs over the mozzarella.

Drizzle with maple syrup and balsamic vinegar. Season with salt and pepper. Place the ramekins in your IP. Put the air fryer lid on top. Select Bake and set the temperature to 350 F and the cooking time to 10 minutes. Push Start. Top with mayonnaise. Serve and enjoy!

Creamy & Cheesy Omelet Cups

Ready in about: 25 minutes | Serves: 4

Ingredients

4 Gouda cheese, sliced
4 crusty rolls
3 strips precooked bacon, chopped

5 eggs, beaten
½ tsp thyme, dried
2 tbsp heavy cream

A pinch of salt

Directions

Cut the tops off the rolls and remove the inside with your fingers. Line the rolls with a slice of cheese and press down, so the cheese conforms to the inside of the roll. In a bowl, mix eggs, heavy cream, bacon, thyme, and salt. Stuff the rolls with the egg mixture. Lay the rolls on the air fryer basket and fit in your IP. Place the air fryer lid on top. Cook for 10 minutes at 350 F on Bake until the eggs become puffy and the roll is golden brown.

Hawaiian Pineapple Breakfast

Ready in about: 15 minutes | Serves: 2

Ingredients

5 pineapple slices
1 tsp cinnamon

½ cup brown sugar
1 tbsp basil, chopped for garnish

1 tbsp honey

Directions

Sprinkle your pineapple slices with sugar and cinnamon. Place them in the air fryer basket and fit it in your IP. Set the air fryer lid on top. Cook for 10 minutes at 350 F on Bake. Serve topped with basil and honey.

Zucchini Cream Cheese Muffins

Ready in about: 20 minutes | Serves: 4

Ingredients

1 cup milk
1 ½ cups flour
1 tsp cinnamon
3 eggs

2 tsp baking powder
2 tbsp sugar
2 tbsp butter, melted
2 tbsp cream cheese

1 tbsp yogurt
½ cup shredded zucchini
A pinch of salt

Directions

In a bowl, whisk the eggs along with the sugar, salt, cinnamon, cream cheese, flour, and baking powder. In another bowl, combine all of the liquid ingredients. Gently mix the dry and liquid mixtures. Stir in zucchini.

Line muffin tins with baking paper and spoon in the batter. Arrange them on the air fryer basket. Place the basket into the IP and put the air fryer lid on top. Select Bake and set the temperature to 350 F and the cooking time to 15 minutes. Push Start. Check with a toothpick; when it comes out clean, the muffins are done.

Greek Breakfast Tart with Feta

Ready in about: 40 minutes | Serves: 2

Ingredients

1 cup crumbled feta cheese	½ cup chopped tomatoes	¼ cup chopped kalamata olives
4 eggs	1 tbsp chopped basil	¼ cup chopped onion
½ cup milk	1 tbsp chopped oregano	Salt and black pepper to taste

Directions

Beat the eggs along with the milk and some salt and pepper. Stir in all of the remaining ingredients. Pour the egg mixture into a greased pie pan. Place the pan into the air fryer basket. Insert the basket into the IP and put the air fryer lid on top. Select Bake and set the temperature to 340 F and the cooking time to 30 minutes. Push Start. Serve and enjoy!

Sweet Blueberry Pancakes

Ready in about: 15 minutes | Serves: 4

Ingredients

½ cup blueberries	1 cup brown sugar	1 ½ tsp vanilla extract
2 cups all-purpose flour	3 eggs, beaten	2 tbsp maple syrup
1 cup milk	1 tsp baking powder	A pinch of salt

Directions

In a bowl, mix the flour, baking powder, salt, milk, eggs, vanilla extract, sugar, and maple syrup until smooth. Stir in the blueberries. Do it gently to avoid coloring the batter. Drop the batter onto a greased baking dish. Just make sure to leave some space between the pancakes. If there is some batter left, repeat the process.

Place the baking dish inside the air fryer basket. Insert the basket into the IP and put the air fryer lid on top. Select Bake and set the temperature to 390 F and the cooking time to 10 minutes. Push Start. Serve and enjoy!

Vanilla Pastry with Berries

Ready in about: 25 minutes | Serves: 3

Ingredients

1 cup cream cheese	2 tbsp mashed strawberries	¼ tsp vanilla extract
3 pastry dough sheets	2 tbsp mashed raspberries	1 tbsp honey

Directions

Divide the cream cheese between the dough sheets and spread it evenly. In a bowl, combine the berries, honey, and vanilla. Divide the mixture between the pastry sheets. Pinch the ends of the sheets to form puff. Place the puffs on a lined baking pan. Place the pan in the air fryer basket and insert the basket into the IP. Put the air fryer lid on top. Select Bake and set the temperature to 380 F and the cooking time to 15 minutes. Push Start.

Turkey & Tomato Sandwich

Ready in about: 15 minutes | Serves: 1

Ingredients

2 tomato slices
1 hamburger bun

⅓ cup shredded leftover turkey
1 tbsp butter, softened

½ tsp red pepper flakes
Salt and black pepper to taste

Directions

Cut the bun in half and spread the butter on the outside of the bun. Place the turkey on one half of the bun. Arrange the tomato slices on top of the turkey. Sprinkle with salt pepper and red pepper flakes. Top with the other bun half. Place the sandwich on the air fryer basket and fit in your IP. Set the air fryer lid on top. Cook for 5 minutes at 350 F on Bake. Serve.

Honey Bread Pudding

Ready in about: 45 minutes | Serves: 3

Ingredients

1 cup milk
2 eggs
8 slices of bread
½ cup buttermilk

¼ cup honey
½ tsp vanilla extract
2 tbsp butter, softened
¼ cup sugar

4 tbsp raisins
2 tbsp chopped hazelnuts
Cinnamon for garnish

Directions

Beat the eggs, buttermilk, honey, milk, vanilla, sugar, and butter in a bowl. Stir in raisins and hazelnuts. Cut the bread into cubes and place them in a baking pan. Pour the milk mixture over the bread. Let soak for 10 minutes. Place the pan into the air fryer basket. Insert the basket into the IP and put the air fryer lid on top. Select Bake and set the temperature to 310 F and the cooking time to 30 minutes. Push Start. Garnish with cinnamon.

Easy Parsnip Rösti with Poached Eggs

Ready in about: 20 minutes | Serves: 2

Ingredients

1 cup flour
1 large parsnip, grated
3 eggs, beaten

½ tsp garlic powder
¼ tsp nutmeg
1 tbsp olive oil

1 tsp horseradish mustard
Salt and black pepper to taste

Directions

In a bowl, combine flour, eggs, parsnip, nutmeg, salt, pepper, and garlic powder. Form patties out of the mixture. Arrange them on the greased air fryer basket and fit in your IP. Place the air fryer lid on top. Select Air Fry and set the temperature to 390 F and the cooking time to 15 minutes. Push Start. Serve with horseradish mustard.

Berry Oatmeal

Ready in about: 30 minutes | Serves: 4

Ingredients

½ tbsp lemon zest
1 cup fresh strawberries
½ cup dried cranberries
1 ½ cups rolled oats

½ tsp baking powder
¼ tsp salt
¼ tsp grated nutmeg
½ tsp ground cinnamon

½ tsp vanilla extract
4 tbsp maple syrup
1 ½ cups apple juice
¼ cup maple syrup

Directions

Spread ½ cup of strawberries on a greased baking pan and top with the cranberries. In a bowl, thoroughly combine the rolled oats, baking powder, salt, lemon zest, nutmeg, cinnamon, vanilla, maple syrup, and apple juice and pour the mixture over the berries; allow to soak for 10 minutes.

Place the pan into the air fryer basket. Insert the basket into the IP and put the air fryer lid on top. Select Bake and set the temperature to 330 F and the time to 12 minutes. Push Start. Top with the remaining strawberries.

Frittata Napolitana

Ready in about: 20 minutes | Serves: 2

Ingredients

1 tbsp olive oil
3 oz salami, chopped
1 beef sausage, chopped

2 slices prosciutto, chopped
1 cup mozzarella cheese, grated
4 eggs

1 tbsp ketchup
1 tbsp chopped onion

Directions

Heat the oil in your IP on Sauté. Fry the onion and sausage for 3 minutes. Remove to a baking pan. In a bowl, whisk the eggs and ketchup until combined. Stir in salami and prosciutto and pour over the sausage; stir. Place the pan into the air fryer basket. Insert the basket into the IP and put the air fryer lid on top.

Select Bake and set the temperature to 380 F and the cooking time to 14 minutes. Push Start. At the 8-minute mark, sprinkle the mozzarella cheese over the frittata and cook for the remaining 6 minutes. When done, the frittata should be lightly browned and puffed. Allow to cool off for 5 minutes. Serve sliced.

Chicken with Green Salad

Ready in about: 20 minutes | Serves: 2

Ingredients

1 chicken breast, cut into cubes
2 tbsp olive oil
½ cup baby spinach

1 cup shredded romaine lettuce
3 large kale leaves, chopped
1 tsp balsamic vinegar

1 garlic clove, minced
Salt and black pepper to taste

Directions

Place the chicken, 1 tbsp olive oil, and garlic in a bowl. Season with salt and pepper and toss to combine. Put on a lined baking dish and place the pan into the air fryer basket. Insert the basket into the IP and put the air fryer lid on top. Select Bake and set the temperature to 380 F and the cooking time to 14 minutes. Push Start.

Meanwhile, place the greens in a large bowl. Add the remaining olive oil and balsamic vinegar. Season with salt and pepper and toss to combine. Serve with the chicken.

Quick Chili Eggs

Ready in about: 20 minutes | Serves: 6

Ingredients

Salt and red chili flakes to taste   6 large eggs

Directions

Lay the eggs in your air fryer basket and place in the IP. Put the air fryer lid on top and cook for 8 minutes for a slightly runny yolk or 12 to 15 minutes for a firmer yolk on Bake at 300 F. Using tongs, place the eggs in an ice-cold water bath to cool for 5 minutes before peeling. Slice into wedges and sprinkle with salt and red chili flakes.

Berry-Flavored Cheese French Toast

Ready in about: 15 minutes | Serves: 4

Ingredients

⅓ cup milk
2 eggs, beaten
4 slices bread

3 tbsp sugar
1 ½ cups corn flakes
¼ tsp nutmeg

4 tbsp berry-flavored cheese
¼ tsp salt

Directions

In a bowl, mix sugar, eggs, nutmeg, salt and milk. In a separate bowl, mix blueberries and cheese. Take 2 bread slices and pour the blueberry mixture over the slices. Top with the milk mixture. Cover with the remaining two slices to make sandwiches. Dredge the sandwiches over cornflakes to coat well. Lay the sandwiches on the air fryer basket and Insert the basket into the IP. Put the air fryer lid on top. Select Air Fry and set the temperature to 400 F and the cooking time to 8 minutes. Push Start. At the 4-minute mark, flip and continue cooking. Serve.

Creamy Shirred Eggs

Ready in about: 25 minutes | Serves: 2

Ingredients

4 slices of ham
4 eggs, divided
2 tbsp heavy cream

3 tbsp Parmesan cheese
¼ tsp paprika
Salt and black pepper to taste

2 tsp butter
2 tsp chopped chives

Directions

Grease a pie pan with butter. Arrange the ham slices on the bottom of the pan to cover it completely. Whisk one egg along with the heavy cream, salt, and pepper in a small bowl. Pour the mixture over the ham slices.

Crack the other eggs over the ham. Sprinkle with Parmesan cheese. Place the pan into the air fryer basket. Insert the basket into the IP and put the air fryer lid on top. Select Bake and set the temperature to 320 F and the cooking time to 14 minutes. Push Start. Season with paprika, garnish with chives and serve with bread.

Creamy Egg Wraps with Spicy Salsa

Ready in about: 15 minutes | Serves: 3

Ingredients

3 bacon slices, cut into strips
3 tortillas

2 previously scrambled eggs
3 tbsp salsa

3 tbsp cream cheese, divided
1 cup grated pepper Jack cheese

Directions

Spread 1 tbsp of cream cheese onto each tortilla. Divide the eggs and bacon between the tortillas evenly. Top with salsa. Sprinkle some grated cheese over. Roll up the tortillas. Arrange them on the greased air fryer basket and fit in your IP. Place the air fryer lid on top. Select Bake and set the temperature to 390 F and the cooking time to 10 minutes. Push Start. Serve and enjoy!

Mom's Strawberry Crepes

Ready in about: 30 minutes | Serves: 4

Ingredients

1 cup milk
1 ½ cups fresh strawberries, sliced

1 cup flour
3 eggs

½ tsp vanilla extract
2 tbsp icing sugar

Directions

In a bowl, mix flour, milk, eggs, and vanilla until fully incorporated. Add the batter to a greased baking. Place the pan into the air fryer basket. Insert the basket into the IP and put the air fryer lid on top. Select Bake and set the temperature to 350 F and the cooking time to 15 minutes. Push Start. Flip the crepes at the 8-minute mark. The crepes should be fluffy and golden brown. Top with icing sugar and sliced strawberries.

Parsley & Sausage Patties

Ready in about: 25 minutes | Serves: 4

Ingredients

1 egg, beaten
1 lb ground Italian sausage
¼ cup breadcrumbs

1 tsp dried parsley
1 tsp red pepper flakes
Salt and black pepper to taste

¼ tsp garlic powder

Directions

Combine all of the ingredients in a large bowl. Line a baking pan with parchment paper. Make patties out of the sausage mixture and arrange them on the baking pan. Place the baking pan inside the air fryer basket. Insert the basket into the IP and put the air fryer lid on top. Select Air Fry and set the temperature to 350 F and the cooking time to 15 minutes. Push Start. Flip the patties halfway through the cooking time. Serve and enjoy!

Honey & Fig Cornbread Cups

Ready in about: 35 minutes | Serves: 4

Ingredients

½ cup fresh figs, chopped
¼ tsp vanilla extract
¼ lime zest
¾ cup flour

1 ¼ cups cornmeal
1 tsp baking powder
½ tsp baking soda
½ tsp salt

3 tbsp honey
2 eggs, well whisked
4 tbsp butter, melted
¾ cup buttermilk

Directions

Sift the flour, baking powder, baking soda, and salt in a bowl. Stir in the cornmeal and lime zest. In a separate bowl, mix the honey, eggs, butter, vanilla, and buttermilk. Mix the wet and dry mixtures and stir to combine well. Fold in the fresh figs. Divide the batter between lightly greased muffin cups and cover with aluminum foil.

Place the cups inside the air fryer basket. Insert the basket into the IP and put the air fryer lid on top. Select Bake and set the temperature to 350 F and the cooking time to 25 minutes. Push Start. At the 15-minute mark, remove the foil and cook for the remaining 10 minutes. Transfer to a wire rack to cool slightly before serving.

Classic Mac 'n' Cheese

Ready in about: 15 minutes | Serves: 2

Ingredients

½ cup warm milk
1 cup cooked macaroni

1 cup grated cheddar cheese
1 tbsp Parmesan cheese, grated

Salt and black pepper to taste

Directions

Add the macaroni to a baking pan. Stir in the cheddar and milk. Season with salt and pepper. Place the pan in the air fryer basket. Insert the basket into the IP and put the air fryer lid on top. Select Bake and set the temperature to 350 F and the cooking time to 10 minutes. Push Start. Sprinkle with Parmesan cheese and serve.

Provençal Apple & Brie Sandwich

Ready in about: 10 minutes | Serves: 1

Ingredients

2 oz brie cheese, thinly sliced
2 bread slices

½ apple, thinly sliced
2 tsp butter

Directions

Spread butter on the outside of the bread slices. Arrange apple slices on the inside of one bread slice. Place brie slices on top of the apple. Top with the other slice of bread. Place in the air fryer basket. Insert the basket into the IP and put the air fryer lid on top. Select Bake and set the temperature to 350 F and the cooking time to 5 minutes. Push Start. Cut diagonally and serve.

Farmer's Kale & Cottage Bake

Ready in about: 15 minutes | Serves: 1

Ingredients

3 eggs
3 tbsp cottage cheese
1 tsp olive oil

3 tbsp chopped kale
½ tbsp chopped basil
½ tbsp chopped parsley

Salt and black pepper to taste

Directions

Beat the eggs, salt, and pepper in a bowl. Stir in the rest of the ingredients. Pour the mixture into a baking pan. Place the pan into the air fryer basket and fit in the IP. Put the air fryer lid on top. Select Bake and set the temperature to 350 F and the cooking time to 10 minutes. Push Start. The cake should be slightly golden.

Quick Parmesan Crostini

Ready in about: 10 minutes | Serves: 1

Ingredients

1 tsp dried parsley
2 tbsp butter, softened

1 tsp dried basil
1 tsp garlic powder

1 tbsp Parmesan cheese
3 baguette slices

Directions

Combine the butter, Parmesan cheese, garlic, basil, and parsley in a small bowl. Spread the mixture onto the baguette slices. Place them in the air fryer basket and fit in the IP. Put the air fryer lid on top. Select Broil and set the temperature to 380 F and the cooking time to 3 minutes. Push Start. Serve.

Easy Choco-Banana Sandwich

Ready in about: 30 minutes | Serves: 2

Ingredients

6 oz milk chocolate, melted

1 banana, sliced

4 slices of brioche

Directions

Spread chocolate and banana on 2 brioche slices. Top with the remaining 2 slices to create 2 sandwiches. Arrange the sandwiches into your air fryer and fit in your IP. Place the air fryer lid on top. Select Air Fry and set the temperature to 400 F and the cooking time to 14 minutes. Push Start. Turn over halfway through the cooking time. Slice in half and serve with vanilla ice cream.

Sweet Porridge with Peanut Butter

Ready in about: 5 minutes | Serves: 4

Ingredients

4 cups milk

2 cups steel-cut oats

1 cup flax seeds

1 tbsp peanut butter

1 tbsp butter

4 tbsp honey

Directions

Mix all the ingredients in a baking pan. Place the pan into the air fryer basket. Insert the basket in the IP and put the air fryer lid on top. Set the temperature to 390 F and the time to 5 minutes on bake. Push Start. Stir and serve.

Ricotta Turnovers

Ready in about: 30 minutes | Serves: 3

Ingredients

5 sheets frozen filo pastry

1 cup ricotta cheese, crumbled

1 whole onion, chopped

2 tbsp parsley, chopped

1 egg yolk

Directions

Cut each of the filo sheets into three equal-sized strips. Brush them with oil. In a bowl, mix onion, ricotta, egg yolk, and parsley. Make triangles using the cut strips; add a little bit of the cheese mixture on top of each triangle. Place the triangles in the air fryer basket and fit in the IP. Put the air fryer lid on top. Select Bake and set the temperature to 400 F and the time to 20 minutes. Push Start. The turnovers should be puffed and golden.

Simple Cinnamon-Orange Toast Casserole

Ready in about: 15 minutes | Serves: 6

Ingredients

2 oranges, zested

12 bread slices

½ cup sugar

1 stick butter

1½ tbsp vanilla extract

1 ½ tbsp cinnamon

Directions

Lay the bread slices in a baking pan on the air fryer basket. Microwave the butter, sugar, and vanilla extract for 30 seconds. Remove and stir in orange zest. Pour the mixture over bread slices. Place the pan into the air fryer basket. Insert the basket into the IP and put the air fryer lid on top. Select Bake and set the temperature to 400 F and the cooking time to 5 minutes. Push Start. Serve with fresh banana and berry sauce if desired.

Roasted Green Bean & Feta Salad

Ready in about: 10 minutes + cooling time | Serves: 4

Ingredients

1 cup feta cheese, crumbled

1 lb trimmed green beans, chopped

Salt and black pepper to taste

1 small red onion, thinly sliced

1 tbsp apple cider vinegar

2 tbsp extra-virgin olive oil

1 tbsp blanched almonds

2 tbsp fresh parsley leaves

Directions

Season the green beans with salt and pepper in the lightly greased air fryer basket. Insert the basket into the IP and put the air fryer lid on top. Select Roast and set the temperature to 380 F and the cooking time to 5 minutes. The green beans should be tender; set aside to cool. In a salad bowl, whisk the apple cider vinegar, olive oil, salt, pepper, and parsley. Add the green beans and onion and toss to coat. Sprinkle with feta and serve.

CHICKEN & TURKEY RECIPES

Effortless Mustard-Honey Thighs

Prep + Cook Time: 30 minutes | Serves: 4

Ingredients

2 tbsp Dijon mustard
4 thighs, skin-on

3 tbsp honey
Salt and black pepper to taste

½ tbsp garlic powder

Directions

In a bowl, mix honey, mustard, garlic, salt, and black pepper. Coat the thighs in the mixture, arrange them in your air fryer basket, and fit in the IP. Place the air fryer lid on top. Select Air Fry and set the temperature to 400 F and the cooking time to 16 minutes. Push Start. Turn over halfway through the cooking time. Serve and enjoy!

Cancun-Style Chicken Drumsticks

Prep + Cook Time: 25 minutes | Serves: 4

Ingredients

½ fresh jalapeño chili, chopped
4 chicken drumsticks

2 tbsp green curry paste
3 tbsp coconut cream

2 tbsp cilantro, chopped
Salt and black pepper to taste

Directions

In a bowl, add drumsticks, paste, cream, salt, pepper, and jalapeño; coat the chicken well. Arrange the drumsticks on the air fryer basket and fit in your IP. Place the air fryer lid on top. Select Air Fry and set the temperature to 400 F and the cooking time to 20 minutes. Push Start. Flip once halfway through. Top with cilantro.

Homemade Chicken Nuggets

Prep + Cook Time: 15 minutes | Serves: 4

Ingredients

4 tbsp sour cream
2 chicken breasts, cut into nuggets

½ cup breadcrumbs
½ tbsp garlic powder

½ tsp cayenne pepper
Salt and black pepper to taste

Directions

In a bowl, add the sour cream and chicken. Stir well. Mix the breadcrumbs, garlic, cayenne, salt, and black pepper and scatter onto a plate. Coat the chicken with the crumb mixture. Arrange the nuggets on the greased air fryer basket in an even layer and fit in your IP. Place the air fryer lid on top. Select Air Fry and set the temperature to 380 F and the cooking time to 16 minutes. Push Start. Turn once halfway through cooking time.

Asian Sticky Chicken Thighs

Prep + Cook Time: 30minutes + marinating time | Serves: 2

Ingredients

½ tsp fish sauce
2 tbsp soy sauce
1 tbsp olive oil
1 tbsp honey

1 tbsp balsamic vinegar
1 tbsp sweet chili sauce
1 lime, juiced
1 garlic clove, minced

1-inch ginger piece, grated
½ pound chicken thighs
1 spring onion, diagonally sliced
2 tsp sesame seeds

Directions

Add the fish sauce, soy sauce, olive oil, honey, balsamic vinegar, sweet chili sauce, lime juice, garlic, and ginger in a bowl and stir. Cover and put in the fridge for at least 30 minutes. Put the fryer basket in your IP and coat with cooking spray. Lay the thighs in the basket and place the air fryer lid on top.

Select Air Fry and set the temperature to 400 F and the cooking time to 20 minutes. Push Start. When cooking is complete, check internal temperature - it should be 165 F. Serve sprinkled with spring onion and sesame seeds.

Chicken Skewers The Eastern Style

Prep + Cook Time: 35 minutes | Serves: 3

Ingredients

2 red peppers, cut into 1-inch pieces
1 green pepper, cut into 1-inch pieces
7 mushrooms, halved
3 chicken breasts, cut into 2-inch cubes

1 tbsp chili powder
¼ cup maple syrup
½ cup soy sauce
2 tbsp sesame seeds
1 garlic clove
2 tbsp olive oil

Zest and juice from 1 lime
¼ cup fresh parsley, chopped
Salt to taste

Directions

Put the chicken, chili powder, salt, maple syrup, soy sauce, and sesame seeds and spray with cooking spray. Toss to coat. Start stacking up the ingredients - stick 1 red pepper, then green, a chicken cube, and a mushroom half. Repeat the arrangement until the skewer is full. Repeat the process until all the ingredients are used.

Brush the skewers with soy sauce mixture and place them into the fryer basket. Grease with cooking spray and fit in your IP. Set the air fryer lid on top. Select Air Fry and set the temperature to 380 F and the cooking time to 16 minutes. Push Start. Flip halfway through. Blend the garlic, olive oil, lime zest, lime juice, parsley, and salt until you obtain a chunky paste. Remove the skewers when ready and serve with prepared salsa verde.

Chicken Cordon Bleu

Prep + Cook Time: 45 minutes | Serves: 4

Ingredients

4 chicken breasts
4 tsp Dijon mustard
4 Swiss cheese slices
4 lean ham slices

1 cup flour
½ tsp garlic powder
½ tsp dried thyme
2 fresh eggs

1 cup panko breadcrumbs
½ cup Parmesan cheese, grated

Directions

On a clean surface, lay the chicken breasts, use a sharp knife parallel to the counter, and cut the chicken to open up like a book. Put the chicken between two pieces of plastic wrap, then beat the chicken with a mallet or rolling pin until it's about ¼ inch thick. Repeat with all chicken. Smear mustard on the breasts, then put a slice of Swiss cheese and ham in the middle. Close "the book" or fold the sides over the cheese and ham. Roll the breast up from the unfolded side to seal and stick a toothpick in it. Repeat with all chicken.

Put flour, garlic powder, and thyme on a plate. Beat the eggs in a bowl. Combine the breadcrumbs and Parmesan in a separate bowl. Roll the chicken in the flour, then place in the eggs, then coat well in the breadcrumb mix.

After spritzing the chicken with cooking oil, put the chicken in the air fryer basket and fit it in your IP. Place the air fryer lid on top. Select Air Fry and set the temperature to 350 F and the cooking time to 25 minutes. Push Start. Flip the chicken halfway through the cooking time. Serve hot.

Cheese Chicken Thighs with Marinara Sauce

Prep + Cook Time: 30 minutes | Serves: 4

Ingredients

4 chicken thighs
½ cup Italian breadcrumbs
2 tbsp grated Parmesan cheese

1 tbsp butter, melted
½ cup marinara sauce

½ cup shredded Monterrey Jack cheese

Directions

Spray the air fryer basket with cooking spray. In a bowl, mix the crumbs and Parmesan cheese. Pour the butter into another bowl. Brush the thighs with butter. Dip each one into the crumbs mixture until well-coated.

Arrange the chicken thighs on the air fryer basket and lightly spray with cooking oil. Insert the basket into the IP and put the air fryer lid on top. Select Air Fry and set the temperature to 380 F and the cooking time to 12 minutes. Push Start. At the 5-minute mark, flip the thighs over, top with marinara sauce and Monterrey Jack cheese, and cook for the remaining 7 minutes. Once the time is done, the thighs should be golden.

Pancetta Whole Chicken

Prep + Cook Time: 70 minutes | Serves: 4

Ingredients

4 slices pancetta, roughly chopped
1 small whole chicken
1 lemon

1 onion, chopped
1 sprig fresh thyme
Olive oil

Salt and black pepper to taste

Directions

In a bowl, mix pancetta, onion, thyme, salt, and black pepper. Pat dry the chicken with a dry paper towel. Insert the pancetta mixture into the chicken's cavity and press tight. Put in the whole lemon and rub the chicken's top and sides with salt and black pepper. Spray the air fryer basket with olive oil and place the chicken inside.

Fit the basket in the IP. Select Air Fry and set the temperature to 400 F and the cooking time to 60 minutes. Push Start. Turn the chicken over halfway through the cooking time. When cooking is complete, the chicken should be golden, and the temperature of a thigh should be around 165 F. Cool the chicken 5 minutes before carving.

Sage & Thyme Stuffed Chicken

Prep + Cook Time: 70 minutes | Serves: 2

Ingredients

2 cloves garlic, crushed
1 brown onion, chopped
1 small chicken
1 ½ tbsp olive oil

1 cup breadcrumbs
⅓ cup chopped sage
⅓ cup chopped thyme
3 tbsp butter

2 eggs, beaten
Salt and black pepper to taste

Directions

Melt the butter in your IP on Sauté. Add the garlic and onion and sauté for 3 minutes. Add the eggs, sage, thyme, pepper, and salt. Cook for 20 seconds and remove. Stuff the chicken cavity with the mixture. Then, tie the legs with a butcher's twine and brush with olive oil. Sprinkle generously with salt and pepper.

Place the chicken into the fryer basket and fit in your IP. Set the air fryer lid on top. Select Air Fry and set the temperature to 380 F and the cooking time to 60 minutes. Push Start. Turn the chicken over halfway through the cooking time. Remove onto a chopping board and let it rest for 10 minutes before carving and serving.

Hot Chicken Wings

Prep + Cook Time: 40 minutes + marinating time | Serves: 4

Ingredients

1 habanero pepper, seeded
2 scallions, chopped
2 lb chicken wings
1 tbsp olive oil
3 cloves garlic, minced

1 tbsp chili powder
½ tbsp cinnamon powder
½ tsp allspice
1 tbsp soy sauce
Salt and white pepper taste

¼ cup red wine vinegar
3 tbsp lime juice
½ tbsp grated ginger
½ tbsp chopped fresh thyme
⅓ tbsp sugar

Directions

In a bowl, add olive oil, soy sauce, garlic, habanero pepper, allspice, cinnamon powder, cayenne pepper, white pepper, salt, sugar, thyme, ginger, scallions, lime juice, and red wine vinegar; mix well. Add the chicken wings to the marinade mixture and coat it well with the mixture. Cover the bowl with cling film and chill for 2 hours.

Next, remove the chicken from the fridge, drain all the liquid, and pat each wing dry using paper towels. Place the wings in the greased air fryer basket and fit in your IP. Set the air fryer lid on top. Select Air Fry and set the temperature to 400 F and the cooking time to 16 minutes. Push Start. Shake halfway through. Serve warm.

Spicy Egg Chicken Breasts

Prep + Cook Time: 35 minutes | Serves: 3

Ingredients

1 red pepper, cut into strips
1 green pepper, cut into strips
2 chicken breasts

1 cup flour
2 eggs, beaten
2 red chilies, minced

1 tbsp paprika
Salt and black pepper to taste

Directions

Put the chicken breasts on a clean flat surface. Cut them into cubes. Pour the flour, eggs, paprika, salt, and pepper into a bowl and stir to combine. Put the chicken in the flour mixture; toss to coat. Place the chicken in the fryer basket, spray with cooking spray, and fit in your IP. Set the air fryer lid on top.

Select Air Fry and set the temperature to 350 F and the cooking time to 15 minutes. Push Start. At the 10-minute mark, flip the chicken, and add the peppers and chilies, and cook for the remaining 5 minutes. When cooking is complete, the chicken should be golden and crispy, and the peppers are sweaty but still crunchy. Serve.

Italian Creamy Chicken

Prep + Cook Time: 25 minutes | Serves: 2

Ingredients

4 slices thin prosciutto
2 chicken breasts

1 tbsp olive oil
1 cup semi-dried tomatoes, sliced

½ cup brie cheese, halved
Salt and black pepper to taste

Directions

Put the chicken on a chopping board, and cut a small incision deep enough to make stuffing on both. Insert one slice of cheese and 4 to 5 tomato slices into each chicken. Lay the prosciutto on the chopping board. Put the chicken on one side and roll the prosciutto over the chicken, ensuring both ends of the prosciutto meet under the chicken. Drizzle olive oil and sprinkle with salt and pepper.

Place the chicken in the air fryer basket. Fit in your IP and set the air fryer lid on top. Select Air Fry and set the temperature to 370 F and the cooking time to 12 minutes. Push Start. Turn once halfway through the cooking time. Slice each chicken breast in half and serve with tomato salad.

Gascon-Style Chicken Drumsticks

Prep + Cook Time: 25 minutes + chilling time | Serves: 4

Ingredients

1 cup crumbled blue cheese
1 cup sour cream
1 ½ tbsp garlic powder
1 lb mini drumsticks
3 tbsp butter
3 tbsp paprika

2 tbsp powdered cumin
¼ cup hot sauce
1 tbsp maple syrup
2 tbsp onion powder
2 tbsp garlic powder
½ cup mayonnaise

2 tbsp buttermilk
1 ½ Worcestershire sauce
1 ½ tbsp onion powder
Salt and black pepper to taste

Directions

Melt the butter in your IP on Sauté and add the hot sauce, paprika, garlic, onion, maple syrup, and cumin; mix well. Cook for 5 minutes or until the sauce reduces. Set aside to cool. Put the drumsticks in a bowl, the marinade over, and mix. Refrigerate the drumsticks for 2 hours.

Meanwhile, make the blue cheese sauce: in a jug, add the sour cream, blue cheese, mayonnaise, garlic powder, onion powder, buttermilk, cayenne pepper, vinegar, Worcestershire sauce, pepper, and salt. Using a stick blender, blend the ingredients until they are well mixed with no large lumps. Adjust the seasoning.

Remove the drumsticks from the fridge and place them in the greased fryer basket. Insert the basket into the IP and put the air fryer lid on top. Select Air Fry and set the temperature to 350 F and the cooking time to 15 minutes. Push Start. Turn the drumsticks halfway through the cooking time. Serve with the blue cheese sauce.

Hot & Sweet Chicken Drumsticks

Prep + Cook Time: 25 minutes | Serves: 3

Ingredients

1 tbsp lime juice
1 tbsp cornstarch
1 lb mini chicken drumsticks
½ tbsp soy sauce
½ tbsp minced garlic

½ tbsp chili powder
½ tbsp chopped cilantro
½ tbsp garlic- ginger paste
1 tbsp vinegar
1 tbsp chili paste

½ tbsp beaten egg
1 tbsp paprika
1 tbsp flour
2 tbsp maple syrup
Salt and black pepper to taste

Directions

Mix garlic ginger paste, chili powder, maple syrup, paprika powder, cilantro, plain vinegar, egg, garlic, and salt, in a bowl. Stir in cornstarch, flour, and lime juice. Add the chicken drumsticks and toss to coat.

Remove the marinade's drumsticks, shake off the excess, and place in a single layer in the air fryer basket. Insert the basket into the IP and put the air fryer lid on top. Select Air Fry and set the temperature to 350 F and the cooking time to 12 minutes. Push Start. At the 6-minute mark, turn over the chicken, spray with cooking spray, and continue to cook for the remaining 6 minutes. Serve with tomato dip, if desired.

Easy Egg-Breaded Turkey Breasts

Prep + Cook Time: 50 minutes | Serves: 3

Ingredients

2 boiled eggs, chopped
1 lb turkey breasts
¼ cup chicken soup cream
¼ cup mayonnaise

2 tbsp lemon juice
¼ cup slivered almonds, chopped
¼ cup breadcrumbs
2 tbsp chopped green onion

2 tbsp chopped pimentos
Salt and black pepper to taste
½ cup diced celery

Directions

Season the turkey breasts with salt and pepper. Grease with cooking spray and place them in the air fryer basket. Insert the basket into the IP and put the air fryer lid on top. Select Air Fry and set the temperature to 350 F and the cooking time to 12 minutes. Push Start. Remove to a chopping board, let cool, and cut into dices.

In a bowl, add the celery, chopped eggs, pimentos, green onions, slivered almonds, lemon juice, mayonnaise, diced turkey, and chicken soup cream and mix well. Scoop the turkey mixture to a greased baking pan, sprinkle with the breadcrumbs, and spray with cooking spray. Put the dish in the air fryer basket and fit it in your IP. Place the air fryer lid on top. Select Bake and cook time to 20 minutes. Serve and enjoy!

Fancy Sesame Seed Wings

Prep + Cook Time: 25 minutes | Serves: 4

Ingredients

3 tbsp sesame seeds
1 lb chicken wings

2 tbsp sesame oil
2 tbsp maple syrup

Salt and black pepper to taste

Directions

In a bowl, add wings, oil, maple syrup, salt, and pepper and stir to coat well. In another bowl, add the sesame seeds and roll the wings in the seeds to coat thoroughly. Arrange the wings in an even layer inside the air fryer basket and fit in your IP. Place the air fryer lid on top. Select Air Fry and set the temperature to 360 F and the cooking time to 12 minutes. Push Start. Turn once halfway through. Serve and enjoy!

Creamy Chicken Tenders

Prep + Cook Time: 25 minutes | Serves: 4

Ingredients

2 chicken breasts, cut into 2 pieces each
1 cup corn flakes, crushed
1 egg

¼ cup buttermilk
Salt and black pepper to taste

Directions

In a bowl, whisk egg and buttermilk. Add in chicken pieces and stir to coat. On a plate, spread the cornflakes out and mix with salt and pepper. Coat the chicken pieces in the cornflakes. Spray the air fryer with cooking spray. Arrange the chicken in an even layer in the air fryer basket and fit it in your IP. Place the air fryer lid on top. Select Air Fry and set the temperature to 360 F and the cooking time to 12 minutes. Push Start. Turn once. Serve.

Cilantro Chicken Burgers

Prep + Cook Time: 25 minutes | Serves: 4

Ingredients

2 garlic cloves, chopped
1 egg, beaten
1 lb ground chicken

½ onion, chopped
½ cup breadcrumbs
½ tbsp ground cumin

½ tbsp paprika
½ tbsp cilantro seeds, crushed
Salt and black pepper to taste

Directions

In a bowl, mix chicken, onion, garlic, egg, breadcrumbs, cumin, paprika, cilantro, salt, and black pepper, with hands; shape into 4 patties. Grease the air fryer basket with oil and arrange the patties inside. Fit in your IP and place the air fryer lid on top. Select Air Fry and set the temperature to 380 F and the cooking time to 12 minutes. Push Start. Turn once halfway through the cooking time. Serve and enjoy!

Simple Chicken Fingers

Prep + Cook Time: 15minutes | Serves: 4

Ingredients

½ cup dried tarragon

1 tbsp butter

2 chicken breasts, sliced lengthwise

Salt and black pepper to taste

Directions

Lay out a 12 X 12 inch cut of foil on a flat surface. Place the chicken breasts on the foil, sprinkle the tarragon on both, and share the butter onto both breasts. Sprinkle with salt and pepper.

Loosely wrap the foil around the breasts to enable airflow. Place the wrapped chicken in the basket and fit in your IP; set the air fryer lid on top. Select Air Fry and set the temperature to 390 F and the cooking time to 12 minutes. Push Start. Remove the chicken and carefully unwrap the foil. Serve with steamed veggies if desired.

Pineapple BBQ Chicken Breast Kabobs

Prep + Cook Time: 20 minutes | Serves: 2

Ingredients

2 green bell peppers, sliced

½ onion, sliced

½ cup barbecue sauce

2 large chicken breasts, cubed

1 can drain pineapple chunks

Directions

Thread the green bell peppers, chicken, onions, and pineapple chunks on the skewers. Brush with barbecue sauce and place in the air fryer basket. Insert the basket into the IP and put the air fryer lid on top. Select Air Fry and set the temperature to 370 F and the cooking time to 16 minutes. Push Start. Turn halfway through the cooking time. When cooking is complete, the kabobs should be cooked through and crispy. Serve warm.

Mexican Chicken Thighs

Prep + Cook Time: 25 minutes | Serves: 4

Ingredients

1 Guajillo chili pepper, chopped

2 garlic cloves, crushed

Salt and black pepper to taste

4 chicken thighs, boneless

4 tbsp chili sauce

Directions

In a bowl, add thighs, garlic, Guajillo pepper, chili sauce, salt, and black pepper, and stir to coat. Arrange the thighs in an even layer inside your air fryer basket. Insert the basket into the IP and put the air fryer lid on top. Select Air Fry and set the temperature to 360 F and the cooking time to 12 minutes. Push Start. Turn over halfway through the cooking time. Serve and enjoy!

Sweet Chicken Fillets

Prep + Cook Time: 20 minutes | Serves: 4

Ingredients

¼ cup honey

2 whole eggs, beaten

1 tbsp red pepper flakes

1 ½ pounds chicken breasts, sliced

½ cup flour

3 tbsp Dijon mustard

1 cup coconut, shredded

½ tsp pepper

Salt to taste

¾ cup breadcrumbs

½ cup orange marmalade

Parsley to taste

Directions

In a bowl, mix honey, orange marmalade, mustard, and pepper flakes. Set aside until ready to use. In a separate bowl, combine coconut, flour, salt, parsley, and pepper. In another bowl, add the beaten eggs. Place breadcrumbs in a third bowl. Dredge the chicken in the egg mix, then in the flour, and finally in the breadcrumbs.

Place the chicken in the air fryer basket and fit it in your IP. Set the air fryer lid on top. Select Air Fry and set the temperature to 400 F and the cooking time to 20 minutes. Push Start. At the 15-minute mark, cover the chicken with marmalade mixture and cook for the remaining 5 minutes. Serve and enjoy!

Italian Chicken Wings

Prep + Cook Time: 35 minutes | Serves: 2

Ingredients

2 cloves garlic, minced

1 lb chicken wings

¼ tsp paprika

2 tsp butter, melted

¼ cup grated Parmesan cheese

1 tsp Italian seasoning

Salt and black pepper to taste

Directions

In a bowl, mix all the ingredients, except for the chicken and Parmesan cheese. Add the chicken and toss to coat. Transfer the wings to the greased air fryer basket. Insert the basket into the IP and put the air fryer lid on top. Select Air Fry and set the temperature to 370 F and the cooking time to 14 minutes. Push Start. At the 10-minute mark, top the chicken wings with Parmesan cheese and cook for the remaining 4 minutes. Serve.

Curried Chicken Breasts

Prep + Cook Time: 20 minutes | Serves: 3

Ingredients

¼ cup sweet chili sauce

3 chicken breasts

1 tsp curry paste

Salt to taste

Directions

In a bowl, add the salt, sweet chili sauce, and curry paste; mix evenly with a spoon. Toss the chicken breasts in the mixture and toss to coat. Place them on the greased fryer basket and fit in your IP. Set the air fryer lid on top. Select Air Fry and set the temperature to 390 F and the cooking time to 18 minutes. Push Start. Turn the breasts halfway through the cooking time. Let them sit for 5 minutes, then slice. Serve and enjoy!

Tomato Chicken Thighs

Prep + Cook Time: 25 minutes | Serves: 2

Ingredients

2 tomatoes, quartered

2 cloves garlic, minced

2 chicken thighs

½ tsp dried tarragon

1 tbsp olive oil

¼ tsp red pepper flakes

Salt and black pepper to taste

Directions

Add the tomatoes, red pepper flakes, tarragon, garlic, and olive oil to a medium bowl. Mix well. In a baking pan, place the chicken and top with the tomato mixture. Place the pan in the air fryer basket and fit it in your IP. Set the air fryer lid on top. Select Bake and set the temperature to 390 F and the cooking time to 16 minutes. Push Start. Remove the pan. Plate the chicken thighs, spoon the cooking juice over, and serve.

Macedonian-Style Chicken Uviaci

Prep + Cook Time: 20 minutes | Serves: 2 to 4

Ingredients

6 turkey bacon
2 chicken breasts
8 oz onion and chive cream cheese

1 tbsp butter
1 tbsp fresh parsley, chopped
juice from ½ lemon

Salt to taste

Directions

Stretch out the bacon slightly and lay them on in 2 sets; 3 bacon strips together on each side. Place the chicken breast on each bacon set and use a knife to smear the cream cheese on both. Share the butter on top and sprinkle with salt. Wrap the bacon around the chicken and secure the ends into the wrap.

Place the wrapped chicken in the air fryer basket and fit it in your IP. Set the air fryer lid on top. Select Air Fry and set the temperature to 390 F and the cooking time to 14 minutes. Push Start. Turn the chicken halfway through. Remove the chicken to a serving plate and top with parsley and lemon juice. Serve and enjoy!

Chicken Fajitas

Prep + Cook Time: 25 minutes | Serves: 4

Ingredients

2 tsp fajita seasoning
¼ tsp chili powder
1 pound chicken breast strips
1 red bell pepper, cut into slices

1 green bell pepper, cut into slices
1 shallot, cut into thin slices
2 tbsp olive oil
8 tortillas, warm

4 tbsp sour cream
2 tbsp pickled jalapeños, chopped
1 cup Boston lettuce, shredded
10 radishes, sliced

Directions

Combine the fajita seasoning and chili powder in a bowl. Add the chicken, bell peppers, onion, and oil and shake until everything is well coated. Distribute the chicken and veggies into a baking pan. Place the baking pan inside the air fryer basket. Insert the basket into the IP and put the air fryer lid on top. Select Air Fry and set the temperature to 380 F and the cooking time to 15 minutes. Shake halfway through the cooking time. Remove and spoon into the tortillas. Top with sour cream, jalapeños, lettuce, and radishes, then roll up to serve.

Austrian Schnitzel with Herbs

Prep + Cook Time: 25 minutes | Serves: 2

Ingredients

2 cups milk
2 chicken breasts
2 eggs, cracked into a bowl

2 tbsp mixed herbs
2 cups mozzarella cheese
1 cup flour

¾ cup shaved ham
1 cup breadcrumbs
4 tbsp tomato sauce

Directions

Place the chicken breast between two plastic wraps and use a rolling pin to pound them to flatten out. Whisk the milk and eggs together in a bowl. Pour the flour into a plate, the breadcrumbs in another dish, and start coating the chicken. Toss the chicken in flour, then in the egg mixture, and then in the breadcrumbs.

Put the chicken in the air fryer basket and fit it in your IP. Place the air fryer lid on top. Select Air Fry and set the temperature to 390 F and the cooking time to 16 minutes. Push Start. Remove them onto a plate and top the chicken with the ham, tomato sauce, mozzarella cheese, and mixed herbs. Return the chicken to the IP and cook further for 5 minutes or until the mozzarella cheese melts. Serve with vegetable fries if desired.

Swedish-Style Squab

Prep + Cook Time: 20 minutes + chilling time | Serves: 4

Ingredients

1 lemon, zested
2 lb cornish hen
¼ tbsp sugar

¼ tsp salt
1 tbsp chopped fresh rosemary
1 tbsp chopped fresh thyme

¼ tsp red pepper flakes
½ cup olive oil

Directions

Place the hen on a chopping board with its back facing you, and use a knife to cut through from the top of the backbone to the bottom of the backbone, making 2 cuts; remove the backbone. Divide the hen into two lengthwise while cutting through the breastplate; set aside.

In a bowl, add the lemon zest, sugar, salt, rosemary, thyme, red pepper flakes, and olive oil; mix well. Add the hen pieces, coat all around with the spoon, and place in the refrigerator to marinate for 4 hours.

After the marinating time, remove the hen pieces from the marinade and pat dry with a paper towel. Place it in the air fryer basket and fit it in your IP. Set the air fryer lid on top. Select Roast and set the temperature to 390 F and the cooking time to 16 minutes. Push Start. Remove to a platter and serve with veggies.

Cheddar Broccoli Bowl

Prep + Cook Time: 45 minutes | Serves: 3

Ingredients

1 broccoli head, chopped
3 chicken breasts

1 cup shredded cheddar cheese
½ cup mushroom soup cream

½ cup croutons
Salt and black pepper to taste

Directions

Place the chicken breasts on a clean flat surface and season with salt and pepper. Grease with cooking spray and place them in the air fryer basket. Insert the basket into the IP and put the air fryer lid on top. Select Air Fry and set the temperature to 390 F and the cooking time to 12 minutes. Push Start. Turn halfway through the cooking time. Remove the chicken to a chopping board, let cool, and cut into bite-size pieces.

In a bowl, add the chicken, broccoli, cheddar cheese, and mushroom soup cream; mix well. Scoop the mixture into a greased baking pan, add the croutons on top, and spray with cooking spray. Put the pan in the basket and cook for 10 minutes on Bake. Serve with a side of steamed greens if desired.

Smoked Mustardy Turkey Breast

Prep + Cook Time: 1 hour | Serves: 6

Ingredients

¼ cup maple syrup
2 lb turkey breasts
1 tbsp butter, melted

1 tbsp Dijon mustard
½ tbsp smoked paprika
1 tbsp thyme

2 tbsp olive oil
½ tbsp sage
Salt and black pepper to taste

Directions

Whisk the butter, maple syrup, and mustard together in a small bowl. Set aside until ready to use. Combine olive oil, all herbs, and seasoning in a small bowl and rub the turkey with the mixture. Place the turkey in the air fryer basket and fit it in your IP. Set the air fryer lid on top. Select Air Fry and set the temperature to 350 F.

Set the cooking time to 25 minutes. Push Start. At the 13-minute mark, flip the turkey, apply the glaze all over, and cook for the remaining 12 minutes. When cooking is complete, the turkey should be golden and crispy.

Golden Chicken Fingers

Prep + Cook Time: 30 minutes + marinating time| Serves: 2

Ingredients

2 cloves garlic, crushed
2 chicken breasts, cut strips
3 tbsp cornstarch

4 tbsp breadcrumbs, like flour bread
4 tbsp grated Parmesan cheese
2 eggs, beaten

Salt and black pepper to taste

Directions

Mix salt, garlic, and pepper in a bowl. Add the chicken and stir to coat. Marinate for an hour in the fridge. Mix the breadcrumbs with cheese evenly; set aside. Remove the chicken from the fridge, lightly toss in cornstarch, dip in eggs, and coat them gently in the cheese mixture.

Place the chicken in the air fryer basket. Insert the basket into the IP and put the air fryer lid on top. Select Air Fry and set the temperature to 360 F and the cooking time to 15 minutes. Push Start. Turn over halfway through the cooking time. When cooking is complete, the fingers should be golden and crispy. Serve and enjoy!

Korean Chicken Breasts

Prep + Cook Time: 25 minutes + chilling time | Serves: 3

Ingredients

1 tsp Gochugaru (Korean chili powder)
2 eggs
2 chicken breasts

1 tbsp mayonnaise
1 tbsp chili pepper

1 tbsp soy sauce
1 tbsp sugar

Directions

Slice the chicken into diagonal pieces. Gently pound them to become thinner using a rolling pin. Place in a bowl and add soy sauce, sugar, curry powder, and chili pepper. Mix well and refrigerate for an hour.

Remove the chicken and crack the eggs on. Add the mayonnaise and mix. Remove each chicken piece and shake well to remove as much liquid as possible. Place them in the air fryer basket and fit it in your IP. Set the air fryer lid on top. Select Air Fry and set the temperature to 360 F and the cooking time to 16 minutes. Push Start. Flip halfway through the cooking time. Serve with a green salad if desired.

Arroz con Pollo (Chicken with Rice)

Prep + Cook Time: 40 minutes | Serves: 4

Ingredients

1 onion, chopped
2 garlic cloves, minced
4 chicken legs

1 cup rice
2 tomatoes, cubed
2 tbsp butter

1 tbsp tomato paste
Salt and black pepper to taste

Directions

Melt the butter in your IP on Sauté. Stir-fry the onion and garlic for 3 minutes. Stir in tomato paste, rice, salt, and pepper for 1 minute. Pour in the tomatoes and 2 cups of water. Place a trivet over the rice and arrange the chicken legs on the trivet. Seal the lid, select Manual, and cook for 14 minutes on High. When ready, do a quick pressure release. Remove the chicken and transfer the rice to a baking pan. Place the chicken on top.

Insert the pan in the air fryer basket and fit the basket in the IP. Put the air fryer lid on top. Select Bake and set the temperature to 350 F and the cooking time to 10 minutes. Push Start. When cooking is complete, the chicken should be golden brown. Serve and enjoy!

Herby Fried Chicken Thighs

Prep + Cook Time: 55 minutes + marinating time| Serves: 3

Ingredients

1 pound chicken thighs	¾ tsp celery salt	½ tsp dried basil
1 cup buttermilk	¾ tsp mustard powder	½ tsp dried tarragon
1 cup flour	½ tsp granulated garlic	¼ tsp dried oregano
1 tsp smoked paprika	Salt and black pepper to taste	3 large eggs

Directions

Put the chicken and buttermilk in a bowl, cover with foil, and marinate in the refrigerator for at least 1 hour. Combine the flour, paprika, mustard powder, granulated garlic, pepper, salt, basil, tarragon, and oregano in a bowl. Whisk the eggs in another bowl. Roll the chicken in the flour mix, then in the eggs, then coat in the flour, making sure the batter is thick on the thighs. Spritz all sides with cooking spray. Place in the air fryer basket.

Insert the basket into the IP and put the air fryer lid on top. Select Air Fry and set the temperature to 375 F and the cooking time to 20 minutes. Push Start. Flip halfway through the cooking time. When cooking is complete, the chicken should be golden and crunchy. Serve and enjoy!

Chicken Tenders with Yogurt

Prep + Cook Time: 25 minutes | Serves: 4

Ingredients

2 beaten eggs	1 lb chicken breasts, cut into strips	½ tsp sweet paprika
1 cup breadcrumbs	½ tsp ground cayenne	1 tsp garlic powder
½ cup yogurt	1 tbsp hot sauce	

Directions

Whisk the eggs with hot sauce and yogurt. In a bowl, combine the breadcrumbs, paprika, pepper, and garlic powder. Line a baking pan with parchment paper. Dip the chicken in the egg/yogurt mixture first, and then coat with breadcrumbs. Arrange on the pan and fit in your IP. Place the baking pan inside the air fryer basket. Set the air fryer lid on top. Select Air Fry and set the temperature to 390 F and the cooking time to 16 minutes. Push Start. Flip the chicken over halfway through.

Tasty Chicken with Shishito Sauce

Prep + Cook Time: 40 minutes | Serves: 4

Ingredients

2 tomatoes, diced	1 large onion, chopped	2 tbsp fresh cilantro, chopped
2 shishito chili peppers, minced	2 tbsp olive oil	Salt and black pepper to taste
1 lb chicken breasts, cut into strips	1 tbsp English mustard	
½ tsp cumin powder	½ tsp ginger powder	

Directions

Heat the olive oil in your IP on Sauté. Add the onion and chili peppers and cook for 2-3 minutes. Stir in the mustard, ginger, cumin, salt, and pepper for 1 minute. Pour in the tomatoes and keep stirring for 3-4 minutes.

Place the chicken into the greased fryer basket and season with salt and pepper; spritz with cooking oil. Insert the basket into the IP and put the air fryer lid on top. Select Air Fry and set the temperature to 380 F and the cooking time to 20 minutes. Push Start. Shake halfway through the cooking time. Pour the sauce over and serve.

Tandoori Chicken Breasts

Prep + Cook Time: 40 minutes + marinating time| Serves: 4

Ingredients

1 cup full-fat yogurt
½ cup onions, chopped
2 tsp tandoori powder

Salt to taste
¼ tsp cayenne powder
4 chicken breasts

2 tbsp fresh cilantro, chopped

Directions

Combine the yogurt, onions, tandoori powder, salt, cayenne, and cilantro and mix well. Toss the chicken in and make sure to coat well. Cover with foil, then put in the fridge for at least 2 hours to marinate.

Shake the extra marinade off the chicken breasts and lay them on the greased air fryer basket. Trash the rest of the marinade. Insert the basket into the IP and put the air fryer lid on top. Select Air Fry and set the temperature to 375 F and the cooking time to 25 minutes. Push Start. Flip the chicken halfway through. Serve and enjoy!

Puebla-Style Chicken Bowl

Prep + Cook Time: 35 minutes | Serves: 4

Ingredients

1 cup red and green pepper stripes
1 can sweet corn

1 cup canned black beans, drained
4 chicken breasts, cubed

2 tbsp vegetable oil
2 tbsp chili powder

Directions

Heat 1 tbsp of olive oil in your IP on Sauté. Stir-fry the peppers for 5 minutes until tender. Stir in the chili powder, corn, and beans. Add a little bit of hot water and keep stirring for 3 more minutes. Set aside until ready to use.

Coat the chicken with salt, black pepper, and remaining olive oil. Place on the air fryer basket and fit in your IP. Set the air fryer lid on top. Select Air Fry and set the temperature to 380 F and the cooking time to 15 minutes. Push Start. Shake once halfway through. Remove the chicken to a plate and serve with bean sauce.

Quick Chicken Tenders

Prep + Cook Time: 25 minutes | Serves: 4

Ingredients

½ cup seasoned breadcrumbs
½ cup all-purpose flour

1 pound chicken tenders
2 tbsp olive oil

2 whole eggs, beaten
1 tbsp black pepper

Directions

Add breadcrumbs, eggs, and flour in three different bowls. Mix breadcrumbs with oil and season with salt and pepper. Dredge the tenders into flour, followed by eggs and crumbs. Add chicken tenders to the air fryer basket and spritz with cooking oil. Insert the basket into the IP and put the air fryer lid on top. Select Air Fry and set the temperature to 380 F and the cooking time to 14 minutes. Push Start. Shake halfway through the cooking time.

Sage Chicken With Romano Cheese

Prep + Cook Time: 15 minutes | Serves: 4

Ingredients

1 cup flour
2 eggs, beaten

4 chicken breasts
1 cup breadcrumbs

2 tbsp grated Romano cheese
1 tbsp fresh sage, chopped

Directions

Place some plastic wrap underneath and on top of the chicken breasts. Using a rolling pin, beat the meat until it becomes skinny. In a bowl, combine the Romano cheese, sage, and breadcrumbs. Dip the chicken in the egg first and then in the sage mixture. Spray with cooking oil and arrange on the air fryer basket.

Insert the basket into the IP and put the air fryer lid on top. Select Air Fry and set the temperature to 370 F and the cooking time to 14 minutes. Push Start. Flip halfway through the cooking time. Serve and enjoy!

Cajun Chicken Strips

Prep + Cook Time: 25 minutes | Serves: 4

Ingredients

2 eggs

1 cup flour

3 lb chicken breast cut into slices

2 tbsp olive oil

½ tsp garlic powder

Salt to taste

¼ cup milk

1 tbsp Cajun seasoning

Directions

Combine the flour, Cajun seasoning, garlic powder, and salt in a bowl. In another bowl, whisk the eggs with the milk and olive oil. Dip the chicken into the egg mixture first, then coat with the flour mixture, shaking the excess. Arrange on the greased air fryer basket. Insert the basket into the IP and place the air fryer lid on top. Select Air Fry and set the temperature to 380 F and the cooking time to 16 minutes. Push Start. Flip halfway through the cooking time. Serve and enjoy!

Chicken Strips with Plum Sauce

Prep + Cook Time: 25 minutes | Serves: 2

Ingredients

1 egg white

2 chicken breasts, cut in stripes

3 tbsp Parmesan cheese, grated

1 tbsp fresh chives, chopped

⅓ cup breadcrumbs

½ tsp fresh thyme, chopped

Black pepper to taste

2 tbsp plum sauce

Directions

Mix the chives, Parmesan cheese, thyme, pepper, and breadcrumbs. In another bowl, whisk the egg white with 1 tbsp of water. Dip the chicken strips into the egg mixture and the breadcrumb mixture. Place the strips in the air fryer basket and fit it in your IP. Set the air fryer lid on top. Select Air Fry and set the temperature to 360 F and the cooking time to 16 minutes. Push Start. Shake halfway through. Serve with plum sauce.

Coconut Chicken Tenders

Prep + Cook Time: 25 minutes | Serves: 4

Ingredients

3 eggs, beaten

4 chicken breasts, cut into strips

½ cup cornstarch

3 cups coconut flakes

Salt and black pepper to taste

Directions

Mix salt, pepper, and cornstarch in a small bowl. Dip the chicken strips in the cornstarch first, then into the eggs, and finally, coat with coconut flakes. Arrange them on the greased fryer basket. Spritz them with cooking oil.

Insert the basket into the IP and put the air fryer lid on top. Select Air Fry and set the temperature to 350 F and the time to 16 minutes. Push Start. Shake halfway through the cooking time. The chicken should be crispy.

Chicken Wings with Cholula Sauce

Prep + Cook Time: 30 minutes + marinating time | Serves: 4

Ingredients

2 pounds chicken wings
1 tsp lime juice
Salt and black pepper to taste

1 tsp red chili flakes
1 tsp granulated garlic
½ tsp shallot powder

2 tbsp olive oil
½ cup Cholula sauce

Directions

In a bowl, combine the lime juice, salt, pepper, red chili flakes, granulated garlic, and olive oil. Add in the chicken wings and toss to coat. Cover with foil and leave in the fridge to marinate for 1 hour.

Place the air fryer basket in your IP. Add the chicken to the air fryer basket. Put the air fryer lid on top. Select Air Fry and set the temperature to 375 F and the cooking time to 20 minutes. Push Start. Flip halfway through the cooking time. When cooking is complete, the chicken should be crispy on the outside. Serve and enjoy!

Mediterranean Turkey Meatball Bake

Prep + Cook Time: 40 minutes | Serves: 4

Ingredients

2 pounds baby potatoes, halved
2 garlic cloves, lightly crushed
2 tbsp olive oil
2 shallots, cut into wedges
1 red bell pepper, sliced

1 pound ground turkey
½ tsp garlic powder
½ tsp onion powder
½ tsp dried thyme
1 cup cherry tomatoes

2 tbsp capers
2 tbsp fresh basil, chopped
Salt and black pepper to taste

Directions

Drizzle the potatoes and crushed garlic with half of the olive oil in a baking pan. Sprinkle with salt and pepper. Place the baking pan inside the air fryer basket. Insert the basket into the IP and put the air fryer lid on top. Select Bake and set the temperature to 350 F and the cooking time to 12 minutes. Push Start.

In a bowl, mix the ground turkey, onion powder, garlic powder, thyme, a pinch of salt and black pepper and shape into balls. Once it beeps, take the lid off, set it down, and add the shallots, bell pepper, and meatballs to the pan. Drizzle with the remaining oil and sprinkle with salt, pepper, and basil. Close the air fryer lid and set the time to 12 minutes. At the 7-minute mark, add the tomatoes and capers and cook for the remaining 5 minutes.

Nutty Chicken with Veggies

Prep + Cook Time: 25 minutes + marinating time | Serves: 4

Ingredients

1 onion, chopped
1 carrot, chopped
1 lb chicken breasts, cubed

2 tbsp soy sauce
1 tbsp cornflour
⅓ cup cashew nuts, chopped

1 bell pepper, chopped
Salt and white pepper to taste
2 tbsp garlic, crushed

Directions

In a bowl, mix the soy sauce, cornflour, salt, and pepper. Add in the chicken cubes and toss to coat. Let it sit for 20 minutes. Transfer the marinated chicken to a greased baking pan. Add the garlic, onion, bell pepper, and carrot and mix to combine. Place the baking pan inside the air fryer basket.

Insert the basket into the IP and put the air fryer lid on top. Select Bake and set the temperature to 380 F and the cooking time to 20 minutes. Push Start. Remove and sprinkle with cashew nuts before serving.

Soul-Style Chicken Wings

Prep + Cook Time: 25 minutes | Serves: 5

Ingredients

8 oz flour	4 tbsp canola oil	2 tbsp honey
1 pound chicken wings	2 tbsp sesame seeds	1 tbsp soy sauce
8 oz breadcrumbs	2 tbsp Korean red pepper paste	Sesame seeds, to serve
3 beaten eggs	1 tbsp apple cider vinegar	Salt and black pepper to taste

Directions

Separate the chicken wings into winglets and drumettes. In a bowl, mix salt, oil, and pepper. Coat the chicken with flour, followed by beaten eggs and breadcrumbs. Place the chicken in your air fryer basket. Spray with a bit of oil, insert the basket into the IP, and put the air fryer lid on top. Select Air Fry and set the temperature to 380 F and the cooking time to 15 minutes. Push Start. Shake halfway through the cooking time.

Mix the red pepper paste, apple cider vinegar, soy sauce, honey, and ¼ cup of water in a saucepan and bring to a boil over medium heat. Transfer the chicken to sauce mixture and toss to coat. Garnish with sesame to enjoy!

Tex-Mex Chicken Drumsticks

Prep + Cook Time: 30 minutes + marinating time | Serves: 4

Ingredients

2 cups buttermilk	Salt and black pepper to taste
6 chicken drumsticks	2 cups all-purpose flour

Tex-Mex seasoning:

1 tsp paprika	½ tsp dried Mexican oregano	½ tsp red chili flakes
1 tsp ancho chile powder	1 tsp garlic powder	½ tsp ground cumin
Sea salt and black pepper to taste	1 tsp onion powder	

Directions

In a bowl, mix all the seasoning ingredients and add the chicken. Toss well to coat. Pour the buttermilk over. Let the chicken chill for 1 hour. Remove the chicken from the marinade and roll it in the flour.

Place into the greased air fryer basket in a single layer. Spritz with cooking oil. Insert the basket into the IP and put the air fryer lid on top. Select Air Fry and set the temperature to 400 F and the cooking time to 20 minutes. Push Start. Flip halfway through the cooking time. Serve and enjoy!

Cayenne Chicken Drumsticks

Prep + Cook Time: 30 minutes | Serves: 4

Ingredients

¼ steamed cauliflower florets	½ tsp oregano	1 tsp ground cayenne
1 egg, beaten	½ tsp thyme	Salt and black pepper to taste
8 chicken drumsticks	2 oz oats	

Directions

Season the drumsticks with salt and pepper. Place all the other ingredients, except the egg, in a food processor. Process until smooth. Dip each drumstick in the egg first and then in the oat mixture. Arrange them on a baking pan and place the pan inside the air fryer basket. Insert the basket into the IP and put the air fryer lid on top. Select Air Fry and set the temperature to 350 F and the cooking time to 20 minutes. Push Start. Serve and enjoy!

Basic Chicken Drumsticks

Prep + Cook Time: 20 minutes + marinating time| Serves: 3

Ingredients

2 tbsp olive oil

2 tbsp honey

3 chicken drumsticks, skin removed

½ tbsp garlic, minced

Directions

Add the garlic, oil, and honey to a sealable zip bag. Add chicken and toss to coat; set aside for 30 minutes. Add the chicken to the air fryer basket and fit in your IP. Set the air fryer lid on top. Select Air Fry and set the temperature to 400 F and the cooking time to 15 minutes. Push Start. Turn over halfway through cooking.

Basil & Oregano Chicken Legs

Prep + Cook Time: 50 minutes | Serves: 5

Ingredients

1 lemon, juiced

5 quarters chicken legs

1 tsp garlic powder

1 tsp dried basil

1 tsp oregano, dried

2 tbsp olive oil

Salt and black pepper to taste

Directions

In a bowl, combine the olive oil, basil, oregano, garlic powder, salt, and pepper. Rub the chicken legs with the mixture and sprinkle with lemon juice. Arrange on the air fryer basket. Insert the basket into the IP and put the air fryer lid on top. Select Air Fry and set the temperature to 350 F and the cooking time to 20 minutes. Push Start. Flip over halfway through the cooking time. Serve and enjoy!

Luscious Oyster Chicken

Prep + Cook Time: 25 minutes + marinating time | Serves: 2

Ingredients

2 rosemary sprigs

½ lemon, cut into wedges

2 chicken breasts

1 tbsp minced ginger

1 tbsp soy sauce

½ tbsp olive oil

1 tbsp oyster sauce

1 tbsp brown sugar

Directions

Mix the ginger, soy sauce, and olive oil in a bowl. Add the chicken and toss to coat. Cover the bowl and refrigerate for 30 minutes. Place the marinated chicken in a greased baking pan. Place the pan inside the air fryer basket.

Insert the basket into the IP and put the air fryer lid on top. Select Air Fry and set the temperature to 370 F and the cooking time to 6 minutes. Push Start. Mix the oyster sauce, rosemary, and brown sugar in a small bowl. Pour the sauce over the chicken. Arrange the lemon wedges on top. Cook for 13 more minutes. Serve .

Drunken Chicken

Prep + Cook Time: 35 minutes | Serves: 4

Ingredients

½ cup olive oil

½ cup white wine

1 lb chicken drumsticks

3 garlic cloves, minced

1 tbsp fresh rosemary, chopped

1 tbsp fresh oregano, chopped

1 tbsp fresh thyme, chopped

Juice from 1 lemon

Salt and black pepper to taste

Directions

In a large bowl, combine garlic, rosemary, thyme, olive oil, lemon juice, oregano, salt, and pepper. Add the chicken and toss to coat. Transfer to a baking pan. Sprinkle with wine. Place the pan inside the air fryer basket.

Insert the basket into the IP and put the air fryer lid on top. Select Bake and set the temperature to 380 F and the cooking time to 25 minutes. Push Start. Serve and enjoy!

Hot Chicken Wings

Prep + Cook Time: 25 minutes | Serves: 2

Ingredients

2 tbsp potato starch	2 tbsp cornstarch	½ tbsp baking powder
8 chicken wings	2 tbsp hot curry paste	

Directions

Combine the hot curry paste and 2 tbsp of water in a small bowl. Place the wings in a large bowl and pour the curry mixture over; toss to coat. Combine the baking powder, cornstarch, and potato starch. Dip each wing in the starch mixture. Place on the greased air fryer basket. Insert the basket into the IP and put the air fryer lid on top. Select Air Fry and set the temperature to 350 F and the cooking time to 16 minutes. Push Start. Flip over halfway through the cooking time. Serve and enjoy!

Winter Creamy Mushroom Chicken

Prep + Cook Time: 25 minutes | Serves: 4

Ingredients

1 (10.5-oz) can condensed cream of mushroom soup

4 chicken breasts, sliced	1 ½ cups onion soup mix	½ cup heavy cream

Directions

Set your IP to Sauté on Low and add the mushroom soup, onion mix, and heavy cream. Stir for 2-3 minutes until heated through. Arrange the chicken slices on a baking pan and spread the mushroom mixture all over them.

Place the baking pan inside the air fryer basket. Insert the basket into the IP and put the air fryer lid on top. Select Bake and set the temperature to 400 F and the cooking time to 15 minutes. Push Start. Serve and enjoy!

Exotic Chicken Breasts

Prep + Cook Time: 20 minutes + marinating time | Serves: 2

Ingredients

1 large mango, cubed	½ tbsp oregano	1 medium avocado, sliced
1 red pepper, chopped	½ tsp mustard powder	1 tbsp parsley, chopped
1 garlic clove, minced	Salt and black pepper to taste	2 tbsp balsamic vinegar
2 tbsp olive oil	2 chicken breasts, cubed	

Directions

In a bowl, mix mango, red pepper, garlic, olive oil, oregano, mustard powder, salt, and pepper. Add the mixture to a blender and pulse until smooth. Pour the mixture over the chicken cubes and allow marinating for 3 hours.

Next, place the chicken cubes in the air fryer basket. Insert the basket into the IP and put the air fryer lid on top. Select Air Fry and set the temperature to 360 F and the cooking time to 14 minutes. Push Start. Shake halfway through the cooking time. Drizzle balsamic vinegar and garnish avocado with parsley. Serve and enjoy!

Buttery Chicken Wings

Prep + Cook Time: 25 minutes | Serves: 4

Ingredients

2 garlic cloves, minced
¾ cup potato starch

16 chicken wings
¼ cup butter

¼ cup honey
½ tbsp salt

Directions

Place the wings in a bowl. Add the starch and toss to coat the chicken. Place the chicken in the greased air fryer basket and fit in your IP. Put the air fryer lid on top. Select Air Fry and set the temperature to 370 F and the cooking time to 15 minutes. Push Start. Whisk the rest of the ingredients together in a bowl. At the 10-minute mark, pour the sauce over the wings and cook for the remaining 5 minutes. Serve and enjoy!

Tropical Chicken Tenders

Prep + Cook Time: 25 minutes + marinating time | Serves: 4

Ingredients

4 scallions, chopped
1 lb chicken tenders
2 cloves garlic, minced

2 tbsp sesame seeds, toasted
⅓ cup sesame oil
1 tbsp fresh ginger, grated

½ cup pineapple juice
½ cup soy sauce
A pinch of black pepper

Directions

Skew each tender and trim any excess fat. Mix the other ingredients in a large bowl. Add the skewered chicken and place it in the fridge for 2 hours. Pat dry the chicken and place it into the greased fryer basket.

Insert the basket into the IP and put the air fryer lid on top. Select Air Fry and set the temperature to 380 F and the cooking time to 14 minutes. Push Start. Shake halfway through the cooking time. Serve and enjoy!

Sicilian Whole Chicken

Prep + Cook Time: 70 minutes | Serves: 6

Ingredients

3 minced cloves of garlic
1 whole chicken, 3 lb
½ cup pitted prunes
2 tbsp capers

2 bay leaves
2 tbsp red wine vinegar
2 tbsp olive oil
1 tbsp dried oregano

¼ cup packed brown sugar
1 tbsp chopped and fresh parsley

Directions

In a large bowl, mix the prunes, olives, capers, garlic, olive oil, bay leaves, oregano, vinegar, salt, and pepper. Spread the mixture on the bottom of a baking pan and place the chicken over. Sprinkle a little bit of brown sugar on top of the chicken. Place the pan inside the air fryer basket. Insert the basket into the IP and put the air fryer lid on top. Select Bake and set the temperature to 360 F and the cooking time to 60 minutes. Push Start. Serve.

Broccoli & Rice Chicken

Prep + Cook Time: 60 minutes | Serves: 3

Ingredients

1 can condensed cream chicken soup
10 oz broccoli florets, chopped
3 chicken legs

1 package instant long grain rice
2 cups water

1 tbsp minced garlic

Directions

Place the chicken legs in the air fryer basket. Season with salt and pepper and drizzle with some olive oil. Insert the basket into the IP and put the air fryer lid on top. Select Air Fry and set the temperature to 390 F and the cooking time to 25 minutes. Push Start. Remove the chicken to a platter. Cover with foil to keep warm.

In a bowl, mix the rice, water, garlic, soup, and broccoli. Combine the mixture very well. Spread the rice mixture on a baking pan and place the pan in the IP. Cook for 20 minutes on Bake. Serve topped with chicken.

Crispy Cayenne Chicken Thighs

Prep + Cook Time: 30 minutes + marinating time | Serves: 6

Ingredients

2 cups flour	Salt and black pepper to taste	2 cups buttermilk
1 ½ lb chicken thighs	1 tbsp paprika	
1 tbsp cayenne pepper	1 tbsp baking powder	

Directions

Place the chicken thighs in a bowl. Add cayenne pepper, salt, black pepper, and buttermilk and stir to coat well. Refrigerate for 2 hours. In another bowl, mix the flour, paprika, salt, and baking powder. Dredge the chicken thighs, one at a time, in the flour and then place on the greased fryer basket. Spritz them with cooking oil.

Insert the basket into the IP and put the air fryer lid on top. Select Air Fry and set the temperature to 380 F and the cooking time to 20 minutes. Push Start. Flip halfway through the cooking time. Serve and enjoy!

Classic Buffalo Chicken Wings

Prep + Cook Time: 35 minutes | Serves: 4

Ingredients

½ cup Buffalo sauce	4 pounds chicken wings	Salt and black pepper to taste
½ cup canola oil	1 tbsp Worcestershire sauce	

Directions

Season the chicken with salt and pepper and place it in the air fryer basket. Insert the basket into the IP and put the air fryer lid on top. Select Air Fry and set the temperature to 380 F and the cooking time to 20 minutes. Push Start. Shake halfway through the cooking time. In a serving bowl, combine Buffalo sauce, canola oil, Worcestershire sauce, and salt. Toss the chicken wings in the prepared sauce. Serve with celery sticks if desired.

Asian Chicken Skewers

Prep + Cook Time: 25 minutes | Serves: 4

Ingredients

4 scallions, chopped	½ cup soy sauce	1 tbsp fresh ginger, grated
4 cloves garlic, chopped	½ cup pineapple juice	2 tbsp toasted sesame seeds
¾ oz chicken tenders	¼ cup sesame oil	Black pepper to taste

Directions

Thread the chicken pieces onto skewers and trim any fat. In a large bowl, mix the remaining ingredients. Coat the skewered chicken with the mixture. Place the chicken in the greased air fryer basket and fit in your IP. Put the air fryer lid on top. Select Air Fry and set the temperature to 390 F and the cooking time to 15 minutes. Push Start. Turn over halfway through the cooking time. Serve and enjoy!

Peanut Chicken Drumsticks

Prep + Cook Time: 20 minutes | Serves: 2

Ingredients

¼ cup satay sauce

1 tbsp peanut butter, melted

½ lime, juiced

1 pound chicken drumsticks

1 garlic clove, sliced

1 green onion, sliced

Directions

In a resealable bag, place the satay sauce, peanut butter, and lime juice. Add the chicken drumsticks and shake to coat on all sides. Arrange the drumsticks on the air fryer basket. Insert the basket into the IP and put the air fryer lid on top. Select Air Fry and set the temperature to 390 F and the cooking time to 20 minutes. Push Start. Turn over halfway through the cooking time. Serve and enjoy!

English-Style Chicken Breasts

Prep + Cook Time: 20 minutes | Serves: 6

Ingredients

2 tbsp olive oil

¼ cup onions, chopped

¼ cup + ½ tbsp flour

1 ½ pounds chicken breasts, sliced

1 tbsp Worcestershire sauce

1 tbsp brown sugar

¼ cup yellow mustard

½ cup ketchup

¾ cup water

Directions

In a bowl, mix the brown sugar, water, ketchup, chopped onion, mustard, Worcestershire sauce, and salt. Add the chicken and toss to coat; set aside for 10 minutes. In a bowl, mix the flour, salt, and pepper. Roll the marinated chicken slices onto the flour mixture, shaking off the excess, and drizzle with olive oil.

Place the chicken in the air fryer basket and fit in your IP. Put the air fryer lid on top. Select Air Fry and set the temperature to 360 F and the cooking time to 15 minutes. Push Start. Shake halfway through the cooking time.

Padrón Pepper & Tomato Chicken

Prep + Cook Time: 30 minutes | Serves: 2

Ingredients

2 tsp olive oil

½ pound chicken breasts

Salt and black pepper to taste

1 padrón or jalapeño pepper, chopped

¼ tsp dried rosemary

¼ tsp dried oregano

1 cup cherry tomatoes, halved

Directions

Rub the chicken with rosemary, oregano, salt, and pepper. Place in the greased air fryer basket and drizzle with some oil. Fit in your IP. Put the air fryer lid on top. Select Air Fry and set the temperature to 380 F and the cooking time to 20 minutes. Push Start. At the 15-minute mark, flip the chicken and add the tomatoes and padrón pepper. Sprinkle with salt, pepper, and the remaining oil and cook for the remaining 5 minutes. Serve.

No-Fuss Chicken Breast

Prep + Cook Time: 20 minutes | Serves: 2

Ingredients

2 lemon, juiced, rind reserved

1 chicken breast

1 tbsp chicken seasoning

1 tbsp garlic puree

A handful of peppercorns

Salt and black pepper to taste

Directions

Place a silver foil sheet on a flat surface. Add all seasonings alongside the lemon rind. Lay out the chicken onto a chopping board and trim any fat and little bones. Season each side with pepper and salt. Rub the chicken seasoning on both sides well. Place on your silver foil sheet and rub. Seal tightly and flatten with a rolling pin.

Place the breast in the air fryer basket and fit it in your IP. Place the air fryer lid on top. Select Air Fry and set the temperature to 360 F and the cooking time 15 minutes. Push Start. Shake the basket halfway through. Serve.

French-Style Chicken Tenders

Prep + Cook Time: 20 minutes | Serves: 4

Ingredients

1 pound chicken breasts, sliced
4 garlic cloves, minced
1 tbsp thyme leaves
½ cup dry champagne

½ cup Dijon mustard
2 cups breadcrumbs
2 tbsp melted butter
1 tbsp lemon zest

2 tbsp olive oil
Salt to taste

Directions

In a bowl, mix garlic, salt, cloves, breadcrumbs, pepper, oil, butter, and lemon zest. In another bowl, mix mustard and champagne. Dip chicken slices into the champagne mixture and then into the crumbs. Place the chicken in the air fryer basket and fit it in your IP. Set the air fryer lid on top. Select Air Fry and set the temperature to 350 F and the cooking time to 15 minutes. Push Start. Turn over halfway through the cooking time. Serve and enjoy!

Fusion Chicken Wings

Prep + Cook Time: 30 minutes | Serves: 2

Ingredients

1 tbsp olive oil
8 chicken wings
½ tsp brown sugar

2 tbsp cornflour
½ tbsp rice wine
1 tbsp shrimp paste

1 tbsp ginger

Directions

In a bowl, mix the olive oil, ginger, rice wine, shrimp paste, and brown sugar. Add the chicken wings and toss to coat. Arrange the wings on the greased air fryer basket and fit in your IP. Place the air fryer lid on top. Select Air Fry and set the temperature to 360 F and the cooking time to 20 minutes. Push Start. Flip halfway through the cooking time. When cooking is complete, the chicken wings should be crispy on the outside. Serve and enjoy!

Ranch Chicken Wings

Prep + Cook Time: 25 minutes | Serves: 2

Ingredients

6 tbsp Romano cheese, grated
1 tsp Ranch seasoning mix

½ cup panko breadcrumbs
2 tsp butter, melted

2 tbsp hoisin sauce
1 pound chicken wings

Directions

In a bowl, combine the Romano cheese, Ranch seasoning, breadcrumbs, butter, and hoisin sauce. Add the chicken wings and toss to coat. Arrange the chicken wings on the air fryer basket. Spritz the wings with cooking spray. Fit the basket in your IP. Place the air fryer lid on top, select Air Fry and set the temperature to 390 F and the cooking time to 18 minutes. Push Start. Shake halfway through cooking. Serve hot and enjoy!

Fatty & Cheesy Chicken Bowl

Prep + Cook Time: 20 minutes | Serves: 4

Ingredients

1 cup mayonnaise

4 chicken breasts, cubed

1 tbsp garlic powder

½ cup soft cheese

Salt and black pepper to taste

Chopped basil for garnish

Directions

In a bowl, mix cheese, mayonnaise, garlic powder, and salt to form a marinade. Cover your chicken with the marinade. Place the marinated chicken in the air fryer basket and fit it in your IP. Place the air fryer lid on top. Select Air Fry and set the temperature to 380 F and the cooking time to 15 minutes. Push Start. Serve and enjoy!

Old-Fashioned Fried Chicken Tenders

Prep + Cook Time: 30 minutes | Serves: 3

Ingredients

2 tsp butter, melted

1 cup flour

½ tsp baking powder

Salt and black pepper to taste

1 tsp garlic powder

1 tsp dried marjoram

2 large eggs

1 pound chicken tenders

1 tbsp fresh chives, chopped

Directions

In a bowl, beat the eggs with salt and pepper until frothy. Mix the flour with baking powder, garlic powder, and marjoram in a separate bowl. Dip the chicken into the beaten eggs and coat with the flour mixture.

Place into the chicken the greased air fryer basket and fit in your IP. Put the air fryer lid on top. Select Air Fry and set the temperature to 390 F and the cooking time to 15 minutes. Push Start. Turn over halfway through the cooking time. Serve warm, sprinkled with chives. Enjoy!

Chinese Sticky Wingettes

Prep + Cook Time: 25 minutes | Serves: 3

Ingredients

1 garlic clove, minced

1 pound chicken wingettes

1 tbsp cilantro leaves, chopped

1 tbsp roasted peanuts, chopped

½ tbsp apple cider vinegar

½ tbsp chili sauce

1 tsp Chiu Chow chili oil

1 ginger, minced

Salt and black pepper to taste

2 tbsp soy sauce

1 tbsp honey

Directions

In a bowl, mix ginger, garlic, chili sauce, chili oil, honey, salt, pepper, soy sauce, cilantro, and vinegar. Add the chicken wingettes and toss to coat; let it rest for 10 minutes. Add the chicken to the air fryer basket and fit in your IP. Place the air fryer lid on top. Select Air Fry and set the temperature to 360 F and the cooking time 20 minutes. Push Start. Shake halfway through the cooking time. Serve sprinkled with peanuts.

Parisian-Style Chicken Escalopes

Prep + Cook Time: 10 minutes | Serves: 6

Ingredients

2 tbsp truffle oil

2 beaten eggs

1 ½ pounds chicken breasts

1 cup flour ounce flour

Salt and black pepper to taste

2 tbsp cranberry jam

Directions

Place the chicken breasts between a cling film, beat well using a rolling pin until a ¼ cm thickness is achieved. Season the chicken with salt and pepper. Roll in the flour, dip in the eggs, then roll again in the flour, shaking off the excess. Place in the air fryer basket and drizzle both sides with truffle oil. Fit the basket in your IP.

Place the air fryer lid on top. Select Air Fry and set the temperature to 390 F and the cooking time to 16 minutes. Push Start. Turn over halfway through the cooking time. The chicken should be golden. Serve with cranberry jam.

Classic Enchilada Chicken Bowl

Prep + Cook Time: 15 minutes | Serves: 6

Ingredients

½ cup salsa

12 flour tortillas

2 lb chicken breasts, chopped

2 cups Mexican cheese, grated

1 can green chilies, chopped

1 (28-oz) can enchilada sauce

Directions

In a bowl, mix salsa and enchilada sauce. Toss in the chopped chicken to coat. Place the chicken on the tortillas and roll; top with cheese. Place the prepared tortillas in the air fryer basket and fit it in your IP. Place the air fryer lid on top. Select Air Fry and set the temperature to 400 F and the cooking time to 5 minutes. Push Start. Serve.

Avocado Chicken Bowls

Prep + Cook Time: 20 minutes | Serves: 2

Ingredients

2 chicken breasts, cubed

1 tbsp chopped parsley

Salt and black pepper to taste

1 avocado, sliced

4 radishes, sliced

½ cup cooked basmati rice

1 carrot, grated

1 zucchini, grated

½ avocado, sliced

2 tbsp canned kidney beans

½ cup baby spinach

2 tbsp canned sweetcorn

1 tsp toasted sesame seed

DIRECTIONS

Season the chicken with salt and pepper and place it in the air fryer basket. Spritz with cooking oil on all sides. Insert the basket into the IP and put the air fryer lid on top. Select Air Fry and set the temperature to 390 F and the cooking time to 12 minutes. Push Start. Shake halfway through the cooking time.

Spoon the cooked rice into the center of two bowls and top with chicken cubes. Arrange the rest of the ingredients around the edge of the bowls. Sprinkle with sesame seeds and serve immediately.

Phillippine-Style Chicken Drumsticks

Prep + Cook Time: 25 minutes | Serves: 4

Ingredients

2 tbsp sesame seeds, toasted

1-inch fresh ginger, grated

2 tbsp cilantro, chopped

8 chicken drumsticks

3 tbsp light soy sauce

2 crushed garlic cloves

1 tbsp olive oil

1 tbsp sesame oil

1 tbsp honey

Directions

Add all ingredients in a freezer bag, except sesame seeds and coriander. Seal up and massage until the drumsticks are coated well. Place the drumsticks in the air fryer basket and fit it in your IP. Place the air fryer lid on top. Select Air Fry and set the temperature to 400 F and the cooking time to 20 minutes. Push Start. Serve.

Almond-Crusted Chicken

Prep + Cook Time: 25 minutes | Serves: 4

Ingredients

3 whole eggs, beaten
3 chicken breasts, cubed

Salt and black pepper to taste
3 cups almond flakes

½ cup cornstarch
1 tbsp cayenne pepper

Directions

In a bowl, mix salt, cornstarch, cayenne pepper, and pepper. In another bowl, add beaten eggs and almond flakes. Cover chicken with pepper mix. Dredge chicken in the egg mix. Brush the chicken with oil. Place the prepared chicken in the air fryer basket and fit it in your IP. Place the air fryer lid on top. Select Air Fry and set the temperature to 350 F and the cooking time to 20 minutes. Push Start. Serve and enjoy!

Mom's Chicken Tenderloins

Prep + Cook Time: 15 minutes | Serves: 2

Ingredients

2 tbsp olive oil
2 oz breadcrumbs

4 chicken tenderloins
1 large whisked egg

Directions

Combine the oil with the crumbs and stir until crumbly. Dip the chicken in the egg, then roll in the crumb mix, making sure it is evenly and fully covered. Arrange them on the greased air fryer basket. Insert the basket into the IP and put the air fryer lid on top. Select Air Fry and set the temperature to 360 F and the cooking time to 12 minutes. Push Start. Serve the dish and enjoy its crispy taste with Dijon mustard.

Cashew Creamed Chicken Wings

Prep + Cook Time: 25 minutes | Serves: 3

Ingredients

2 tbsp honey
½ tbsp vinegar
½ tbsp garlic chili sauce
½ tbsp ginger, minced

1 pound chicken wings
1 tbsp cilantro
Salt and black pepper to taste
1 tbsp cashews cream

1 garlic clove, minced
1 tbsp yogurt

Directions

Season the wings with salt and pepper. Place them in the air fryer. Insert the basket into the IP and put the air fryer lid on top. Select Bake and set the temperature to 360 F and the cooking time to 15 minutes. Push Start.

In a bowl, mix the remaining ingredients. At the 10-minute mark, top the chicken with the sauce and cook for the remaining 5 minutes. Serve and enjoy!

Air Fried BBQ Chicken Pizza

Prep + Cook Time: 15 minutes | Serves: 1

Ingredients

¼ cup shredded Monterrey Jack cheese
½ chicken sausage
¼ cup barbeque sauce

¼ cup shredded mozzarella cheese
2 tbsp red onion, thinly sliced

1 piece naan bread
Chopped cilantro for garnish

Directions

Spray naan's bread bottom with cooking spray and arrange it in the air fryer. Brush well with barbeque sauce, sprinkle mozzarella cheese, Monterrey Jack cheese, and red onion on top. Top with the sausage over and spray the crust with cooking spray. Cook in your IP for 8 minutes at 400 F on Air Fry mode. Serve and enjoy!

Simple Turkey Meatballs

Prep + Cook Time: 40 minutes | Serves: 4

Ingredients

1 egg
1 lb ground turkey
½ cup breadcrumbs

1 tbsp garlic powder
1 tbsp Italian seasoning
1 tbsp onion powder

Salt and black pepper to taste
¼ cup Parmesan cheese, grated

Directions

In a bowl, add the ground turkey, crack the egg onto it, add the breadcrumbs, garlic powder, onion powder, Italian seasoning, Parmesan, salt, and pepper. Use your hands to mix them well. Spoon out portions and make bite-size balls out of the mixture. Grease the air fryer basket with cooking spray and add in the turkey balls.

Insert the basket into the IP and put the air fryer lid on top. Select Bake and set the temperature to 400 F and the cooking time to 12 minutes. Push Start. Flip the meatballs halfway through the cooking time. Serve.

Panko-Crispy Turkey

Prep + Cook Time: 25 minutes | Serves: 6

Ingredients

2 lb turkey breasts, boneless and skinless
1 stick butter, melted
2 cups panko breadcrumbs

½ tsp Poblano chili pepper, ground
Salt and black pepper to taste

Directions

In a bowl, combine the breadcrumbs, black pepper, chili pepper, and salt. In another bowl, combine the melted butter with salt and pepper. Brush the butter mixture over the turkey breasts. Coat the turkey with the panko mixture. Arrange them on the greased fryer basket. Insert the basket into the IP and put the air fryer lid on top. Select Air Fry and set the temperature to 390 F and the cooking time to 25 minutes. Push Start. Turn halfway through the cooking time. Let cool for a few minutes before slicing and serving. Enjoy!

Parmesan Turkey Bites

Prep + Cook Time: 20 minutes | Serves: 2

Ingredients

8 oz turkey breast, boneless and skinless
1 cup breadcrumbs
1 egg, beaten

1 tbsp grated Parmesan cheese
1 tbsp dried thyme

½ tbsp dried parsley
Salt and black pepper to taste

Directions

Cut the turkey into bite-sized pieces and place them in a bowl. Toss with thyme, parsley, salt, and pepper. Combine the breadcrumbs with Parmesan cheese in a bowl. Dip the turkey pieces into the crumbs first, then into the egg, and finally into the crumbs again. Arrange them on the air fryer basket and spritz with cooking oil.

Insert the basket into the IP and put the air fryer lid on top. Select Air Fry and set the temperature to 380 F and the cooking time to 20 minutes. Push Start. Shake halfway through the cooking time. Serve and enjoy!

BEEF, LAMB AND PORK RECIPES

Easy Rib Eye Steak

Prep + Cook Time: 20 minutes | Serves: 6

Ingredients

1 tbsp olive oil	2 lb rib eye steak	1 tbsp steak rub

Directions

Rub the steak with the steak seasoning and olive oil. Place in the air fryer basket and fit it in your IP. Place the air fryer lid on top. Select Air Fry and set the temperature to 400 F and the cooking time to 18 minutes. Push Start. Turn over halfway through the cooking time. Serve and enjoy!

Quick Cayenne Beef Steaks

Prep + Cook Time: 15 minutes | Serves: 2

Ingredients

1 tbsp olive oil	2 beef steaks, 1-inch thick	½ tsp cayenne pepper
½ tsp ground paprika	½ tsp black pepper	Salt and black pepper to taste

Directions

Mix olive oil, black pepper, cayenne, paprika, salt, and pepper and rub onto steaks. Spread evenly. Put the steaks in the fryer basket and fit in your IP. Place the air fryer lid on top. Select Air Fry and set the temperature to 390 F and the cooking time to 18 minutes. Push Start. Turn them halfway through. Serve and enjoy!

Homemade Beef Meatloaf

Prep + Cook Time: 30 minutes | Serves: 4

Ingredients

2 garlic cloves, crushed	2 eggs, lightly beaten	1 tsp mixed dried herbs
1 onion, finely chopped	½ cup breadcrumbs	
1 lb ground beef	2 tbsp tomato puree	

Directions

In a bowl, mix beef, eggs, breadcrumbs, garlic, onion, puree, and herbs. Gently press the mixture into a greased loaf pan and slide in the fryer basket. Insert the basket into the IP and put the air fryer lid on top. Select Bake and set the temperature to 380 F and the cooking time to 25 minutes. Push Start. Cool for 5 minutes before slicing.

Asian-Style Roasted Beef

Prep + Cook Time: 20 minutes + chilling time | Serves: 2

Ingredients

Thumb-sized piece of ginger, chopped

3 chilies, deseeded and chopped	1 tsp brown sugar	2 tbsp basil, chopped
4 garlic cloves, chopped	Juice of 1 lime	2 tbsp oil
1 lb ground beef	2 tbsp mirin	2 tbsp fish sauce
2 tbsp soy sauce	2 tbsp coriander, chopped	Salt and black pepper to taste

Directions

Place all ingredients, except the beef, salt, and pepper, in a blender; process until smooth. Season the beef with salt and pepper. Place all in a zipper bag; shake well to combine. Marinate in the fridge for 4 hours.

Place the beef in the air fryer basket and fit it in your IP. Place the air fryer lid on top. Select Air Fry and set the temperature to 380 F and the cooking time to 12 minutes. Push Start. Let sit for a couple of minutes before serving. Serve with cooked rice and fresh veggies if desired. Enjoy!

Awesome Peanut Butter & Beef Bowl

Prep + Cook Time: 55 minutes | Serves: 4

Ingredients

Hoisin Sauce:

3 cloves garlic, minced	1 tbsp peanut butter	1 tsp sugar
2 tbsp soy sauce	½ tsp sriracha hot sauce	1 tsp rice vinegar

Beef Veggie Mix:

1 red onion, chopped	2 green peppers, cut into strips	½ cup water
2 lb broccoli, chopped	2 white onions, chopped	2 tsp sesame oil
2 lb beef sirloin, cut into strips	2 tbsp soy sauce	1 tbsp olive oil
2 yellow peppers, cut into strips	3 tsp minced garlic	
2 green peppers, cut into strips	2 tsp ground ginger	

Directions

Set your IP to Sauté and add the soy sauce, peanut butter, sugar, hot sauce, rice vinegar, and minced garlic. Bring to simmer until reduced, about 15 minutes. Stir occasionally using a vessel and let it cool. Let cool. To the chilled hoisin sauce, add the garlic, sesame oil, soy sauce, ginger, and water; mix well. Add in the meat, mix with a spoon, and refrigerate for 20 minutes to marinate.

Meanwhile, add the florets, peppers, onions, and olive oil to a bowl; mix to coat well. Add the veggies to the fryer basket and fit in your IP. Place the air fryer lid on top. Select Air Fry and set the temperature to 400 F and the cooking time to 5 minutes. Push Start. Remove the veggies to a serving plate and set aside.

Remove the meat from the fridge and drain the liquid into a bowl. Add the beef into the air fryer basket and place in the IP. Insert the basket into the IP and put the air fryer lid on top. Select Air Fry and set the temperature to 380 F and the cooking time to 15 minutes. Push Start. Shake once. Remove to the veggie plate; season with salt and pepper and pour the cooking sauce over to serve.

Easy Beef Meatballs in Red Sauce

Prep + Cook Time: 20 minutes | Serves: 4

Ingredients

10 oz of tomato sauce	1 egg	½ tbsp thyme leaves, chopped
½ lb ground beef	4 tbsp breadcrumbs	Salt and black pepper to taste
1 medium onion	1 tbsp fresh parsley, chopped	

Directions

Place all ingredients into a bowl and mix very well. Shape the mixture into 10 to 12 balls. Place the meatballs in the air fryer basket and fit it in your IP. Place the air fryer lid on top. Select Air Fry and set the temperature to 380 F and the cooking time to 18 minutes. Push Start. At the 12-minute mark, add the tomato sauce and cook for the remaining 6 minutes. Serve and enjoy!

Simple Beef Empanadas

Prep + Cook Time: 25 minutes | Serves: 4

Ingredients

2 tbsp olive oil	½ onion, diced	½ tbsp olive oil
4 empanada shells	1 garlic clove, minced	½ tsp cumin
1 egg yolk	¼ cup tomato salsa	Salt and black pepper to taste
1 lb ground beef	2 tsp milk	

Directions

Heat the olive oil in your IP on Sauté and add the beef, onion, cumin, and garlic. Stir-fry for 8-10 minutes. Season with salt and pepper. Stir in the tomato salsa and set aside.

In a small bowl, combine the milk and yolk. Place the empanada shells on a dry and clean surface. Divide the beef mixture between the shells. Fold the shells and seal the ends with a fork. Brush with the egg wash.

Place on a lined baking sheet and fit in the air fryer basket. Insert the basket into the IP and put the air fryer lid on top. Select Bake and set the temperature to 350 F and the cooking time to 10 minutes. Push Start. Serve.

Ground Beef & Cannellini Bake

Prep + Cook Time: 50 minutes | Serves: 6

Ingredients

1 onion, chopped	½ cup finely chopped bell peppers	½ cup chopped celery
2 garlic cloves, minced	1 can (8 oz) cannellini beans	1 ½ cup vegetable broth
1 lb ground beef	1 tsp chopped cilantro	Salt and black pepper to taste
½ tbsp chili powder	3 tbsp olive oil	
1 can diced tomatoes	½ tsp parsley	

Directions

Heat the olive oil in your IP on Sauté and add the garlic, onion, bell peppers, and celery. Stir-fry for 5 minutes. Add the beef and cook for 6 more minutes. Stir in broth, tomatoes, chili, parsley, and cilantro. Transfer the mixture to a baking pan. Stir in the beans and adjust the seasoning with salt and pepper.

Place the pan in the air fryer basket and fit it in your IP. Place the air fryer lid on top. Select Air Fry and set the temperature to 350 F and the cooking time to 20 minutes. Push Start. Sprinkle with parsley and serve.

American-Style Flank Steaks

Prep + Cook Time: 25 minutes | Serves: 4

Ingredients

2 tbsp chopped cilantro	2 tbsp fish sauce	2 tbsp minced garlic
½ cup roasted peanuts, chopped	2 tbsp soy sauce	2 tbsp minced ginger
2 lb flank steaks, cut in long strips	2 tbsp sugar	2 tsp hot sauce

Directions

In a zipper bag, add the beef, fish sauce, sugar, garlic, soy sauce, ginger, and hot sauce. Zip the bag and massage the ingredients with your hands to mix well. Open the bag, remove the beef, shake off the excess marinade, and place the beef strips in the air fryer basket in a single layer, avoid overlapping.

Insert the basket into the IP and put the air fryer lid on top. Select Air Fry and set the temperature to 400 F and the cooking time to 14 minutes. Push Start. Turn once halfway through. Garnish with peanuts and cilantro.

Beef Tenderloin with Green Sauce

Prep + Cook Time: 30 minutes | Serves: 3

Ingredients

Beef:
½ cup flour   2 lb beef tenderloin, cut into strips

Sauce:
1 tbsp minced garlic   ½ cup soy sauce   1 tsp cornstarch
½ cup chopped green onions   ½ cup water   ½ tsp red chili flakes
1 tbsp minced ginger   ¼ cup vinegar   Salt and black pepper to taste
2 tbsp olive oil   ¼ cup sugar

Directions

To make the sauce, pour the cornstarch in a bowl and mix it with 3 to 4 teaspoons of water until well dissolved. Set your IP to Sauté and add the olive oil, garlic, and ginger. Stir continually for 10 seconds. Add the soy sauce, vinegar, and remaining water. Stir well and bring to boil for 2 minutes. Stir in the sugar, chili flakes, and cornstarch mixture. Stir in the green onions and cook for 1 to 2 minutes. Season with pepper and salt. Set aside.

Dredge the beef in the flour. Arrange them on the greased air fryer basket; spray with cooking spray. Insert the basket into the IP and put the air fryer lid on top. Select Air Fry and set the temperature to 400 F and the cooking time to 12 minutes. Push Start. Toss halfway through cooking. Pour the sauce over the strips and serve.

English-Style Beef Meatballs

Prep + Cook Time: 30 minutes | Serves: 4

Ingredients

⅓ cup rice, cooked   2 tbsp Worcestershire sauce   1 green bell pepper, finely chopped
1 lb ground beef   2 cups tomato sauce   1 tsp celery salt
1 tbsp minced onion   1 tsp oregano

Directions

Combine the rice, ground beef, onion, celery salt, green pepper, and garlic. Shape into balls of 1-inch each. Arrange the balls on the air fryer basket and fit in your IP. Place the air fryer lid on top. Select Air Fry and set the temperature to 320 F and the cooking time to 25 minutes. Push Start. Mix the tomato juice, oregano, and Worcestershire sauce in a small bowl. Serve the balls warm with the sauce. Enjoy!

Quick Herby Beef Loin

Prep + Cook Time: 70 minutes | Serves: 6

Ingredients

2 lb beef loin   ½ tsp oregano   1 tbsp olive oil
1 tsp thyme   ½ tsp garlic powder   Salt and black pepper to taste
1 tsp rosemary   1 tsp onion powder

Directions

In a bowl, combine olive oil and seasonings. Rub the mixture onto the beef. Place the beef in the air fryer basket and fit it in your IP. Place the air fryer lid on top. Select Air Fry and set the temperature to 350 F and the cooking time to 60 minutes. Push Start. Turn the roast over halfway through the cooking time. When cooking is complete, the meat should be well-roasted. Serve with mushroom sauce if desired.

Easy Stuffed Cabbage Rolls

Prep + Cook Time: 35 minutes | Serves: 3

Ingredients

2 cloves garlic, minced
1 lb ground beef
8 savoy cabbage leaves
1 small onion, chopped

1 tsp chopped cilantro
¼ packet Taco seasoning
1 tbsp cilantro-lime rotel
⅔cup shredded Mexican cheese

2 tsp olive oil
Salt and black pepper to taste

Directions

Heat the olive oil in your IP on Sauté. Add the onions and garlic and sauté until fragrant, about 3 minutes. Add the beef, pepper, salt, and taco seasoning. Cook until the beef browns while breaking the meat with a vessel as it cooks. Add the cilantro rotel and stir well to combine. Remove to a bowl.

Lay 4 of the savoy cabbage leaves on a flat surface, scoop the beef mixture in the center and sprinkle with the Mexican cheese. Wrap diagonally and double wrap with the remaining 4 cabbage leaves. Arrange the rolls on the air fryer basket and spray with cooking spray. Insert the basket into the IP and put the air fryer lid on top. Select Air Fry and set the temperature to 400 F and the cooking time to 12 minutes. Push Start. Flip the rolls halfway through the cooking time. Remove, garnish with cilantro and allow them to cool. Serve and enjoy!

Classic Jalapeño Mozzarella Beef Tacos

Prep + Cook Time: 25 minutes | Serves: 4

Ingredients

1 cup corn kernels, canned
8 soft round taco shells
1 beefsteak, sliced

1 cup mozzarella cheese, grated
½ cup fresh cilantro, chopped
1 jalapeño pepper, minced

Salt and black pepper to taste

Directions

Season the beef slices with salt and pepper and arrange them on the greased air fryer basket. Insert the basket into the IP and put the air fryer lid on top. Select Air Fry and set the temperature to 360 F and the cooking time to 16 minutes. Push Start. Turn over halfway through the cooking time.

Divide the beef between the taco shells, top with cheese, cilantro, jalapeño, corn, salt, and pepper. Fold gently in half and secure with toothpicks if necessary. Spritz the tacos with cooking oil and arrange them on the basket. Bake in the IP at 380 F for 12 minutes on Bake, turning once. Serve with guacamole if desired.

British Meatloaf

Prep + Cook Time: 35 minutes | Serves: 6

Ingredients

1 onion, diced
4 lb ground beef
1 tbsp Worcestershire sauce
3 tbsp ketchup

1 tbsp basil
1 tbsp oregano
1 tbsp parsley
½ tsp salt

1 tsp ground peppercorns
10 whole peppercorns
1 cup breadcrumbs

Directions

Place all of the ingredients, except the whole peppercorns, in a large bowl. Mix with your hand until well combined. Place the meatloaf on a lined baking dish. Place in the air fryer basket and fit it in your IP. Place the air fryer lid on top. Select Air Fry and set the temperature to 350 F and the cooking time to 25 minutes. Push Start. Garnish the meatloaf with the whole peppercorns and let cool slightly before serving. Serve and enjoy!

Avocado Rib Eye Steak

Prep + Cook Time: 35 minutes | Serves: 4

Ingredients

1 avocado, diced
Juice from ½ lime

1 ½ lb rib-eye steak
2 tsp olive oil

1 tbsp chipotle chili pepper
Salt and black pepper to taste

Directions

Place the steak on a chopping board. Pour the olive oil over and sprinkle with chipotle pepper, salt, and black pepper. Use your hands to rub the spices on the meat. Leave it to sit and marinate for 10 minutes.

Place in the meat the greased air fryer basket. Insert the basket into the IP and put the air fryer lid on top. Select Air Fry and set the temperature to 400 F and the cooking time to 18 minutes. Push Start. Turn over halfway through the cooking time. Remove the steak, cover with foil, and let it sit for 5 minutes before slicing.

Meanwhile, prepare the avocado salsa by mashing the avocado with potato mash. Add in the lime juice and mix until smooth. Taste, adjust the seasoning, slice, and serve with salsa.

Classic Beef Burgers

Prep + Cook Time: 25 minutes | Serves: 4

Ingredients

1 ½ tbsp Worcestershire sauce
1 ½ lb ground beef
¼ tsp liquid smoke
2 tsp onion powder

1 tsp garlic powder
Salt and black pepper to taste
4 cheddar cheese slices
4 buns

4 trimmed lettuce leaves
4 tbsp mayonnaise
1 large tomato, sliced

Directions

In a bowl, combine the beef, salt, pepper, liquid smoke, onion powder, garlic powder, and Worcestershire sauce and mix to combine. Form 4 patties out of the mixture. Place the patties in the air fryer basket making sure to leave enough space between them. Insert the basket into the IP and put the air fryer lid on top.

Select Air Fry and set the temperature to 370 F and the cooking time to 14 minutes. Push Start. Turn over halfway through cooking. Place the patties on a plate. Assemble burgers with lettuce, mayonnaise, cheese, and tomato.

Sherry Beef Steak with Broccoli

Prep + Cook Time: 35 minutes + marinating time | Serves: 4

Ingredients

1 pound broccoli, cut into florets
1 lb circular beef steak, cut into strips
1 garlic clove, minced
⅓ cup oyster sauce

2 tbsp sesame oil
⅓ cup sherry
1 tsp soy sauce
1 tsp white sugar

1 tsp cornstarch
1 tbsp sesame oil

Directions

In a large bowl, mix the cornstarch, sherry, oyster sauce, sesame oil, soy sauce, sugar, and beef strips. Set aside for 45 minutes. Rub the garlic, sesame oil, and ginger onto the steaks. Place the steaks in the air fryer basket and fit it in your IP. Place the air fryer lid on top.

Select Air Fry and set the temperature to 390 F and the cooking time to 18 minutes. Push Start. At the 10-minute mark, shake the strips, add the broccoli, and cook for the remaining 8 minutes. Serve.

Parsley Ragu Meatballs

Prep + Cook Time: 25 minutes | Serves: 6

Ingredients

1 ¾ pound grounded beef
1 small onion, chopped
1 tbsp fresh parsley, chopped

½ tbsp fresh thyme leaves, chopped
1 whole egg, beaten
3 tbsp breadcrumbs

2 cups tomato sauce
Salt and black pepper to taste

Directions

In a mixing bowl, mix all the ingredients except tomato sauce. Roll the mixture into 10-12 balls. Place the balls in the air fryer basket and fit it in your IP. Place the air fryer lid on top. Select Air Fry and set the temperature to 390 F and the cooking time to 16 minutes. Push Start. At the 8-minute mark, shake the meatballs, add the tomato sauce, and toss to coat and cook for the remaining 5 minutes. Serve and enjoy!

Quick Beef Roast with Potatoes

Prep + Cook Time: 50 minutes | Serves: 3

Ingredients

1 pound red potatoes, halved
2 tbsp olive oil

1 pound top round roast beef
Salt and black pepper to taste

1 tsp dried thyme
½ tsp fresh rosemary, chopped

Directions

In a small bowl, mix 1 tbsp of olive oil, rosemary, salt, pepper, and thyme. Rub the mixture onto the beef. Place it in the air fryer basket and fit it in your IP. Place the air fryer lid on top. Select Air Fry and set the temperature to 360 F and the cooking time to 40 minutes. Push Start. At the 15-minute mark, give the meat a turn and add potatoes, salt, pepper, and remaining oil; cook for the remaining 25 minutes. Let cool for 5 minutes. Serve.

Beef & Mushrooms Noodles

Prep + Cook Time: 35 minutes | Serves: 6

Ingredients

1 can (14.5 oz) cream mushroom soup
2 cups mushrooms, sliced
1 ½ pounds beef steak
1 package egg noodles, cooked

1 ounce dry onion soup mix
1 whole onion, chopped
½ cup beef broth

3 garlic cloves, minced

Directions

Rub the dry onion soup mix all over the meat and place it in a baking pan. In a bowl, mix the cream mushroom soup, garlic, broth, chopped onion, and mushrooms. Top the meat with the prepared sauce mixture. Place the pan in the air fryer basket and fit it in your IP. Place the air fryer lid on top. Select Bake and set the temperature to 360 F and the cooking time to 25 minutes. Push Start. Serve with cooked egg noodles.

Parsley Beef Balls

Prep + Cook Time: 25 minutes | Serves: 6

Ingredients

¾ pound grounded beef
1 small onion, chopped
1 tbsp fresh parsley, chopped

½ tbsp fresh thyme, chopped
1 whole egg, beaten
3 tbsp breadcrumbs

Salt and black pepper to taste
Tomato sauce for coating

Directions

In a bowl, mix all ingredients, except the tomato sauce in a bowl; roll the mixture into balls. Place the balls in the air fryer basket and fit it in your IP. Place the air fryer lid on top. Select Air Fry and set the temperature to 390 F and the cooking time to 14 minutes. Push Start. At the 10-minute mark, add tomato sauce and toss the balls to coat. Cook for the remaining 4 minutes. When ready, stir gently and serve with spaghetti. Enjoy!

Homemade Beef Roast

Prep + Cook Time: 50 minutes | Serves: 2

Ingredients

½ lb beef roast
2 tsp olive oil

½ tsp dried rosemary
½ tsp dried thyme

Salt and black pepper to taste
½ tsp dried oregano

Directions

Drizzle oil over the beef and sprinkle with salt, pepper, and herbs in the greased air fryer basket. Rub onto the meat with hands. Insert the basket into the IP and put the air fryer lid on top.

Select Air Fry and set the temperature to 40 F and the cooking time to 45 minutes for medium-rare and 50 minutes for well-done. Push Start. Flip halfway through. Wrap the beef in foil for 10 minutes after cooking to allow the juices to reabsorb into the meat. Slice the beef and serve with a side of steamed asparagus.

Gourmet Garlic Beef Schnitzel

Prep + Cook Time: 22 minutes | Serves: 1

Ingredients

1 thin beef cutlet
1 egg, beaten
2 oz breadcrumbs

2 tbsp olive oil
1 tsp paprika
¼ tsp garlic powder

Salt and black pepper to taste

Directions

Combine olive oil, breadcrumbs, paprika, garlic powder, and salt in a bowl. Dip the beef in with the egg first, and then coat it with the breadcrumb mixture completely. Place the breaded meat in the greased air fryer basket.

Insert the basket into the IP and put the air fryer lid on top. Select Air Fry and set the temperature to 350 F and the cooking time to 12 minutes. Push Start. Turn over halfway through the cooking time. Serve and enjoy!

Healthy Beef Steak with Broccoli & Green Beans

Prep + Cook Time: 40 minutes | Serves: 2

Ingredients

½ lb beef steak, cut into strips
Salt and black pepper to taste
5 oz broccoli florets

¼ cup green beans, chopped
1 ½ tbsp soy sauce
2 tsp sesame oil

2 tsp minced ginger
2 tsp vinegar
1 clove garlic, minced

Directions

In a bowl, mix the broccoli, green beans, garlic, ginger, sesame oil, vinegar, and soy sauce and set aside. Sprinkle the beef with pepper and salt. Add the beef to the air fryer basket and fit in your IP. Place the air fryer lid on top.

Select Air Fry and set the temperature to 400 F and the cooking time to 18 minutes. Push Start. At the 10-minute mark, turn the beef strips, add the broccoli/green bean mixture, and cook for the remaining 8 minutes. Serve.

Bulgogi Beef with Mushrooms

Prep + Cook Time: 15 minutes + chilling time | Serves: 2

Ingredients

½ cup sliced mushrooms
2 beef steaks

4 tbsp bulgogi marinade
½ diced onion

Directions

Place the beef in a bowl. Add the bulgogi and mix to coat. Cover the bowl and place it in the fridge for 3 hours. Transfer the beef to a baking pan and stir in the mushrooms and onion. Place the pan inside the air fryer basket. Insert the basket into the IP and put the air fryer lid on top. Select Bake and set the temperature to 350 F and the cooking time to 14 minutes. Push Start. When cooking is complete, the beef should be tender. Serve.

Alpine-Style Beef Schnitzel

Prep + Cook Time: 25 minutes | Serves: 4

Ingredients

2 eggs, beaten
4 beef schnitzel cutlets

½ cup flour
Salt and black pepper to taste

1 cup breadcrumbs

Directions

Coat the cutlets with flour, shaking off any excess. Dip the coated cutlets into the beaten eggs. Sprinkle with salt and black pepper. Then dip into the crumbs and coat well. Spray them generously with oil and place in the air fryer basket. Insert the basket into the IP and put the air fryer lid on top. Select Air Fry and set the temperature to 360 F and the cooking time to 16 minutes. Push Start. Turn over halfway through the cooking time. Serve.

Mom's Beef Balls

Prep + Cook Time: 15 minutes | Serves: 5

Ingredients

2 whole eggs, beaten
1 pound ground beef

1 large red onion, chopped
1 tsp garlic, minced

Salt and black pepper to taste

Directions

Add the onion, garlic, cook ground beef, and eggs in a bowl, and mix well. Season with salt and pepper. Roll the mixture into golf ball shapes. Place the balls in the air fryer basket and fit it in your IP. Place the air fryer lid on top. Select Air Fry and set the temperature to 350 F and the cooking time to 16 minutes. Push Start. Serve.

Italian Beef Rolls

Prep + Cook Time: 30 minutes | Serves: 4

Ingredients

6 mozzarella cheese slices
2 pounds beef steak, sliced

¾ cup spinach, chopped
3 oz bell peppers, and sliced

3 tbsp pesto
Salt and black pepper to taste

Directions

Top the steak slices with pesto, cheese, spinach, and bell pepper. Roll up the slices and secure with toothpicks. Season with salt and pepper. Place the prepared slices in the air fryer basket and fit it in your IP. Place the air fryer lid on top. Select Air Fry and set to 400 F and the time to 16 minutes. Push Start. When ready, serve warm.

Effortless Beef Escalopes

Prep + Cook Time: 25 minutes | Serves: 2

Ingredients

1 whole egg, whisked   1 lemon, juiced   2 oz breadcrumbs
1 thin beef schnitzel, cut into strips   2 tbsp vegetable oil

Directions

Mix the breadcrumbs with oil. Dip schnitzel in egg, then coat with the breadcrumbs. Place them in the air fryer basket and fit it in your IP. Place the air fryer lid on top. Select Air Fry and set the temperature to 360 F and the time to 16 minutes. Push Start. Turn over halfway through the cooking time. Drizzle with lemon juice. Serve.

Classic Beef Stroganoff

Prep + Cook Time: 25 minutes | Serves: 3

Ingredients

16 oz egg noodles, cooked   1 whole onion, chopped   2 cups beef broth
1 pound thin steak   1 cup sour cream
4 tbsp butter, melted   8 oz mushrooms, sliced

Directions

In a bowl, mix the butter, mushrooms, cream, onion, and broth. Place the steak on a baking pan and pour the mushroom mixture all over steak. Place the pan in the air fryer basket and fit it in your IP. Place the air fryer lid on top. Select Air Fry and set the temperature to 400 F and the time to 16 minutes. Push Start. Serve and enjoy!

Lebanese Lamb Chops

Prep + Cook Time: 30 minutes | Serves: 4

Ingredients

1 garlic clove, minced   2 tsp olive oil   ½ tbsp oregano
4 lamb chops   Salt and black pepper to taste   ½ tbsp thyme

Directions

Coat the lamb chops with garlic, olive oil, oregano, thyme, salt, and pepper and arrange them on the air fryer basket. Insert the basket into the IP and put the air fryer lid on top. Select Air Fry and set the temperature to 390 F and the cooking time to 12 minutes. Push Start. Turn over halfway through the cooking time. Serve warm.

Minty Lamb Steaks with Potatoes

Prep + Cook Time: 25 minutes | Serves: 2

Ingredients

4 red potatoes, cubed   2 tbsp olive oil   A bunch of fresh mint leaves
2 lamb steaks   2 garlic cloves, crushed   Salt and black pepper to taste

Directions

Rub the steaks with oil, garlic, salt, and pepper. Cover a greased baking pan with mint leaves and place the steaks on top of them. Oil the potato chunks and sprinkle with salt and pepper. Arrange the potatoes next to the steaks. Place the baking pan inside the air fryer basket. Insert the basket into the IP and put the air fryer lid on top. Select Air Fry and set the temperature to 350 F and the time to 14 minutes. Push Start. Turn once.

Parmesan Lamb Meatloaf

Prep + Cook Time: 40 minutes | Serves: 6

Ingredients

2 tsp cayenne pepper
½ tsp dried basil
⅓ cup chopped parsley
2 egg whites

1 cup tomato basil sauce
1 ½ lb ground lamb
1 ¼ cup diced onion
2 tbsp minced garlic

2 tbsp minced ginger
½ cup breadcrumbs
½ cup grated Parmesan cheese
Salt and black pepper to taste

Directions

In a bowl, add the lamb, half of the tomato sauce, onion, garlic, ginger, breadcrumbs, cheese, salt, pepper, cayenne pepper, dried basil, parsley, and egg whites; mix well. Shape the mixture into a greased meatloaf while pressing firmly. Spread the remaining tomato sauce all over. Place the pan in the fryer basket and fit in your IP.

Place the air fryer lid on top. Select Bake and set the temperature to 360 F and the cooking time to 25 minutes. Push Start. Let meatloaf cool for 20 minutes before slicing. Serve with a side of sautéed green beans if desired.

Eastern-Style Lamb Rack

Prep + Cook Time: 30 minutes | Serves: 4

Ingredients

1 ½ lb rack of lamb
1 garlic clove, minced
3 oz chopped cashews

1 tbsp chopped rosemary
1 tbsp breadcrumbs
1 egg, beaten

1 tbsp olive oil
Salt and black pepper to taste

Directions

Rub the lamb with olive oil and garlic. Combine the rosemary, cashews, and crumbs in a bowl. Brush the egg over the lambs and coat it with the cashew mixture. Place the lamb into the air fryer basket. Insert the basket into the IP and put the air fryer lid on top.

Select Air Fry and set the temperature to 300 F and the cooking time to 30 minutes. Push Start. At the 10-minute mark, increase the temperature to 390 F and cook for the remaining 5 minutes. Cover with a foil and let sit for a couple of minutes before serving.

African Lamb Kofta

Prep + Cook Time: 30 minutes | Serves: 6

Ingredients

3 garlic cloves, minced
1 ½ lb ground lamb
½ cup minced onion
2 tbsp chopped mint leaves

2 tsp paprika
2 tsp coriander seeds
½ tsp cayenne pepper
1 tbsp chopped parsley

2 tsp cumin
½ tsp ground ginger
1 tsp salt

Directions

Combine all ingredients in a large bowl. Mix well with your hands until the herbs and spices are evenly distributed, and the mixture is well incorporated. Shape the lamb mixture into 12 sausage shapes around skewers.

Arrange on the greased air fryer basket. Insert the basket into the IP and put the air fryer lid on top. Select Air Fry and set the temperature to 350 F and the cooking time to 16 minutes. Push Start. Turn once.

Easy Stuffed Pork Tenderloin

Prep + Cook Time: 45 minutes | Serves: 4

Ingredients

1 pound pork tenderloin
4 oz bacon slices
1 cup spinach
3 oz cream cheese

1 small onion, sliced
1 tbsp olive oil
1 clove garlic, minced
½ tsp dried thyme

Salt and black pepper to taste
½ tsp dried rosemary

Directions

Place the pork on a chopping board, cover it with a plastic wrap and pound it using a kitchen hammer to a 2-inches flat and square piece. Trim the uneven sides with a knife to have a perfect square. Set aside. On the same chopping board, place and weave the bacon slices into a square of the pork's size. Place the pork on the bacon.

Heat the olive oil in your IP on Sauté and add the onion and garlic. Sauté for 3 minutes. Add the spinach, rosemary, thyme, salt, and pepper. Stir and allow the spinach to wilt. Stir in the cream cheese, set aside.

Spoon and spread the spinach mixture onto the pork loin. Roll up the bacon and pork over the spinach stuffing. Secure the ends with as many toothpicks as necessary. Season with more salt and pepper.

Place it in the air fryer basket and fit it in your IP. Place the air fryer lid on top. Select Air Fry and set the temperature to 360 F and the cooking time to 25 minutes. Push Start. Flip halfway through the cooking time. Remove to a clean chopping board. Let sit for 4 minutes before slicing. Serve with steamed veggies. Enjoy!

Sticky Homemade Pork Ribs

Prep + Cook Time: 55 minutes + chilling time | Serves: 6

Ingredients

4 garlic cloves, minced
2 lb pork ribs
1 tbsp honey

1 tbsp soy sauce
2 tbsp char siew sauce
2 tbsp minced ginger

2 tbsp hoisin sauce
2 tbsp sesame oil

Directions

Whisk together all the ingredients, except the ribs, in a bowl. Add in the ribs and toss to coat. Cover and refrigerate for 4 hours. Remove the ribs from the marinade, reserving the marinade. Place them into a baking pan and fit in the air fryer basket. Insert the basket into the IP and put the air fryer lid on top.

Select Air Fry and set the temperature to 350 F and the cooking time to 30 minutes. Push Start. At the 20-minute mark, pour the reserved marinade over the ribs and cook for the remaining 10 minutes. Serve and enjoy!

Apple & Pork Burgers

Prep + Cook Time: 25 minutes | Serves: 2

Ingredients

1 apple, peeled and grated
12 oz ground pork
1 cup breadcrumbs

2 eggs, beaten
Salt and black pepper to taste
½ tsp ground cumin

½ tsp ground cinnamon

Directions

In a bowl, add the pork, apple, breadcrumbs, cumin, eggs, cinnamon, salt, and pepper; mix well. Shape into 4 even-sized burger patties. Arrange them on the greased air fryer basket and fit in your IP. Place the air fryer lid on top. Select Air Fry and set the temperature to 380 F and the cooking time to 14 minutes. Push Start. Serve.

Sichuan Pork Belly

Preparation 65 minutes | Serves: 6

Ingredients

1 lemon, halved
1 ½ lb pork belly
1 ½ tsp garlic powder

1 ½ tsp coriander powder
Salt and black pepper to taste
1 ½ dried thyme

1 ½ tsp dried oregano
1 ½ tsp cumin powder

Directions

In a small bowl, add the garlic powder, coriander powder, salt, black pepper, thyme, oregano, and cumin powder. Poke holes all around the pork, using a fork. Smear the spicy rub thoroughly on all sides with your hands and squeeze the lemon juice all over. Let sit for 5 minutes. Put the pork in the air fryer basket and fit it in your IP. Place the air fryer lid on top. Select Air Fry and set the temperature to 350 F and the time to 55 minutes.

Push Start. At the 30-minute mark, turn the pork with the help of two spatulas, increase the temperature to 390 F and continue cooking for the remaining 25 minutes. Once ready, remove it and place it on a chopping board to sit for 4 minutes before slicing. Serve the pork slices with a side of sautéed asparagus and hot sauce.

Smoking Hot Pork Skewers

Prep + Cook Time: 20 minutes + marinating time | Serves: 4

Ingredients

¼ cup soy sauce
1 lb pork steak, cubed
2 tsp smoked paprika

1 tsp powdered chili
1 tsp garlic salt
1 tsp red chili flakes

1 tbsp white wine vinegar
3 tbsp steak sauce

Skewing:

1 yellow squash, seeded and cubed
1 green squash, seeded and cubed

1 green pepper, cut into cubes
1 red pepper, cut into cubes

Salt and black pepper to taste

Directions

In a mixing bowl, add the pork cubes, soy sauce, smoked paprika, powdered chili, garlic salt, red chili flakes, white wine vinegar, and steak sauce. Mix well. Marinate them in the fridge for 1 hour.

After one hour, remove the marinated pork from the fridge. On each skewer, stick the pork cubes and vegetables in the order that you prefer. Have fun doing this. Once the pork cubes and vegetables are finished, arrange the skewers on the air fryer basket and fit in your IP. Place the air fryer lid on top. Select Air Fry and set the temperature to 380 F and the cooking time to 16 minutes. Turn over halfway through the cooking time. Serve.

Very Hot Rack Ribs

Prep + Cook Time: 40 minutes | Serves: 2

Ingredients

½ cup hot sauce
1 rack rib steak
1 tsp white pepper

1 tsp garlic powder
½ tsp red pepper flakes
1 tsp ginger powder

Salt to taste

Directions

Season the ribs with salt, garlic, ginger, white pepper, and red pepper flakes. Place them in the air fryer basket and fit it in your IP. Place the air fryer lid on top. Select Air Fry and set the temperature to 360 F and the cooking time to 30 minutes. Push Start. Turn over halfway through the cooking time. Remove the ribs onto a chopping board and let sit for 3 minutes before slicing. Plate and drizzle hot sauce over and serve. Enjoy!

Easy Pork Chops with Shallots

Prep + Cook Time: 20 minutes + marinating time | Serves: 3

Ingredients

2 shallots, chopped
2 garlic cloves, minced
3 pork chops

1 ½ tbsp sugar
4 stalks lemongrass, chopped
2 tbsp olive oil

1 ¼ tsp soy sauce
1 ¼ tsp fish sauce
1 ½ tsp black pepper

Directions

In a bowl, add the garlic, sugar, lemongrass, shallots, olive oil, soy sauce, fish sauce, and black pepper; mix well. Add the pork chops, coat them with the mixture and allow to marinate for 2 hours to get nice and savory.

Remove and shake the pork chops from the marinade and place them in the air fryer basket. Insert the basket into the IP and put the air fryer lid on top. Select Air Fry and set the temperature to 400 F and the cooking time to 12 minutes. Push Start. Turn over halfway through the cooking time. Serve and enjoy!

Asian-Style Pork Ribs

Prep + Cook Time: 30 minutes + marinating time | Serves: 3

Ingredients

2 cloves garlic, minced
1 lb pork ribs
1 tsp oregano

1 tbsp + 1 tbsp maple syrup
3 tbsp barbecue sauce
1 tbsp cayenne pepper

1 tsp sesame oil
1 tsp soy sauce
Salt and black pepper to taste

Directions

Put the chops on a chopping board and use a knife to cut them into smaller pieces of desired sizes. Put them in a mixing bowl, add the soy sauce, salt, pepper, oregano, one tablespoon of maple syrup, barbecue sauce, garlic, cayenne pepper, and sesame oil. Mix well and place the pork in the fridge to marinate in the spices for 2 hours.

Place the ribs in the air fryer basket. Insert the basket into the IP and put the air fryer lid on top. Select Air Fry and set the temperature to 350 F and the cooking time to 25 minutes. Push Start. At the 10-minute mark, turn the ribs using tongs, apply the remaining maple syrup, and continue cooking for the remaining 10 minutes. Serve.

Happy Macadamia Pork Rack

Prep + Cook Time: 50 minutes | Serves: 3

Ingredients

1 clove garlic, minced
1 lb pork rack
2 tbsp olive oil

1 cup macadamia nuts, chopped
1 tbsp breadcrumbs
1 egg, beaten

1 tbsp rosemary, chopped
Salt and black pepper to taste

Directions

Add the olive oil and garlic to a bowl. Mix vigorously with a spoon to make garlic oil. Place the rack of pork on a chopping board and brush it with the garlic oil using a brush. Sprinkle with salt and pepper. In a bowl, add breadcrumbs, nuts, and rosemary. Brush the meat with the egg on all sides and sprinkle the nut mixture generously over the pork. Press with hands. Put the coated pork in the air fryer basket fit in your IP.

Place the air fryer lid on top. Select Air Fry and set the temperature to 320 F and the cooking time to 35 minutes. Push Start. At the 30-minute mark, increase the temperature to 390 F, and cook for the remaining 5 minutes. Remove the meat onto a chopping board. Allow a sitting time of 10 minutes before slicing. Serve and enjoy!

British-Style Pulled Pork with Cheddar

Prep + Cook Time: 50 minutes | Serves: 2

Ingredients

5 thick bacon slices, chopped
1 cup grated Cheddar cheese
½ pound pork steak

1 tsp steak seasoning
2 bread buns, halved
Salt and black pepper to taste

½ tbsp Worcestershire sauce

Directions

Place the pork steak on a plate and season with pepper, salt, and steak seasoning. Place the pork in the greased air fryer basket. Insert the basket into the IP and put the air fryer lid on top. Select Air Fry and set the temperature to 400 F and the cooking time to 22 minutes. Push Start. Turn over halfway through the cooking time.

Once ready, remove the steak onto a chopping board and use two forks to shred the pork into small pieces. Place the chopped bacon in a small heatproof bowl and place the bowl in the air fryer basket. Put the air fryer lid and cook the bacon at 370 F for 10 minutes on Air Fry. Remove the bacon into a large bowl, add the pulled pork, Worcestershire sauce, and cheddar cheese. Season with salt and pepper. Spoon to scoop the meat into the halved buns and serve with a cheese or tomato dip. Enjoy!

Fall Pork Chops with Apples

Prep + Cook Time: 30 minutes | Serves: 3

Ingredients

Topping:

1 cup sliced apples
1 small onion, sliced
2 tbsp olive oil

1 tbsp apple cider vinegar
2 tsp thyme
¼ tsp brown sugar

2 tsp rosemary

Meat:

3 pork chops
¼ tsp smoked paprika

1 tbsp olive oil
1 tbsp apple cider vinegar

Salt and black pepper to taste

Directions

Mix all the topping ingredients in a bowl and set aside. Place the pork chops in the air fryer basket. Coat them with olive oil, vinegar, paprika, salt, and pepper. Add the basket to the IP. Put the air fryer lid on top. Select Air Fry and set the temperature to 350 F and the cooking time to 16 minutes. Push Start. At the 10-minute mark, turn over the chops, and pour the topping over; cook for the remaining 6 minutes. Serve immediately.

Creamy Pork Chops

Prep + Cook Time: 25 minutes | Serves: 4

Ingredients

4 pork chops, center-cut
½ cup breadcrumbs

2 tbsp flour
2 tbsp sour cream

Salt and black pepper to taste

Directions

Coat the chops with flour. Drizzle the cream over and rub gently to coat well. Spread the breadcrumbs onto a bowl, and coat each pork chop with crumbs. Spray the chops with oil and arrange them in the air fryer basket.

Fit the basket in your IP. Place the air fryer lid on top. Select Air Fry and set the temperature to 380 F and the cooking time to 14 minutes. Push Start. Turn once halfway through. Serve and enjoy!

Homemade Cheddar Pork Patties

Prep + Cook Time: 35 minutes | Serves: 2

Ingredients

2 bread buns, halved	2 tsp garlic powder	Salt and black pepper to taste
½ lb ground pork	1 tbsp tomato puree	
1 tbsp mixed herbs	1 tsp mustard	

Assembling:

1 large tomato, sliced in 2-inch rings	2 small lettuce leaves, cleaned
1 large onion, sliced in 2-inch rings	4 slices cheddar cheese

Directions

In a bowl, add the ground pork, mixed herbs, garlic powder, tomato puree, mustard, salt, and pepper and mix evenly. Form two patties out of the mixture and place them in the air fryer basket. Insert the basket into the IP and put the air fryer lid on top. Select Air Fry and set the temperature to 370 F and the cooking time to 15 minutes. Push Start. Turn over halfway through the cooking time.

Remove them onto a plate and start assembling the burger. Place two halves of the bun on a clean flat surface. Add the lettuce in both, then a patty each, followed by an onion ring each, a tomato ring each, and then 2 slices of cheddar cheese each. Cover the buns with their other halves. Serve with ketchup and french fries.

Easy Teriyaki Pork Ribs

Prep + Cook Time: 20 minutes + marinating time | Serves: 3

Ingredients

1 garlic clove, minced	1 tsp five-spice powder	1 tbsp water
1 pound pork ribs	1 tbsp teriyaki sauce	1 tbsp tomato sauce
1 tbsp sugar	1 tbsp light soy sauce	Salt and black pepper to taste
1 tsp ginger juice	2 tbsp honey	

Directions

In a bowl, mix the black pepper, sugar, five-spice powder, salt, ginger juice, and teriyaki sauce. Add in the pork ribs and toss to coat. Let marinate for 2 hours. Add pork ribs to the air fryer basket and fit in your IP. Place the air fryer lid on top. Select Air Fry and set the temperature to 380 F and the cooking time to 16 minutes. Push Start.

Turn over halfway through the cooking time. In a separate mixing bowl, mix the soy sauce, garlic, honey, water, garlic, and tomato sauce. Remove the pork ribs and pour the prepared sauce over. Serve and enjoy!

Chinese-Style Pork Belly

Prep + Cook Time: 60 minutes | Serves: 4

Ingredients

1 tsp five-spice seasoning	½ tsp white pepper	1 tsp salt
1 ½ lb pork belly, blanched	¾ tsp garlic powder	

Directions

Pierce the belly's skin with a skewer as many times as you can so you can ensure crispiness. Combine the seasonings in a small bowl and rub the spice mixture onto the pork. Place the pork into the air fryer basket and fit in your IP. Place the air fryer lid on top. Select Air Fry and set the temperature to 360 F and the cooking time to 50 minutes. Push Start. Let cool slightly before serving.

Effortless BBQ Pork Ribs

Prep + Cook Time: 35 minutes + chilling time | Serves: 2

Ingredients

3 garlic cloves, chopped
1 lb pork ribs
½ tsp five-spice powder

1 tsp soy sauce
1 tsp black pepper
1 tsp sesame oil

1 tbsp honey + for brushing
4 tbsp barbecue sauce
1 tsp salt

Directions

In a bowl, whisk together all of the ingredients, except for the pork. Chop the ribs into smaller pieces and add them to the bowl. Mix until the pork is fully coated. Cover the bowl and place it in the fridge for about 4 hours.

Arrange the ribs on the greased air fryer basket and fit in your IP. Place the air fryer lid on top. Select Air Fry and set the temperature to 370 F and the cooking time to 25 minutes. Push Start. At the 15-minute mark, brush the ribs with some honey and cook for the remaining 10 minutes. Serve and enjoy!

Sweet Pork Chops

Prep + Cook Time: 15 minutes | Serves: 3

Ingredients

1 tbsp yellow mustard
3 pork chops, ½-inch thick

1 tbsp maple syrup
1 ½ tbsp minced garlic

Salt and black pepper to taste

Directions

In a bowl, add maple syrup, garlic, mustard, salt, and pepper; mix well. Add the pork and toss it in the mustard sauce to coat well. Place the chops in the air fryer basket and fit it in your IP. Place the air fryer lid on top. Select Air Fry and set the temperature to 350 F and the cooking time to 14 minutes. Push Start. Turn once. Serve.

Pear Pork Tenderloins

Prep + Cook Time: 60 minutes | Serves: 4

Ingredients

1 tbsp olive oil
1 tbsp soy sauce

4 pork tenderloins
1 pear, wedged

1 cinnamon quill
Salt and black pepper to taste

Directions

In a bowl, add pork, pear, cinnamon, olive oil, soy sauce, salt, and black pepper; stir to coat well. Let sit at room temperature for 25-35 minutes. Put the pork, pear, and a little bit of marinade into a baking pan and fit in the air fryer basket. Place the basket in your IP. Place the air fryer lid on top. Select Air Fry and set the temperature to 380 F and the cooking time to 14 minutes. Push Start. Serve hot.

French Pork Chops

Prep + Cook Time: 25 minutes | Serves: 3

Ingredients

1 lemon, zested
3 lean pork chops
2 eggs
½ tsp garlic powder

3 tsp paprika
1 ½ tsp oregano
½ tsp cayenne pepper
¼ tsp dry mustard

1 tbsp water
1 cup breadcrumbs
Salt and black pepper to taste

Directions

in a bowl, beat the eggs with 1 tbsp of water. In another bowl, add the breadcrumbs, salt, pepper, garlic powder, paprika, oregano, cayenne pepper, lemon zest, and dry mustard and mix to combine.

Dip each pork chop in the eggs and then in the breadcrumb mixture. Place the breaded chops in the greased air fryer basket. Insert the basket into the IP and put the air fryer lid on top. Select Air Fry and set the temperature to 360 F and the cooking time to 16 minutes. Push Start. Turn over halfway through the cooking time. Serve.

Pork Chops with Caramelized Potatoes

Prep + Cook Time: 35 minutes + marinating time | Serves: 4

Ingredients

4 pork chops
2 whole caramelized potatoes
2 tbsp tamarind paste
1 tbsp garlic, minced

½ cup green mole sauce
3 tbsp corn syrup
1 tbsp olive oil
2 tbsp molasses

4 tbsp southwest seasoning
2 tbsp ketchup
2 tbsp water

Directions

In a bowl, mix all the ingredients except potatoes, pork chops, and mole sauce. Let the pork chops marinate in the mixture for 30 minutes. Place the pork chops in the air fryer basket and fit in your IP. Place the air fryer lid on top. Select Air Fry and set the temperature to 350 F and the cooking time to 25 minutes. Push Start. Turn over halfway through the cooking time. Serve with caramelized potatoes and mole sauce. Enjoy!

Classic Pork Ribs

Prep + Cook Time: 30 minutes | Serves: 4

Ingredients

2 pounds pork ribs
2 tbsp olive oil

½ tsp mixed peppercorns, cracked
1 tsp red pepper flakes

1 tsp mustard powder
Sea salt to taste

Directions

In a bowl, mix the olive oil, cracked peppercorns, red pepper flakes, and mustard powder. Rub the mixture over the ribs. Arrange them on the greased air fryer basket. Insert the basket into the IP and put the air fryer lid on top. Select Air Fry and set the temperature to 400 F and the cooking time to 30 minutes. Push Start. At the 12-minute mark, turn the heat to 330 F and cook for the remaining 18 minutes. Serve and enjoy!

Sicilian Herby Pork Chops

Prep + Cook Time: 30 minutes | Serves: 4

Ingredients

1 whole egg, beaten
1 tbsp flour
4 slices pork chops, sliced

3 tbsp olive oil
Salt and black pepper to taste
Breadcrumbs as needed

A bunch of Italian herbs

Directions

Mix oil, salt, and pepper to form a marinade. Place the beaten egg in a bowl. On a separate plate, add the breadcrumbs. Add pork to the marinade and allow to rest for 15 minutes. Add one slice in egg and then to breadcrumbs; repeat with all slices. Place the prepared slices in the air fryer basket and fit it in your IP.

Place the air fryer lid on top. Select Air Fry and set the temperature to 400 F and the cooking time to 20 minutes. Push Start. Turn over halfway through the cooking time. Serve and enjoy!

Dutch-Style Pork Meatballs

Prep + Cook Time: 25 minutes | Serves: 4

Ingredients

1 large onion, chopped
1 lb ground pork
½ tsp maple syrup

2 tsp mustard
½ cup chopped basil leaves
2 tbsp cheddar cheese, grated

Salt and black pepper to taste

Directions

In a mixing bowl, add the ground pork, onion, maple syrup, mustard, basil leaves, salt, pepper, and cheddar cheese; mix well. Form balls. Place them in the air fryer basket and fit it in your IP. Place the air fryer lid on top. Select Air Fry and set the temperature to 380 F and the cooking time to 16 minutes. Push Start. Shake halfway through the cooking time. Serve and enjoy!

Hot Chili Pork Chops with Rice

Prep + Cook Time: 40 minutes | Serves: 4

Ingredients

1 onion, chopped
3 garlic cloves, minced
2 pork chops
1 tsp garlic powder

1 ½ cups white rice, cooked
2 tbsp olive oil
1 can (14.5 oz) tomato sauce
½ tsp oregano

1 tsp chipotle chili
1 lime juice
Salt and black pepper to taste

Directions

Season pork chops with salt, pepper, and garlic powder. In a bowl, mix onion, garlic, chipotle, oregano, and tomato sauce. Add the pork to the mixture. Let marinate for 1 hour. Remove the meat from the mixture and allow the mixture to sit for 15 minutes. After, place them into the air fryer basket and fit in your IP.

Place the air fryer lid on top. Select Air Fry and set the temperature to 350 F and the cooking time to 25 minutes. Push Start. Turn over halfway through the cooking time. Serve and enjoy!

Traditional Ratatouille with Sausage

Prep + Cook Time: 35 minutes | Serves: 4

Ingredients

4 pork sausages

For Ratatouille

15 oz tomatoes, chopped
2 garlic cloves, minced
1 bell pepper, chopped
2 zucchinis, chopped

1 eggplant, chopped
1 medium red onion, chopped
1 tbsp olive oil
1-ounce butter beans, drained

2 sprigs fresh thyme
1 tbsp balsamic vinegar
1 red chili, chopped

Directions

Drizzle the bell pepper, eggplant, onion, and zucchinis with olive oil and add to the air fryer basket. Insert the basket into the IP and put the air fryer lid on top. Select Roast and set the temperature to 390 F and the cooking time to 14 minutes. Push Start.

Press Sauté on your IP and mix the roasted vegetables and the remaining ratatouille ingredients and bring to a boil. Simmer for 10 minutes; season with salt and pepper. Remove to a baking pan ad add in the sausage. Place the pan in the air fryer basket. Fit the basket in the IP. Place the air fryer lid on top. Select Air Fry and set the temperature to 380 F and the cooking time to 10 minutes. Push Start. Serve warm.

Bacon & Sausage Rolls

Prep + Cook Time: 45 minutes | Serves: 4

Ingredients

Sausage:

8 pork sausages   8 bacon strips

Relish:

8 large tomatoes   3 tbsp chopped parsley   1 tbsp white wine vinegar
1 clove garlic, peeled   2 tbsp sugar   Salt and black pepper to taste
1 small onion, peeled   1 tsp smoked paprika

Directions

Start with the relish; add the tomatoes, garlic, and onion in a food processor. Blitz them for 10 seconds until the mixture is pulpy. Set your IP to Sauté and pour in the pulp, vinegar, salt, and pepper. Bring to simmer for 10 minutes; add the paprika and sugar. Stir with a spoon and simmer for 10 minutes until pulpy and thick. Transfer the relish to a bowl and place in the refrigerator to chill while preparing the sausage rolls.

Wrap each sausage with a bacon strip neatly and stick in a bamboo skewer at the end of the sausage to secure the bacon ends. Place the sausages in the air fryer basket and fit it in your IP. Put the air fryer lid on top. Select Air Fry and set the temperature to 350 F and the cooking time to 12 minutes. Push Start. The bacon should be golden and crispy. Remove the relish from the refrigerator. Serve the sausages and relish with turnip mash.

Cheesy Ham Muffins

Prep + Cook Time: 25 minutes | Serves: 6

Ingredients

1 cup milk   1 ½ cups Swiss cheese, grated   Salt and black pepper to taste
3 whole eggs, beaten   ¼ cup green onion, chopped
6 ham slices   ½ tsp thyme

Directions

In a bowl, mix beaten eggs, thyme, onion, salt, Swiss cheese, pepper, and milk. Prepare baking forms and place ham slices in each baking form. Top with the egg mixture. Place the prepared muffin forms in the air fryer basket and fit it in your IP. Place the air fryer lid on top. Select Air Fry and set the temperature to 350 F and the cooking time to 15 minutes. Push Start. Serve and enjoy!

Nutty Pork Bites

Prep + Cook Time: 40 minutes | Serves: 6

Ingredients

1 whole egg, beaten   2 tbsp dried sage   3 ½ oz apple, sliced
3 ½ oz onion, chopped   2 tbsp almonds, chopped   ½ tsp salt
16 oz sausage meat   ½ tsp pepper

Directions

In a bowl, mix the onion, almonds, apples, egg, pepper, and salt. Add the almond mixture and sausage in a Ziploc bag; mix to coat. Shape the mixture into cutlets. Add them to your fryer basket and fit in your IP. Place the air fryer lid on top. Select Air Fry and set the temperature to 350 F and the cooking time to 25 minutes. Push Start. Serve with heavy cream and enjoy!

Garlic Sausages Balls

Prep + Cook Time: 25 minutes | Serves: 4

Ingredients

1 cup onion, chopped
1 pound sausages, sliced

3 tbsp breadcrumbs
½ tsp garlic puree

1 tsp thyme
Salt and black pepper to taste

Directions

In a bowl, mix onions, sausage, thyme, garlic puree, salt, and pepper. Add breadcrumbs to a plate. Form balls from the mixture and roll them in breadcrumbs. Add the balls to the air fryer basket and fit in your IP. Place the air fryer lid on top. Select Air Fry and set the temperature to 360 F and the cooking time to 15 minutes. Push Start.

Fancy Stuffed Pork Chops

Prep + Cook Time: 40 minutes | Serves: 4

Ingredients

4 garlic cloves, minced
8 pork chops

4 cups stuffing mix
Salt and black pepper to taste

2 tbsp olive oil
2 tbsp sage leaves

Directions

Cut a hole in pork chops and fill them with the stuffing mix. In a bowl, mix sage leaves, garlic cloves, oil, salt, and pepper. Cover chops with marinade and let marinate for 10 minutes. Place the chops in the air fryer basket and fit it in your IP. Place the air fryer lid on top. Select Air Fry and set the temperature to 350 F and the cooking time to 25 minutes. Push Start. Flip halfway through the cooking time. Serve and enjoy!

"Yes Sir" Franks in Blanket

Prep + Cook Time: 20 minutes | Serves: 4

Ingredients

8 oz can crescent rolls

12 oz cocktail franks

Directions

Use a paper towel to pat the cocktail franks to drain completely. Cut the dough in 1 by 1.5-inch rectangles using a knife. Gently roll the franks in the strips, making sure the ends are visible. Place in freezer for 5 minutes.

Take the franks out of the freezer. Place them in the air fryer basket and fit it in your IP. Place the air fryer lid on top. Select Air Fry and set the temperature to 350 F and the cooking time to 12 minutes. Push Start. Serve.

Easy Brunch H&C Sandwich

Prep + Cook Time: 15 minutes | Serves: 4

Ingredients

8 tomato slices
8 whole-wheat bread slices

4 lean pork ham slices
4 cheddar cheese slices

Directions

Lay four slices of bread on a flat surface. Cover 4 bread slices with cheese, tomatoes, turkey, and ham. Cover with the remaining bread slices to form sandwiches. Add the sandwiches to the air fryer basket and fit in your IP. Place the air fryer lid on top. Select Air Fry and set the temperature to 360 F and the cooking time to 10 minutes. Push Start. Flip halfway through the cooking time. Serve and enjoy!

SEAFOOD & FISH RECIPES

Homemade Crab Croquettes

Prep + Cook Time: 30 minutes | Serves: 4

Ingredients

Filling:

1 red pepper, chopped finely
⅓ cup chopped red onion
1 ½ lb lump crab meat
3 egg whites, beaten

⅓ cup sour cream
⅓ cup mayonnaise
1 ½ tbsp olive oil
2 ½ tbsp chopped celery

½ tsp chopped tarragon
½ tsp chopped chives
1 tsp chopped parsley
1 tsp cayenne pepper

Breading:

4 eggs, beaten
1 ½ cup breadcrumbs

2 tsp olive oil
1 cup flour

Salt to taste

Directions

Heat 1 tbsp of olive oil in your IP on Sauté and add the red pepper, onion, and celery. Sauté for 5 minutes or until sweaty and translucent; remove. Add the breadcrumbs, the remaining olive oil, and salt to a food processor. Blend to mix evenly; set aside. In 2 separate bowls, add the flour and 4 eggs, respectively.

In a separate bowl, add the crabmeat, mayo, egg whites, sour cream, tarragon, chives, parsley, cayenne pepper, and the sautéed vegetables and mix evenly. Form into croquettes shapes from the mixture.

Dip the crab croquettes into the egg mixture and press them in the breadcrumb mixture. Place the croquettes in the fryer basket; avoid overcrowding. Insert the basket into the IP and put the air fryer lid on top. Select Air Fry and set the temperature to 390 F and the cooking time to 12 minutes. Push Start. Turn over halfway through the cooking time. When cooking is complete, the croquettes should be golden brown. Serve and enjoy!

Awesome Seafood Pie

Prep + Cook Time: 60 minutes | Serves: 3

Ingredients

1 small tomato, diced
1 cup seafood marinara mix
1 lb russet potatoes, quartered
1 carrot, grated
½ head baby fennel, grated

1 bunch dill sprigs, chopped
1 sprig parsley, chopped
A handful of baby spinach
½ celery sticks, grated
2 tbsp butter

1 tbsp milk
1 small red chili, minced
½ lemon, juiced
Salt and black pepper to taste
½ cup grated Cheddar cheese

Directions

Set your IP to Sauté. Add the potatoes and cover with water. Seal the lid, select manual, and cook for 12 minutes. Once the cooking process ends, use a quick pressure release. Drain the water and use a potato masher to mash. Add the butter, milk, salt, and pepper. Mash until smooth and well mixed; set aside.

In a bowl, add the celery, carrots, cheese, chili, fennel, parsley, lemon juice, seafood mix, dill, tomato, spinach, salt, and pepper; mix well. Onto a baking pan, spread half of the carrot mixture. Top with half of the potato mash and level. Place the dish in the air fryer basket and fit it in your IP. Place the air fryer lid on top.

Select Air Fry and set the temperature to 360 F and the cooking time to 20 minutes. Push Start. Remove the dish and add the remaining seafood mixture and level out. Top with the remaining potato mash and level it too. Place the dish back to the fryer and cook at 330 F for 20 minutes. Slice the pie and serve with salad if desired.

Cheesy Shrimp Risotto

Prep + Cook Time: 25 minutes | Serves: 4

Ingredients

½ cup cooked shrimp, chopped
4 whole eggs, beaten

½ cup rice, cooked
½ cup baby spinach

½ cup Monterey Jack cheese, grated
Pinch of salt

Directions

In a small bowl, add the eggs, salt, and basil and stir until frothy. Add the cooked rice, spinach, and shrimp to a greased baking pan. Pour egg mixture over and top with cheese. Place the pan in the air fryer basket and fit in your IP. Place the air fryer lid on top. Select Bake and set the temperature to 350 F and the cooking time to 14 minutes. Push Start. Serve immediately.

American-Style Calamari

Prep + Cook Time: 20 minutes + chilling time | Serves: 3

Ingredients

2 large eggs, beaten
½ lb calamari rings

½ cup cornmeal or cornstarch
2 garlic cloves, mashed

1 cup breadcrumbs
2 tbsp lemon juice

Directions

In a bowl, mix the eggs and garlic. Coat the calamari rings with the cornmeal. Dip the calamari in the egg mixture. Then dip them in the breadcrumbs. Put the rings in the fridge for 2 hours. Then, line them on the air fryer basket and fit in your IP. Place the air fryer lid on top. Select Air Fry and set the temperature to 390 F and the cooking time to 12 minutes. Push Start. Shak once. Serve topped with lemon juice.

Air Fried Bacon Prawns

Prep + Cook Time: 30 minutes + chilling time | Serves: 4

Ingredients

8 jumbo prawns, peeled and deveined
8 bacon slices   Lemon Wedges for garnishing

Directions

Wrap each prawn from head to tail with each bacon slice overlapping to keep the bacon in place. Secure the end of the bacon with a toothpick. It's ok not to cover the ends of the cheese with bacon. Refrigerate for 15 minutes. Arrange the bacon-wrapped prawns in the fryer basket fit in your IP. Place the air fryer lid on top.

Select Air Fry and set the temperature to 400 F and the cooking time to 7 minutes. Push Start. Flip halfway through the cooking time. The wrapped prawns should be browned and crispy. Serve with lemon wedges.

Ligurian Octopus

Prep + Cook Time: 30 minutes | Serves: 3

Ingredients

2 garlic cloves, minced
1 lb baby octopus, cleaned
1 ½ tbsp olive oil
1 ½ tbsp capers
1 ¼ tbsp balsamic glaze

1 bunch parsley, chopped roughly
1 bunch baby fennel, chopped
1 cup semi-dried tomatoes, chopped
¼ cup chopped grilled Halloumi
1 long red chili, minced

1 red onion, sliced
A handful of arugula
Salt and black pepper to taste

Directions

Set your IP to Sauté and pour 2 cups of water and bring to boil. Cut the octopus into bite sizes and add them to the boiling water. Cook for 5 minutes. Then drain. Place it in the fryer basket and coat it with garlic and olive oil. Insert the basket into the IP and put the air fryer lid on top. Select Air Fry and set the temperature to 390 F and the cooking time to 12 minutes. Push Start. Remove to a plate.

In a salad bowl, add the capers, halloumi, chili, tomatoes, olives, parsley, red onion, fennel, octopus, arugula, and balsamic glaze. Season with salt and pepper and mix. Top with the octopus and serve.

Hot Mayo Crab Cakes

Prep + Cook Time: 20 minutes | Serves: 8

Ingredients

2 eggs, beaten	⅓ cup finely chopped green onion	1 tsp sweet chili sauce
1 lb crabmeat, shredded	¼ cup parsley, chopped	Salt and black pepper to taste
½ cup breadcrumbs	1 tbsp mayonnaise	½ tsp paprika

Directions

In a bowl, add meat, eggs, crumbs, green onion, parsley, mayo, chili sauce, paprika, salt, and black pepper and mix well with hands. Shape into 8 cakes and grease them lightly with oil. Arrange the cakes into the air fryer basket without overcrowding. Insert the basket into the IP and put the air fryer lid on top. Select Bake and set the temperature to 400 F and the cooking time to 8 minutes. Push Start. Turn over halfway through cooking.

Honey Coconut Shrimp

Prep + Cook Time: 30 minutes | Serves: 2

Ingredients

2 tbsp coconut milk	½ cup orange jam	¼ tsp hot sauce
½ pound large shrimp	1 tsp mustard	Salt and black pepper to taste
½ cup breadcrumbs	1 tbsp honey	
½ cup shredded coconut	½ tsp cayenne pepper	

Directions

Combine breadcrumbs, cayenne pepper, shredded coconut, salt, and pepper in a bowl. Dip the shrimp in the coconut milk and then in the coconut crumbs. Arrange them on the greased air fryer basket and fit in your IP. Place the air fryer lid on top. Select Air Fry and set the temperature to 350 F and the cooking time to 20 minutes. Push Start. Meanwhile, whisk the jam, honey, hot sauce, and mustard. Serve shrimp drizzled with the sauce.

Old-Fashioned Tiger Shrimp

Prep + Cook Time: 15 minutes | Serves: 4

Ingredients

1 tbsp olive oil	½ a tbsp old bay seasoning	¼ a tbsp smoked paprika
5-6 oz tiger shrimp, 12 to 16 pieces	¼ a tbsp cayenne pepper	A pinch of sea salt

Directions

Mix all ingredients in a large bowl. Coat the shrimp with a little bit of oil and spices. Place the shrimp in the air fryer basket and fit it in your IP. Place the air fryer lid on top. Select Air Fry and set the temperature to 380 F and the cooking time to 7 minutes. Push Start. Serve with rice or salad if desired.

Crunchy Crab Balls with Mustard

Prep + Cook Time: 20 minutes | Serves: 4

Ingredients

¼ tsp Dijon mustard
Zest of ½ lemon
½ pound jumbo crab

Lemon juice to taste
2 tbsp parsley, chopped
Old bay seasoning as needed

1 tbsp basil, chopped
3 tbsp real mayo
¼ cup panko breadcrumbs

Directions

In a bowl, mix the mayo, lemon zest, old bay seasoning, mustard, and oil. Blend crab meat in a food processor and season with salt. Fold into the mayo mixture. Form cakes from the mixture and dredge them into breadcrumbs. Place the cakes in the air fryer basket and fit it in your IP. Place the air fryer lid on top. Select Air Fry and set the temperature to 400 F and the cooking time to 15 minutes. Push Start. Serve topped with basil and lemon juice.

Easy Crab Cakes

Prep + Cook Time: 55 minutes | Serves: 4

Ingredients

¼ cup chopped red onion
¼ cup chopped celery
½ cup cooked crab meat
1 tbsp chopped basil

¼ cup chopped red pepper
3 tbsp mayonnaise
Zest of half a lemon
¼ cup breadcrumbs

2 tbsp chopped parsley
½ tsp Old bay seasoning

Directions

Place all ingredients in a large bowl and mix well. Make 4 large crab cakes from the mixture and place them on a lined sheet. Refrigerate for 30 minutes to set. Spay the air basket with cooking spray and arrange the crab cakes inside it. Place the baking pan inside the air fryer basket. Insert the basket into the IP and put the air fryer lid on top. Select Bake and set the temperature to 390 F and the cooking time to 14 minutes. Push Start. Serve warm.

Spicy Jumbo Shrimp

Prep + Cook Time: 10 minutes | Serves: 3

Ingredients

1 tbsp olive oil
1 lb jumbo shrimp

¼ tsp old bay seasoning
¼ tsp chili powder

⅓ tsp smoked paprika
Salt to taste

Directions

In a bowl, add the shrimp, paprika, oil, salt, old bay seasoning, and chili powder; mix well. Place the shrimp in the air fryer basket and fit it in your IP. Place the air fryer lid on top. Select Air Fry and set the temperature to 390 F and the cooking time to 5 minutes. Push Start. Serve with mayo and rice.

Air Fried Mussels in White Wine

Prep + Cook Time: 25 minutes | Serves: 4

Ingredients

2 garlic cloves
4 bread slices
4 pounds mussels
2 tbsp olive oil

1 cup white wine
2 tsp salt
2 bay leaves
1 tbsp pepper

1 ½ cup flour
1 tbsp fenugreek
2 tbsp vinegar
½ cup mixed nuts

Directions

Add bay leaves, wine, and mussels to your IP. Seal the lid, select manual, and cook for 3 minutes on High. Once the cooking process ends, use a quick pressure release. Take the mussels out and drain; discard any unopened. Remove from shells and place them into a baking pan.

Add oil, garlic, vinegar, salt, nuts, fenugreek, pepper, and bread to a food processor and process until you obtain a creamy texture. Stir in the flour. Pour the mixture over the mussels and insert the pan in the air fryer basket.

Put the air fryer lid on top. Select Bake and set the temperature to 350 F and the cooking time to 10 minutes. Push Start. Serve with fenugreek and enjoy.

Chinese Shrimp with Peanut Butter

Prep + Cook Time: 30 minutes | Serves: 5

Ingredients

4 garlic cloves
1 ½ pound shrimp
2 scallions, chopped
Juice of 1 lemon

1 tsp sugar
3 tbsp peanut oil, melted
2 tbsp cornstarch
¼ tsp Chinese powder

1 chili pepper, minced
Salt and black pepper to taste

Directions

In a Ziploc bag, mix the lemon juice, sugar, pepper, peanut oil, cornstarch, Chinese powder, and salt. Add in the shrimp and massage to coat evenly. Let sit for 10 minutes. Place the marinated shrimp, garlic, chili, and scallions in a baking pan and insert the pan in the air fryer basket. Put the air fryer lid on top.

Select Bake and set the temperature to 370 F and the cooking time to 10 minutes. Push Start. When cooking is complete, the shrimp should be nice and crispy. Serve and enjoy!

Shrimp Medley Asian-Style

Prep + Cook Time: 20 minutes | Serves: 4

Ingredients

2 cloves garlic, chopped
2 whole onions, chopped
1 pound shrimp

3 tbsp butter
1 ½ tbsp sugar
2 tbsp soy sauce

1 tsp ginger, chopped
2 tsp lime juice

Directions

Place the shrimp in a baking pan. In a bowl, mix the onions, lime juice, soy sauce, ginger, garlic, sugar, and butter. Pour the mixture over shrimp. Place the pan in the air fryer basket and fit it in your IP. Place the air fryer lid on top. Select Air Fry and set the temperature to 350 F and the cooking time to 12 minutes. Push Start. Serve.

Simple Crispy Salmon

Prep + Cook Time: 20 minutes | Serves: 2

Ingredients

2 salmon fillets

Zest of a lemon

Salt to taste

Directions

Spray the fillets with olive oil and rub them with salt and lemon zest. Place them in your air fryer basket. Insert the basket into the IP and put the air fryer lid on top. Select Air Fry and set the temperature to 360 F and the cooking time to 10 minutes. Push Start. Turn halfway through. Serve drizzled with lemon juice.

Rosemary Prawns in Butter

Prep + Cook Time: 15 minutes + chilling time | Serves: 2

Ingredients

3 garlic cloves, minced
8 large prawns

1 rosemary sprig, chopped
½ tbsp melted butter

Salt and black pepper to taste

Directions

Combine the garlic, butter, rosemary, salt, and pepper in a bowl. Add the prawns to the bowl and mix to coat them well. Cover the bowl and refrigerate for 1 hour. Transfer the prawns to the greased air fryer basket and fit in your IP. Place the air fryer lid on top. Select Air Fry and set the temperature to 350 F and the cooking time to 6 minutes. Push Start. Shake halfway through the cooking time. Serve and enjoy!

Fancy Fried Scallops

Prep + Cook Time: 15 minutes | Serves: 6

Ingredients

1 egg, lightly beaten
12 fresh scallops

3 tbsp flour
Salt and black pepper to taste

1 cup breadcrumbs

Directions

Coat the scallops with flour. Dip into the egg, then into the breadcrumbs. Spray them with olive oil and arrange them on the air fryer basket and fit in your IP. Place the air fryer lid on top. Select Air Fry and set the temperature to 360 F and the cooking time to 6 minutes. Push Start. Turn over halfway through cooking. Serve and enjoy!

Effortless Crispy Crab Legs

Prep + Cook Time: 25 minutes | Serves: 3

Ingredients

2 cups butter, melted

3 pounds crab legs

1 cup salted water

Directions

Dip the crab legs in salted water; let stay for a few minutes. Place the crab legs in the air fryer basket and fit it in your IP. Place the air fryer lid on top. Select Air Fry and set the temperature to 380 F and the cooking time to 10 minutes. Push Start. Pour the butter over the crab legs to serve.

Cayenne-Spiced Calamari Rings

Prep + Cook Time: 25 minutes | Serves: 5

Ingredients

1 large egg, beaten
1 cup all-purpose flour
12 oz frozen squid

1 tsp ground coriander seeds
1 tsp cayenne pepper
½ tsp pepper

½ tsp salt
olive oil for spray
Lemon wedges, to garnish

Directions

In a bowl, mix the flour, ground pepper, paprika, cayenne pepper, and salt. Dredge calamari in eggs, followed by the floured mixture. Place the in the greased air fryer basket. Insert the basket into the IP and put the air fryer lid on top. Select Air Fry and set the temperature to 390 F and the cooking time to 15 minutes. Push Start. Garnish with lemon wedges, and enjoy!

The Quickest Shrimp Bowl

Prep + Cook Time: 15 minutes | Serves: 6

Ingredients

1 tbsp olive oil
1 ¼ pound tiger shrimp

¼ tsp cayenne pepper
½ tsp old bay seasoning

¼ tsp smoked paprika
A pinch of salt

Directions

In a bowl, mix all the ingredients. Place the mixture in the air fryer basket and fit it in your IP. Place the air fryer lid on top. Select Air Fry and set the temperature to 390 F and the cooking time to 5 minutes. Push Start. Serve.

Air Fried Mixed Seafood

Prep + Cook Time: 15 minutes | Serves: 4

Ingredients

1 lb fresh scallops, mussels, fish fillets, prawns, shrimp
1 cup breadcrumbs mixed with zest of 1 lemon
2 eggs, lightly beaten   Salt and black pepper to taste

Directions

Clean the seafood as needed. Dip each piece into the egg and season with salt and pepper. Coat in the crumbs and spray with oil. Arrange in the air fryer basket and fit it in your IP. Place the air fryer lid on top. Select Air Fry and set the temperature to 400 F and the cooking time to 6 minutes. Push Start. Flip halfway through. Serve.

Classic Calamari Rings

Prep + Cook Time: 10 minutes + chilling time | Serves: 4

Ingredients

1 lb calamari (squid), cut in rings
2 large beaten eggs

1 cup breadcrumbs
¼ cup flour

Directions

Coat the calamari rings with the flour and dip them in the eggs. Then, roll in the breadcrumbs. Refrigerate for 2 hours. Line them in the air fryer basket and apply oil generously. Fit the basket in your IP. Place the air fryer lid on top. Select Air Fry and set the temperature to 380 F and the cooking time to 9 minutes. Push Start. Serve.

Sour Salmon Fillets with Broccoli

Prep + Cook Time: 25 minutes | Serves: 2

Ingredients

1 head broccoli, cut into florets
1 tsp olive oil
1 tbsp soy sauce

2 salmon fillets
1 tsp olive oil
Juice of 1 lime

1 tsp chili flakes
Salt and black pepper to taste

Directions

In a bowl, add oil, lime juice, flakes, salt, and black pepper; rub the mixture onto fillets. Lay the florets into the air fryer basket and fit in your IP. Place the air fryer lid on top. Select Air Fry and set the temperature to 380 F and the cooking time to 20 minutes. Push Start. At the 10-minute mark, arrange the fillets on top of the broccoli and cook for the remaining 10 minutes. Drizzle the florets with soy sauce and serve!

Savona Cod Sandwich with Pesto

Prep + Cook Time: 20 minutes | Serves: 4

Ingredients

4 lettuce leaves
½ cup capers
4 cod fillets

2 tbsp flour
4 bread rolls
2 oz breadcrumbs

4 tbsp pesto sauce
Salt and black pepper to taste

Directions

Season the fillets with salt and pepper, coat them with flour, and then roll them in the breadcrumbs. Arrange the fillets on the air fryer basket and fit in your IP. Place the air fryer lid on top. Select Air Fry and set the temperature to 370 F and the cooking time to 14 minutes. Push Start. Cut the bread rolls in half. Divide the lettuce leaves between the bread bottom halves; put the fillets over. Spread the pesto sauce on the fillets and cover with the remaining bread halves.

Breaded Haddock Fillets

Prep + Cook Time: 15 minutes | Serves: 4

Ingredients

1 egg, beaten
4 haddock fillets
1 cup breadcrumbs

2 tbsp lemon juice
Salt and black pepper to taste
¼ cup dry potato flakes

¼ cup Parmesan cheese, grated
3 tbsp flour

Directions

Combine the flour, black pepper, and salt in a small bowl. In another bowl, combine the lemon, breadcrumbs, Parmesan cheese, and potato flakes. Dip the fillets in the flour first, then in the beaten egg, and coat them with the lemony crumbs. Arrange on the air fryer basket and fit in your IP. Place the air fryer lid on top. Select Air Fry and set the temperature to 380 F and the cooking time to 10 minutes. Push Start. Serve and enjoy!

Healthy Salmon with Dill-Yogurt Sauce

Prep + Cook Time: 25minutes | Serves: 4

Ingredients

4 (6-oz) salmon pieces
2 tsp olive oil

3 tbsp chopped dill
1 cup sour cream

Salt and black pepper to taste

Directions

In a bowl, mix well the sour cream, yogurt, dill, and salt. Set aside until ready to use. Drizzle the olive oil over the salmon and rub it with salt and pepper. Arrange the salmon pieces on the fryer basket and fit in your IP. Place the air fryer lid on top. Select Air Fry and set the temperature to 350 F and the cooking time to 12 minutes. Push Start. Turn over halfway through the cooking time. Serve the salmon with the yogurt sauce.

Fried Fish Fillets

Prep + Cook Time: 20 minutes | Serves: 5

Ingredients

5 biscuits, crumbled
5 frozen fish fillets
3 tbsp flour

1 egg, beaten
¼ tsp rosemary
3 tbsp olive oil divided

A handful of sesame seeds
Salt and black pepper to taste

Directions

Combine the flour, pepper, and salt in a shallow bowl. In another shallow bowl, combine the sesame seeds, crumbled biscuits, oil, and rosemary. Dip the fish fillets into the flour mixture first, then into the beaten egg, and finally, coat them with the sesame mixture. Arrange them on the air fryer basket and fit in your IP.

Place the air fryer lid on top. Select Air Fry and set the temperature to 390 F and the cooking time to 12 minutes. Push Start. Flip the fillets over halfway through the cooking time. Serve and enjoy.

Cheesy Tuna Sandwich

Prep + Cook Time: 10 minutes | Serves: 2

Ingredients

2 small tins of tuna, drained
4 white bread slices

½ onion, finely chopped
2 tbsp mayonnaise

1 cup mozzarella cheese, shredded

Directions

Lay the bread out onto a board. In a bowl, mix tuna, onion, mayonnaise. Spoon the mixture over two bread slices. Top with cheese and put the other piece of bread on top. Spray with oil on each side and arrange the sandwiches on the air fryer basket. Insert the basket into the IP and put the air fryer lid on top. Select Air Fry and set the temperature to 350 F and the cooking time to 6 minutes. Push Start. Turn once. Serve.

French Trout en Papillote

Prep + Cook Time: 30 minutes | Serves: 2

Ingredients

½ brown onion, sliced
¾ lb whole trout, scaled and cleaned
¼ bulb fennel, sliced

3 tbsp chopped dill
2 tbsp olive oil
1 lemon, sliced

3 tbsp chopped parsley
Salt and black pepper to taste

Directions

In a bowl, add the onion, parsley, dill, fennel, and garlic. Mix and drizzle the olive oil over. Open the cavity of the fish and fill it with the fennel mixture. Wrap the fish completely in parchment paper and then in foil. Place the fish on the fryer basket and fit in your IP. Place the air fryer lid on top. Select Air Fry and set the temperature to 380 F and the cooking time to 10 minutes. Push Start. Remove the paper and foil and top with lemon slices.

Milanese Salmon with Parmesan & Pistachios

Prep + Cook Time: 20 minutes | Serves: 1

Ingredients

1 tsp mustard
3 tbsp pistachios, finely chopped
1 salmon fillet

1 tsp lemon juice
1 tsp grated Parmesan cheese
1 tsp olive oil

A pinch of sea salt
A pinch of garlic powder
A pinch of black pepper

Directions

Whisk the mustard and lemon juice in a bowl. Season the salmon with salt, pepper, and garlic powder. Drizzle with olive oil. Rub the mustard mixture onto the salmon. Combine the pistachios with Parmesan cheese and sprinkle the mixture over the salmon. Place the salmon in the air fryer basket with the skin side down.

Put the baking pan inside the air fryer basket. Insert the basket into the IP and put the air fryer lid on top. Select Bake and set the temperature to 350 F and the cooking time to 12 minutes. Push Start. Serve and enjoy!

Mountain-Style Trout in Dill Sauce

Prep + Cook Time: 30 minutes | Serves: 3

Ingredients

3 tbsp olive oil

3 trout fillets, 5-6 oz each

1 pinch salt

Dill Sauce:

½ cup sour cream

½ cup mayonnaise

2 tbsp finely chopped dill

1 pinch salt

Directions

Drizzle the trout with oil and season with salt. Place the seasoned trout into the air fryer basket. Insert the basket into the IP and put the air fryer lid on top. Select Air Fry and set the temperature to 350 F and the cooking time to 12 minutes. Push Start. In a large bowl, mix all the sauce ingredients. Serve with the trout.

Mashed Potatoes & Salmon Patties

Prep + Cook Time: 15 minutes + chilling time | Serves: 4

Ingredients

14 oz boiled and mashed potatoes

2 oz flour

10 oz cooked salmon

A handful of capers

A handful of chopped parsley

Zest of 1 lemon

Directions

Place the mashed potatoes in a large bowl and flake the salmon over. Stir in capers, parsley, and lemon zest. Shape small cakes out of the mixture. Dust them with flour and place in the fridge to set for 1 hour.

Add the cakes to the greased air fryer basket. Insert the basket into the IP and put the air fryer lid on top. Select Bake and set the temperature to 350 F and the cooking time to 8 minutes. Push Start. Serve and enjoy!

Celery Salmon Cakes

Prep + Cook Time: 13 minutes | Serves: 2

Ingredients

1 large egg

4 oz tinned salmon

4 tbsp celery, chopped

1 spring onion, sliced

½ tsp garlic powder

4 tbsp wheat germ

1 tbsp olive oil

1 tbsp dill, chopped

Directions

In a large bowl, mix the tinned salmon, egg, celery, spring onion, dill, and garlic. Shape the mixture into 2-inch-sized balls and roll them in the wheat germ, flatten them. Then add the balls to the air fryer greased basket and drizzle them with olive oil; fit in your IP. Place the air fryer lid on top. Select Air Fry and set the temperature to 390 F and the cooking time to 12 minutes. Push Start. Turn over halfway through the cooking time. Serve.

Miami Fish Tacos

Prep + Cook Time: 15 minutes | Serves: 4

Ingredients

1 halibut fillet

4 corn tortillas

2 tbsp olive oil1

½ cup flour, divided

4 tbsp peach salsa

4 tsp chopped cilantro

1 tsp baking powder

1 can of beer

1 tsp salt

Directions

Combine 1 cup of flour, baking, powder, and salt in a bowl. Pour in some of the beer, enough to form a batter-like consistency. Save the rest of the beer to gulp with the taco. Slice the fillet into 4 strips and toss them in the flour. Dip them into the beer batter and arrange on a lined baking sheet.

Place the baking sheet inside the air fryer basket. Insert the basket into the IP and put the air fryer lid on top. Select Bake and set the temperature to 390 F and the cooking time to 8 minutes. Push Start. Spread the peach salsa on the tortillas. Top each tortilla with fish strips and chopped cilantro. Serve and enjoy!

Gingery Cod Fillet with Honey

Prep + Cook Time: 20 minutes | Serves: 1

Ingredients

1 tsp olive oil	A few drops of sesame oil	A pinch of sea salt
1 cod fillet	¼ tsp ginger powder	A pinch of pepper
1 tbsp soy sauce	¼ tsp honey	

Directions

Rub the the cod with olive oil, salt, and pepper. Place the cod onto an aluminum sheet and into the air fryer basket. Insert the basket into the IP and put the air fryer lid on top. Select Air Fry and set the temperature to 370 F and the cooking time to 12 minutes. Push Start. Combine soy sauce, ginger, honey, and sesame oil. At the 6-minute mark, flip the fish, brush it with the glaze, and cook for the remaining 3 minutes.

Homemade Tuna Cakes

Prep + Cook Time: 50 minutes | Serves: 2

Ingredients

1 small onion, diced	1 tsp lime juice	½ cup milk
2 eggs	1 tsp paprika	1 tsp chili powder, optional
5 oz of canned tuna	¼ cup flour	½ tsp salt

Directions

Place all ingredients in a bowl and mix well to combine. Make two large patties out of the mixture. Place them on a lined sheet and refrigerate for 30 minutes. Place the baking pan inside the air fryer basket. Insert the basket into the IP and put the air fryer lid on top. Select Bake and set the temperature to 350 F and the cooking time to 14 minutes. Push Start. Turn over halfway through the cooking time. Serve and enjoy!

Air Fried Cod Nuggets

Prep + Cook Time: 25 minutes | Serves: 4

Ingredients

1 ¼ lb cod fillets, cut into 4 chunks each

½ cup flour	1 tbsp water	1 tbsp olive oil
1 egg	1 cup cornflakes	Salt and black pepper to taste

Directions

Place the oil and cornflakes in a food processor and process until crumbed. Season the fish chunks with salt and pepper. In a bowl, beat the egg along with water. Dredge the chunks in flour first, then dip in the egg, and coat with cornflakes. Arrange on the greased air fryer basket and fit in your IP. Place the air fryer lid on top. Select Air Fry and set the temperature to 350 F and the cooking time to 15 minutes. Push Start. Serve and enjoy!

Easy Fish Nuggets

Prep + Cook Time: 25 minutes | Serves: 4

Ingredients

28 oz fish fillets	1 tsp drilled dill	1 tbsp paprika
1 whole egg, beaten	4 tbsp mayonnaise	Lemon juice to taste
1 tbsp garlic powder	3 ½ oz breadcrumbs	Salt and black pepper to taste

Directions

Season the fish fillets with salt and pepper. In a bowl, mix the beaten egg, lemon juice, and mayonnaise. In a separate bowl, mix breadcrumbs, paprika, dill, and garlic powder. Dredge fillets in the egg mixture and then the garlic-paprika mix; repeat until all fillets are prepared. Place the fillets in the air fryer basket and fit it in your IP.

Place the air fryer lid on top. Select Air Fry and set the temperature to 400 F and the cooking time to 16 minutes. Push Start. Flip halfway through the cooking time. Serve and enjoy!

Sweet Cod in Soy Sauce

Prep + Cook Time: 20 minutes | Serves: 4

Ingredients

3 tbsp oil	5 tbsp light soy sauce	1 cup water
1 ¼ pounds cod fish fillets	1 tsp dark soy sauce	Salt to taste
4 tbsp chopped cilantro	5 cubes rock sugar	
5 slices of ginger	3 green onions, chopped	

Directions

Sprinkle the codfish with salt and cilantro; drizzle with oil. Place the fish fillet in the air fryer basket and fit it in your IP. Place the air fryer lid on top. Select Air Fry and set the temperature to 360 F and the cooking time to 15 minutes. Push Start. Place the remaining ingredients in a frying pan over medium heat; cook for 5 minutes. Serve the fish with the sauce and enjoy.

Quick & Crispy Salmon

Prep + Cook Time: 20 minutes | Serves: 2

Ingredients

2 salmon fillets	Salt and black pepper to taste

Directions

Coat the fish generously on both sides with cooking spray. Season with salt and pepper. Arrange the fillets skin-side-down on the air fryer basket and fit in your IP. Place the air fryer lid on top. Select Air Fry and set the temperature to 350 F and the cooking time to 10 minutes. Push Start. Turn once halfway through cooking.

Onion Frittata with Trout

Prep + Cook Time: 30 minutes | Serves: 6

Ingredients

2 smoked trout fillets, flaked	6 tbsp crème fraiche	A handful of fresh dill
1 onion, sliced	½ tbsp horseradish sauce	
1 egg, beaten	2 tbsp olive oil	

Directions

In a bowl, mix the egg, crème fraiche, horseradish, onion, and trout and mix well. Place the mixture in a baking pan and insert it in the air fryer basket. Put the air fryer lid on top. Select Bake and set the temperature to 320 F and the cooking time to 20 minutes. Push Start. Serve and enjoy!

Cod Fillets with Grapes

Prep + Cook Time: 25 minutes | Serves: 4

Ingredients

1 cup grapes, halved
1 small fennel bulb, sliced
2 black cod fillets

½ cup pecans
2 tsp white balsamic vinegar
2 tbsp extra virgin olive oil

Salt and black pepper to taste

Directions

Season the fillets with salt and pepper; drizzle oil on top. Place the fillet in the air fryer basket and fit it in your IP. Place the air fryer lid on top. Select Air Fry and set the temperature to 400 F and the time to 12 minutes.

Push Start. In a bowl, add grapes, pecans, and fennels. Drizzle oil over the grape mixture, and season with salt and pepper. At the 9-minute mark, add the mixture to the basket and cook for the remaining 3 minutes. Whisk the balsamic vinegar, oil, salt, and pepper in a bowl. Drizzle over the fish and serve.

Quick Salmon with Vegetables

Prep + Cook Time: 25 minutes | Serves: 2

Ingredients

2 sockeye salmon fillets (6 oz each)
8 cherry tomatoes, halved
2-3 fingerling potatoes, thinly sliced

½ bulb fennel, thinly sliced
4 tbsp melted butter
Salt and black pepper to taste

2 tsp fresh dill

Directions

Microwave the potatoes for 2 minutes and set aside. Cut 2 large-sized rectangles of parchment paper of 13x15 inch size. In a large bowl, mix potatoes, melted butter, fennel, fresh ground pepper, and salt. Divide the mixture between parchment paper pieces. Place fillet on top of veggie piles; season with salt and pepper.

Add cherry tomato on top of each veggie pile and drizzle with butter. Fold the squares and seal them. Place on the air fryer basket. Garnish with dill and enjoy!

Smoked Fish Tart

Prep + Cook Time: 35 minutes | Serves: 5

Ingredients

1 cup smoked mackerel, flaked
1 cup shredded mozzarella cheese
1 quiche pastry case

5 eggs, lightly beaten
4 tbsp heavy cream
¼ cup finely chopped green onions

2 tbsp chopped parsley
1 tsp baking powder
Salt and black pepper to taste

Directions

In a bowl, whisk eggs, cream, scallions, parsley, baking powder, salt, and pepper. Add in fish and cheese and stir to combine. Line the air fryer basket with baking paper. Pour the mixture into the pastry case and place it gently inside the air fryer. Insert the basket into the IP and put the air fryer lid on top. Select Bake and set the temperature to 360 F and the cooking time to 25 minutes. Push Start. Serve and enjoy!

White Fish with Parmesan & Nuts

Prep + Cook Time: 25 minutes | Serves: 6

Ingredients

6 white fish fillet
2 tbsp olive oil
1 bunch of basil

2 garlic cloves, minced
1 tbsp olive oil
2 tbsp pine nuts

1 tbsp Parmesan cheese, grated
Salt and black pepper to taste

Directions

Season the fillets with salt and pepper. Place the on the greased air fryer basket. Insert the basket into the IP and put the air fryer lid on top. Select Air Fry and set the temperature to 350 F and the cooking time to 8 minutes. Push Start. In a bowl, mix the basil, oil, pine nuts, garlic, and Parmesan cheese. Serve with the fish.

Alaskan Salmon with Parsley Sauce

Prep + Cook Time: 30 minutes | Serves: 4

Ingredients

2 tsp olive oil
4 Alaskan wild salmon fillets

Salt and pepper to taste
½ cup milk

½ cup heavy cream
2 tbsp chopped parsley

Directions

Add the salmon to the frying basket and drizzle with some oil. Season with salt and pepper. Fit the basket in your IP. Place the air fryer lid on top. Select Air Fry and set the temperature to 310 F and the cooking time to 25 minutes. Push Start. In a bowl, mix the remaining oil, heavy cream, milk, and parsley. Serve the salmon with the sauce.

Buttery Catfish Fillets

Prep + Cook Time: 20 minutes | Serves: 2

Ingredients

1 garlic clove, mashed
2 catfish fillets

2 tsp blackening seasoning
Juice of 1 lime

2 tbsp butter, melted
2 tbsp cilantro

Directions

In a bowl, blend the garlic, lime juice, cilantro, and butter. Divide the sauce into two parts, pour 1 part of the sauce over the fillets; Sprinkle the fillets with seasoning. Place the fillets in the air fryer basket and fit it in your IP. Place the air fryer lid on top. Select Air Fry and set the temperature to 360 F and the cooking time to 15 minutes. Push Start. Serve the cooked fish with the remaining sauce.

Old Bay Tilapia Fillets

Prep + Cook Time: 20 minutes | Serves: 4

Ingredients

2-3 butter buds
1 pound tilapia fillets

1 tbsp Old bay seasoning
2 tbsp canola oil

2 tbsp lemon pepper
Salt to taste

Directions

Drizzle the canola oil over tilapia fillets. In a bowl, mix salt, lemon pepper, butter buds, and seasoning; spread on the fish. Place the fillets in the air fryer basket and fit it in your IP. Place the air fryer lid on top. Select Air Fry and set the temperature to 400 F and the cooking time to 10 minutes. Push Start. Serve and enjoy!

Easy Catfish Fillets

Prep + Cook Time: 25 minutes | Serves: 4

Ingredients

¼ cup seasoned fish fry   4 catfish fillets, rinsed and dried   1 tbsp olive oil

Directions

Add fry and fillets in a large Ziploc bag; massage well to coat. Place the fillets in the air fryer basket and fit it in your IP. Place the air fryer lid on top. Select Air Fry and set the temperature to 400 F and the cooking time to 14 minutes. Push Start. Flip halfway through the cooking time. Serve and enjoy!

Capers, Potato & Salmon Fried Cakes

Prep + Cook Time: 15 minutes + chilling time | Serves: 2

Ingredients

1 ½ oz potatoes, mashed   1 ¾ oz plain flour   A handful of parsley, chopped
8 oz cooked salmon, flaked   A handful of capers   Zest of 1 lemon

Directions

In a bowl, mix the salmon, zest, capers, dill, and mashed potatoes. Form small cakes using the mixture and dust the cakes with flour; refrigerate for 60 minutes. Arrange the cakes on the greased air fryer basket. Insert the basket into the IP and put the air fryer lid on top. Select Air Fry and set the temperature to 380 F and the cooking time to 14 minutes. Push Start. Turn over halfway through the cooking time. Serve and enjoy!

Simple Catfish Fillets with Parsley

Prep + Cook Time: 40 minutes | Serves: 2

Ingredients

2 sprigs parsley, chopped   3 tbsp breadcrumbs   1 tsp dry dill
2 catfish fillets   1 tsp cayenne pepper   Salt to taste, optional

Directions

Pour all the dry ingredients, except the parsley, in a zipper bag. Add the catfish fillets and shake to coat. Arrange them on the air fryer basket, lightly spray the fish with cooking oil, and fit in your IP. Place the air fryer lid on top. Select Air Fry and set the temperature to 40 F and the cooking time to 12 minutes. Push Start. Flip the fish halfway through the cooking time. When cooking is complete, the fish should be crispy. Garnish with parsley.

Effortless Cod Fish Nuggets

Prep + Cook Time: 20 minutes | Serves: 4

Ingredients

2 eggs, beaten   2 tbsp olive oil   1 cup breadcrumbs
4 cod fillets   1 cup flour   A pinch of salt

Directions

Place the breadcrumbs, olive oil, and salt in a bowl and mix until evenly combined. Place the eggs into another bowl and the flour into a third bowl. Toss the cod fillets in the flour, then in the eggs, and then in the breadcrumb mixture. Place them in the fryer basket and fit in your IP. Place the air fryer lid on top. Select Air Fry and set the temperature to 390 F and the cooking time to 14 minutes. Push Start. Turn the chicken nuggets over. Serve.

Easy Salmon Quiches

Prep + Cook Time: 20 minutes | Serves: 5

Ingredients

6 oz cream cheese, divided into 15 pieces

3 oz smoked salmon

4 eggs, lightly beaten

15 mini tart cases

½ cup heavy cream

Salt and black pepper to taste

6 fresh dill

Directions

Mix together eggs and cream in a pourable measuring container. Arrange the tarts on the air fryer basket. Spoon the mixture into the tarts, about halfway up the side, and top with a piece of salmon and cheese.

Insert the basket into the IP and put the air fryer lid on top. Select Bake and set the temperature to 340 F and the cooking time to 10 minutes. Push Start. Sprinkle with dill and serve chilled.

Parmesan Tilapia Fillets

Prep + Cook Time: 15 minutes | Serves: 4

Ingredients

4 tilapia fillets

¾ cup grated Parmesan cheese

1 tbsp olive oil

2 tsp paprika

1 tbsp chopped parsley

¼ tsp garlic powder

¼ tsp salt

Directions

Mix the Parmesan cheese, garlic, salt, and paprika in a shallow bowl. Brush the olive oil over the fillets, and then coat them with the Parmesan mixture. Place the tilapia onto a lined baking sheet.

Insert the sheet in the air fryer basket and fit it in your IP. Place the air fryer lid on top. Select Air Fry and set the temperature to 380 F and the cooking time to 8 minutes. Push Start. Turn over halfway through the cooking time. Sprinkle the fried tilapia fillets with parsley. Serve and enjoy!

Classic Fish & Fries

Prep + Cook Time: 25 minutes | Serves: 4

Ingredients

4 white fish fillets

4 potatoes, cut into thin slices

2 tbsp flour

1 egg, beaten

1 cup breadcrumbs

Salt and black pepper to taste

Directions

Spray the potato slices with olive oil and season with salt and black pepper. Place them in the air fryer basket fit in your IP. Place the air fryer lid on top. Select Air Fry and set the temperature to 400 F and the cooking time to 20 minutes. Push Start. Spread flour on a plate and coat the fish. Dip them in the egg, then into the crumbs.

Season with salt and black pepper. At the 10-minute mark, add the fish to the fryer and cook for the remaining 6 minutes. When cooking is complete, the fish and chips should be crispy. Serve and enjoy!

VEGETARIAN & VEGAN

Air Fried Veggies

Prep + Cook Time: 30 minutes | Serves: 4

Ingredients

3 tbsp olive oil
2 lb chopped veggies: potatoes, parsnips, zucchini, pumpkin, carrot

1 tbsp balsamic vinegar
1 tbsp maple syrup
Salt and black pepper to taste

Directions

In a bowl, add oil, balsamic vinegar, agave syrup, salt, and black pepper; mix well with a fork. Arrange the veggies on the air fryer basket, drizzle with the dressing and massage with hands until well-coated. Insert the basket into the IP and put the air fryer lid on top. Select Air Fry and set the temperature to 360 F and the cooking time to 25 minutes. Push Start. Toss halfway through the cooking time. Serve and enjoy!

Veggies with Sweet Asian Sauce

Prep + Cook Time: 20 minutes | Serves: 4

Ingredients

2 lb chopped veggies: carrot, parsnip, green beans, zucchini, onion rings, asparagus, cauliflower
1 ½ cups plain flour
1 ½ tbsp cornstarch

Salt and black pepper to taste
¾ cup cold water

Dipping sauce:

½ tsp sesame oil
½ tsp sugar

4 tbsp soy sauce
Juice of 1 lemon

½ garlic clove, chopped
½ tsp sweet chili sauce

Directions

Line the Air fryer basket with baking paper. In a bowl, mix flour, salt, pepper, and cornstarch; whisk to combine. Keep whisking as you add water into the dry ingredients into a smooth batter is formed. Dip each veggie piece into the batter and place into the air fryer basket. Insert the basket into the IP and put the air fryer lid on top.

Select Air Fry and set the temperature to 360 F and the cooking time to 12 minutes. Push Start. Turn over halfway through the cooking time. Mix all the dipping ingredients in a bowl. Serve on the side of crispy veggies.

Stuffed Butternut Squash

Prep + Cook Time: 50 minutes | Serves: 3

Ingredients

2 tsp olive oil
½ butternut squash

6 grape tomatoes, halved
1 poblano pepper, cut into strips

¼ cup grated mozzarella
Salt and black pepper to taste

Directions

Trim the ends and cut the squash lengthwise in half. Scoop the flash out, so you make room for the filling. Brush 1 tsp oil over the squash. Place in the air fryer basket. Insert the basket into the IP and put the air fryer lid on top. Select Roast and set the temperature to 350 F and the cooking time to 30 minutes. Push Start.

Combine the remaining olive oil with tomatoes and poblanos; season with salt and pepper. Spoon the peppers and tomatoes into the squash halves. Top with mozzarella. Cook for 15 more minutes in the IP on Bake.

Corn Cakes with Green Onions

Prep + Cook Time: 25 minutes | Serves: 6

Ingredients

2 eggs, lightly beaten
2 cups corn kernels
⅓ cup finely chopped green onions

¼ cup roughly chopped parsley
½ cup all-purpose flour
½ cup self-raising flour

½ tsp baking powder
Salt and black pepper to taste

Directions

In a bowl, add corn, eggs, parsley, and onion, and season with salt and pepper; mix well to combine. Sift flour and baking powder into the bowl and stir. Line the air fryer basket with baking paper and spoon batter dollops, making sure they are separated by at least an inch. Work in batches if needed. Insert the basket into the IP.

Put the air fryer lid on top. Select Air Fry and set the temperature to 400 F and the cooking time to 10 minutes. Push Start. Turn over halfway through the cooking time. Serve with sour cream and chopped scallions.

Friendly Veggie Bites

Prep + Cook Time: 30 minutes | Serves: 13 to 16 bites

Ingredients

6 medium carrots, diced
½ cup garden peas
1 medium cauliflower, cut in florets
1 medium broccoli, cut in florets
1 onion, diced
2 leeks, sliced thinly

1 small zucchini, chopped
⅓ cup flour
1 tbsp garlic paste
2 tbsp olive oil
1 tbsp curry paste
2 tsp mixed spice

1 tsp coriander
1 tsp cumin powder
1 ½ cups milk
1 tsp ginger paste
Salt and black pepper to taste

Directions

Heat the olive oil in your IP on Sauté. Add the onion, ginger, garlic, and olive oil. Stir-fry for 3 minutes. Add in the leeks, zucchini, and curry paste. Stir and cook for 5 minutes. Add all spices and milk, stir, and simmer for 5 minutes. Throw in the remaining vegetables and 1 cup of water. Seal the lid and cook on Manual for 8 minutes. Once the time is done, use a quick pressure release. Remove the veggies; let them cool.

Mash the mixture and mold it into bite-sized balls. Arrange the veggie bites on the air fryer basket and fit in your IP. Place the air fryer lid on top. Select Air Fry and set the temperature to 350 F and the cooking time to 10 minutes. Push Start. Toss halfway through the cooking time. Serve and enjoy!

Spanish-Style Brussels Sprouts with Aioli

Prep + Cook Time: 25 minutes | Serves: 4

Ingredients

1 lb brussels sprouts, halved
1 ½ tbsp olive oil
2 tsp lemon juice

1 tsp powdered chili
3 garlic cloves, unpeeled
¾ cup mayonnaise

Salt and black pepper to taste
2 cups water

Directions

Add the brussels sprouts and garlic to the air fryer basket. Coat with olive oil, salt, and pepper. Insert the basket into the IP and put the air fryer lid on top. Select Air Fry and set the temperature to 350 F and the time to 12 minutes. Push Start. Toss halfway through the cooking time. Spoon the brussels sprouts onto a serving bowl.

Squeeze the garlic into a bowl and mash it with a fork. Stir in the mayonnaise, lemon juice, powdered chili, pepper, and salt until smooth and uniform. Serve the chili-garlic aioli on the side of the brussels sprouts.

Homemade Vegan Falafels

Prep + Cook Time: 25 minutes | Serves: 6

Ingredients

1 onion, chopped
1 cup fresh parsley, chopped
2 cups cooked chickpeas
½ cup chickpea flour

Juice of 1 lemon
4 garlic cloves, chopped
2 tsp ground cumin
2 tsp ground coriander

1 tsp chili powder
Salt and black pepper to taste

Directions

In a blender, add chickpeas, flour, parsley, lemon juice, garlic, onion, cumin, coriander, chili, turmeric, salt, and pepper and blend until well-combined but not too battery; there should be some lumps. Shape the mixture into 15 balls, press them with your hands, and make sure they are still around. Spray them with oil.

Arrange them on the greased air fryer basket. Insert the basket into the IP and put the air fryer lid on top. Select Air Fry and set the temperature to 360 F and the cooking time to 14 minutes. Push Start. Turn halfway through the cooking time. When cooking is complete, they should be crunchy and golden. Serve.

Quick Pasta with Roasted Vegetables

Prep + Cook Time: 25 minutes | Serves: 6

Ingredients

½ cup Kalamata olives, pitted and halved

1 zucchini, sliced
1 acorn squash, sliced
1 lb penne, cooked
1 bell pepper, sliced

4 oz mushrooms, sliced
¼ cup olive oil
1 tsp Italian seasoning
1 cup grape tomatoes, halved

3 tbsp balsamic vinegar
2 tbsp chopped basil
Salt and black pepper to taste

Directions

Combine the bell pepper, zucchini, squash, mushrooms, and olive oil in the air fryer basket. Season with salt and pepper. Insert the basket into the IP and put the air fryer lid on top. Select Air Fry and set the temperature to 380 F and the cooking time to 15 minutes. Push Start. Toss halfway through the cooking time.

Once the cooking process ends, remove the veggies to a serving bowl. Add in the cooked penne, olives, tomatoes, Italian seasoning, and vinegar. Toss to combine. Sprinkle the basil on top and enjoy!

Indian-Style Veggie Skewers

Prep + Cook Time: 20 minutes | Serves: 4

Ingredients

3 garlic cloves
1 cup canned beans
⅓ cup grated carrots
2 boiled and mashed potatoes

¼ cup chopped fresh mint leaves
½ tsp garam masala powder
½ cup paneer
1 green chili

2 tbsp cornflour
1-inch piece of fresh ginger
Salt to taste

Directions

Place the beans, carrots, garlic, ginger, chili, paneer, and mint in a food processor; process until smooth, then transfer to a bowl. Add the mashed potatoes, cornflour, salt, and garam masala powder to the bowl; mix until fully incorporated. Divide the mixture into 12 equal pieces. Shape the pieces around skewers.

Arrange them on the greased air fryer basket. Insert the basket into the IP and put the air fryer lid on top. Select Air Fry and set the temperature to 350 F and the cooking time to 10 minutes. Push Start. Turn once. Serve.

Veggie Tacos with Guacamole

Prep + Cook Time: 30 minutes | Serves: 3

Ingredients

3 soft taco shells
1 cup black beans, drained
1 cup kidney beans, drained
½ cup tomato puree

1 fresh jalapeño pepper, chopped
1 cup fresh cilantro, chopped
1 cup corn kernels
½ tsp ground cumin

½ tsp cayenne pepper
1 cup grated mozzarella cheese
Guacamole to serve
Salt and black pepper to taste

Directions

In a bowl, add the beans, tomato puree, chili, cilantro, corn, cumin, cayenne, salt, and pepper; stir well. Spoon the mixture onto the tacos, sprinkle the cheese over the top, and fold over. Lay the tacos inside the air fryer basket. Insert the basket into the IP and put the air fryer lid on top. Select Air Fry and set the temperature to 360 F and the cooking time to 12 minutes. Push Start. Serve hot with guacamole.

Easy Quinoa Stuffed Peppers

Prep + Cook Time: 25 minutes | Serves: 2

Ingredients

2 bell peppers, cored and cleaned
1 diced tomato
2 tomato slices

½ cup cooked quinoa
½ diced onion
¼ tsp smoked paprika

1 tbsp olive oil
¼ tsp dried basil
Salt and black pepper to taste

Directions

In a bowl, combine the remaining ingredients, except the tomato slices and olive oil. Stuff the peppers with the filling and top with the tomato slices. Brush the tomato slices and peppers with olive oil. Arrange the peppers on a baking pan. Place the baking pan into the air fryer basket. Insert the basket into the IP and put the air fryer lid on top. Select Bake and set the temperature to 350 F and the cooking time to 10 minutes. Push Start. Serve.

Parsley & Garlic Mushrooms

Ready in about: 15 minutes | Serves: 2

Ingredients

2 tsp olive oil
2 cups small mushrooms

2 slices white bread
1 garlic clove, crushed

2 tbsp parsley, finely chopped
Salt and black pepper to taste

Directions

In a food processor, grind the bread into fine crumbs. Add garlic, parsley, and pepper; mix and stir in the olive oil. Cut off the mushroom stalks and fill the caps with the breadcrumbs. Pat the crumbs inside the caps to ensure there are no loose crumbs. Place the mushroom caps inside the air fryer basket and carefully slide the basket into your IP. Select Bake and set the temperature to 360 F and the time to 10 minutes. Push Start. Serve.

Veggie Stuffed Tomatoes

Prep + Cook Time: 25 minutes | Serves: 3

Ingredients

½ cup portobello mushrooms, chopped
1 small red onion, diced
3 tomatoes

1 green bell pepper, diced
½ cup grated mozzarella cheese

½ tsp garlic powder
Salt and black pepper to taste

Directions

Cut the tops of the tomatoes and scoop out the flesh; reserve the tops of the tomatoes. Chop the tomato flesh and add it to a bowl. Add in the remaining ingredients, except mozzarella, and stir to combine. Divide the filling between the tomatoes. Top with mozzarella. Arrange the tomatoes on a greased baking pan.

Place the baking pan inside the air fryer basket. Insert the basket into the IP and put the air fryer lid on top. Select Bake and set the temperature to 350 F and the cooking time to 15 minutes. Push Start. Serve and enjoy!

Quick Vegetable Pizza

Prep + Cook Time: 15 minutes | Serves: 1

Ingredients

1 tortilla
4 eggplant slices
4 red onion rings
1 ½ tbsp tomato paste

¼ cup grated cheddar cheese
¼ cup grated mozzarella cheese
1 tbsp cooked sweet corn
4 zucchini slices

½ green bell pepper, chopped
3 cherry tomatoes, quartered
¼ tsp basil
¼ tsp oregano

Directions

Spread the tomato paste on the tortilla. Arrange the zucchini and eggplant slices first, then green peppers and onion rings. Arrange the cherry tomatoes and sprinkle the sweet corn over. Sprinkle with oregano and basil and top with cheddar and mozzarella. Place in the greased air fryer basket and fit in your IP. Place the air fryer lid on top. Select Bake and set the temperature to 350 F and the cooking time to 10 minutes. Push Start. Serve.

Bell Pepper & Tomato Dip

Prep + Cook Time: 25 minutes | Serves: 6

Ingredients

1 tbsp olive oil
¾ lb green bell pepper
¾ lb tomatoes

1 medium onion
1 tbsp lemon juice
1 tbsp cilantro powder

½ tbsp salt

Directions

Line the peppers, tomatoes, and onion on the greased air fryer basket. Insert the basket into the IP and put the air fryer lid on top. Select Air Fry and set the temperature to 360 F and the cooking time to 10 minutes. Push Start. Toss halfway through the cooking time. Remove them from the fryer and peel the skin. Place the vegetables in a blender and sprinkle with salt and coriander powder. Blend until smooth and drizzle with oil.

Party Pepper & Potato Skewers

Prep + Cook Time: 20 minutes | Serves: 2

Ingredients

1 tbsp olive oil
1 beetroot
2 large sweet potatoes

1 red bell pepper
1 tsp chili flakes
½ tsp turmeric

¼ tsp garlic powder
¼ tsp paprika
Salt and black pepper to taste

Directions

Peel the veggies and cut them into bite-sized chunks. Place the piece in a bowl along with the remaining ingredients; mix until fully coated. Thread the veggies in this order: potato, pepper, beetroot. Place in the greased air fryer basket and fit in your IP. Place the air fryer lid on top. Select Air Fry and set the temperature to 360 F and the cooking time to 15 minutes. Push Start. Turn over halfway through the cooking time. Serve.

Simple Air Fried Cauliflower

Prep + Cook Time: 20 minutes | Serves: 4

Ingredients

2 tbsp olive oil   1 head of cauliflower, cut into florets   Salt and black pepper to taste

Directions

In a bowl, toss cauliflower, oil, salt, and black pepper, until the florets are well-coated. Arrange the florets on the air fryer basket and fit in your IP. Place the air fryer lid on top. Select Air Fry and set the temperature to 360 F and the cooking time to 14 minutes. Push Start. Serve the crispy cauliflower with your favorite dip.

Chinese-Style Tofu Sandwich

Prep + Cook Time: 20 minutes | Serves: 1

Ingredients

2 tsp olive oil   1-inch thick tofu slice   ¼ tsp vinegar
2 slices of bread   ¼ cup red cabbage, shredded   Salt and black pepper to taste

Directions

Brush the tofu with some olive oil and place in the greased air fryer basket. Insert the basket into the IP and put the air fryer lid on top. Select Air Fry and set the temperature to 350 F and the cooking time to 10 minutes. Push Start. Turn over halfway through the cooking time. Combine the cabbage, remaining oil, and vinegar, salt, and pepper. Place the tofu on top of one bread slice, top with the cabbage, and cover with the other bread slice. Eat.

Easy Avocado Rolls

Prep + Cook Time: 15 minutes | Serves: 5

Ingredients

3 ripe avocados, pitted and peeled   1 tomato, diced
10 egg roll wrappers   Salt and black pepper to taste

Directions

Place the avocado and tomato in a bowl; mash with a fork until smooth. Season with salt and pepper. Divide the feeling between the egg wrappers. Wet your finger and brush along the edges so the wrappers can seal well. Roll and seal the wrappers. Arrange them on a baking sheet and place the sheet in the air fryer basket. Cook in your IP at 350 F for 5 minutes on Bake mode. Serve and enjoy.

Italian Cheese Ravioli

Prep + Cook Time: 15 minutes | Serves: 6

Ingredients

1 cup buttermilk   1 package cheese ravioli   ¼ cup Parmesan cheese, grated
1 tsp olive oil   2 cup Italian breadcrumbs   ¼ tsp garlic powder

Directions

In a small bowl, combine the breadcrumbs, Parmesan cheese, garlic powder, and olive oil. Dip the ravioli in the buttermilk and then coat them with the breadcrumb mixture. Line a baking pan with parchment paper and arrange the ravioli on it. Place in the greased air fryer basket and fit in your IP. Place the air fryer lid on top. Select Air Fry and set the temperature to 390 F and the cooking time to 5 minutes. Push Start. Serve and enjoy!

Potato Stuffed Bread Rolls

Prep + Cook Time: 25 minutes | Serves: 4

Ingredients

5 large potatoes, boiled and mashed
8 bread slices
2 green chilies, chopped

1 medium onion, finely chopped
½ tsp mustard seeds
1 tbsp olive oil

½ tsp turmeric
2 sprigs curry leaf
Salt to taste

Directions

Combine the olive oil, onion, curry leaves, and mustard seed in a baking dish. Place the baking pan inside the air fryer basket. Insert the basket into the IP and put the air fryer lid on top. Select Bake and set the temperature to 350 F and the cooking time to 5 minutes. Push Start. Remove the onion mixture to a bowl and mix with the mashed potatoes, chilies, turmeric, and salt. Divide the mixture into 8 equal pieces.

Trim the sides of the bread, and wet with some water. Make sure to get rid of the excess water. Take one wet bread slice in your palm and place one of the potato pieces in the center. Roll the bread over the filling, sealing the edges. Place the rolls in a baking dish and cook in the IP for 12 minutes on Bake. Serve and enjoy!

Warm Veggie Salad

Prep + Cook Time: 25 minutes | Serves: 1

Ingredients

1 carrot, sliced diagonally
1 cup cherry tomatoes
1 potato, peeled and chopped
¼ onion, sliced
½ small beetroot, sliced

2 tbsp olive oil
Juice of 1 lemon
A handful of rocket salad
A handful of baby spinach
3 tbsp canned chickpeas

½ tsp cumin
½ tsp turmeric
¼ tsp sea salt
Parmesan shavings

Directions

Combine the onion, potato, cherry tomatoes, carrot, beetroot, cumin, sea salt, turmeric, and 1 tbsp of olive oil in a bowl. Place in the fryer basket and fit in your IP. Place the air fryer lid on top. Select Air Fry and set the temperature to 370 F and the cooking time to 20 minutes. Push Start. Let cool for 2 minutes.

Place the rocket salad, spinach, lemon juice, and remaining olive oil into a serving bowl; mix to combine. Stir in the roasted veggies. Top with chickpeas and Parmesan shavings. Serve and enjoy!

Effortless Blooming Onion

Prep + Cook Time: 20 minutes | Serves: 4

Ingredients

2 pounds cipollini onions, cut into flowers
2 cups flour
Olive oil as needed
1 tsp cayenne pepper
1 tsp garlic powder

1 tbsp paprika
1 tbsp ketchup
¼ cup mayonnaise
¼ cup mayonnaise

¼ cup sour cream
Salt and black pepper to taste

Directions

In a bowl, mix salt, pepper, paprika, flour, garlic powder, and cayenne pepper. Add mayonnaise, ketchup, sour cream to the mixture and stir. Coat the onions with the prepared mixture and spray with oil. Add the coated onions to the air fryer basket and fit in your IP. Place the air fryer lid on top. Select Air Fry and set the temperature to 360 F and the cooking time to 15 minutes. Push Start. Serve and enjoy!

Spicy Chili Nachos

Prep + Cook Time: 20 minutes | Serves: 2

Ingredients

1 tbsp butter
1 cup sweet corn

1 cup all-purpose flour
½ tsp chili powder

Salt to taste
3 tbsp water

Directions

Add a small amount of water to the sweet corn and grind until you obtain a fine paste. In a bowl, add the flour, salt, chili powder, butter and mix very well; add corn and stir well. Start to knead with your palm until you obtain a stiff dough. Dust a little bit of flour and spread the dough with a rolling pin. Make it around ½ inch thick.

Cut it in any shape you want and place them into the frying basket. Insert the basket into the IP and put the air fryer lid on top. Select Air Fry and set the temperature to 350 F and the cooking time to 10 minutes. Push Start.

Garlic Paneer Cutlet

Prep + Cook Time: 15 minutes | Serves: 1

Ingredients

¼ small onion, finely chopped
2 cup grated paneer
1 tsp butter

1 cup grated cheese
½ tsp chai masala
½ tsp garlic powder

½ tsp oregano
½ tsp salt

Directions

Mix all ingredients in a bowl until well incorporated. Make cutlets out of the mixture and place them in a greased baking dish. Place the dish in the air fryer basket, insert the basket into the IP, and put the air fryer lid on top. Select Air Fry and set the temperature to 350 F and the cooking time to 10 minutes. Push Start. Serve.

Cheddar English Muffins

Prep + Cook Time: 15 minutes | Serves: 3

Ingredients

1 tomato, chopped
1 sweet onion, chopped
3 split English muffins, toasted

1 cup cheddar cheese, smoked and shredded
1 mashed avocado

1 cup alfalfa sprouts
¼ cup ranch-style salad dressing
¼ cup sesame seeds, toasted

Directions

Arrange the muffins open-faced in the air fryer basket. Spread the mashed avocado on each half of the muffin. Place the halves close to each other. Cover the muffins with sprouts, tomatoes, onion, dressing, sesame seeds, and cheese. Place them into the greased air fryer basket and put the air fryer lid on top. Select Bake and set the temperature to 350 F and the cooking time to 8 minutes. Push Start. Serve and enjoy!

Punjabi Ginger Cheese Balls

Prep + Cook Time: 12 minutes | Serves: 2

Ingredients

1 green chili, chopped
2 oz paneer cheese
2 tbsp flour

2 medium onions, chopped
1 tbsp cornflour
1-inch ginger piece, chopped

1 tsp red chili powder
A few leaves of cilantro, chopped
Salt to taste

Directions

Mix all the ingredients, except the oil and cheese, in a bowl. Take a small part of the mixture, roll it up, and slowly press it to flatten. Stuff in 1 cube of cheese and seal the edges. Repeat with the rest of the mixture. Arrange the balls on the air fryer basket and fit in your IP. Place the air fryer lid on top. Select Air Fry and set the temperature to 370 F and the cooking time to 12 minutes. Push Start. Turn once. Serve hot with ketchup!

Spicy Cheese Lings

Prep + Cook Time: 15 minutes | Serves: 4

Ingredients

1 cup all-purpose flour	1 tbsp butter	¼ tsp sal
4 cups grated cheese, any	1 tbsp baking powder	¼ tsp chili powder

Directions

In a bowl, mix the flour and baking powder. Add in the chili powder, salt, butter, cheese, and 1-2 tbsp of water. Make a stiff dough. Knead the dough for a while and sprinkle about 1 tbsp of flour on the table. With a rolling pin, roll the dough into ½-inch thickness. Cut into any shape and place in a greased baking sheet.

Place the sheet inside the air fryer basket. Insert the basket into the IP and put the air fryer lid on top. Select Bake and set the temperature to 370 F and the cooking time to 6 minutes. Push Start. Serve and enjoy!

Air Fried Potato Pancakes

Prep + Cook Time: 15 minutes | Serves: 4

Ingredients

1 medium onion, chopped	¼ cup milk	3 tbsp flour
1 beaten egg	2 tbsp unsalted butter	Salt and black pepper to taste
4 medium potatoes, shredded	½ tsp garlic powder	

Directions

In a bowl, mix egg, potatoes, onion, milk, butter, pepper, garlic powder, and salt; add flour and form batter. Forms cakes about ¼ cup of batter. Place the cakes in the air fryer basket and fit it in your IP. Place the air fryer lid on top. Select Air Fry and set the temperature to 390 F and the cooking time to 12 minutes. Push Start. Serve.

Bengali Air Fried Potatoes

Prep + Cook Time: 20 minutes | Serves: 3

Ingredients

1 bell pepper, sliced	¼ fennel bulb	2 tbsp cilantro, chopped
1 small onion, chopped	5 tbsp flour	Salt and black pepper to taste
4 potatoes, cubed	2 tbsp ginger-garlic paste	
3 tbsp lemon juice	½ tbsp mint leaves, chopped	

Directions

In a bowl, mix cilantro, mint, fennel, ginger garlic paste, flour, salt, and lemon juice. Blend to form a paste and add in the potato cubes, bell pepper, onion, and fennel mixture; mix well until you have a thick mix. Divide the mixture evenly into 6 patties. Add the prepared potato cakes to the greased air fryer basket.

Insert the basket into the IP and put the air fryer lid on top. Select Air Fry and set the temperature to 360 F and the cooking time to 15 minutes. Push Start. Turn over halfway through the cooking time. Serve with ketchup.

Thai Coconut & Spinach Chickpeas

Prep + Cook Time: 20 minutes | Serves: 4

Ingredients

1 pound spinach
4 garlic cloves, minced
1 can coconut milk
2 tbsp olive oil

1 onion, chopped
1 tbsp ginger, minced
1 can chickpeas
1 lemon, juiced

1 hot pepper
½ cup dried tomatoes, chopped
Salt and black pepper to taste

Directions

In a bowl, mix the lemon juice, tomatoes, pepper, ginger, coconut milk, garlic, salt, hot pepper, and onion. Rinse chickpeas under running water to get rid of all the gunk. Put them in a large bowl. Cover with spinach. Pour the air fryer basket. Insert the basket into the IP and put the air fryer lid on top. Select Bake and set the temperature to 350 F and the cooking time to 15 minutes. Push Start. Serve and enjoy!

Rosemary Air Fried Beet Bowl

Prep + Cook Time: 20 minutes | Serves: 2

Ingredients

1 tbsp olive oil
1 tbsp honey

4 beets, cubed
⅓ cup balsamic vinegar

2 springs rosemary
Salt and black pepper to taste

Directions

In a bowl, mix rosemary, pepper, salt, vinegar, and honey. Cover beets with the prepared sauce and then coat with oil. Place in a baking pan and fit in the air fryer basket. Insert the basket into the IP and put the air fryer lid on top. Select Air Fry and set the temperature to 400 F and the cooking time to 10 minutes. Push Start. Serve.

Sicilian Brussels Sprouts

Prep + Cook Time: 25 minutes | Serves: 6

Ingredients

15 oz brussels sprouts, stems cut off and cut in half
1 tbsp olive oil
1 ¾ oz toasted pine nuts

1 ¾ oz raisins, soaked
Juice of 1 orange

Salt to taste

Directions

In a bowl, pop the sprouts with oil and salt and stir to combine well. Add the sprouts to the greased air fryer basket and fit in your IP. Place the air fryer lid on top. Select Air Fry and set the temperature to 380 F and the cooking time to 16 minutes. Push Start. Toss halfway through the cooking time. Remove the Brussel sprouts. Mix with toasted pine nuts and soaked raisins. Drizzle with remaining orange juice and serve.

Mediterranean Air Fried Veggies

Prep + Cook Time: 10 minutes | Serves: 6

Ingredients

15 oz bell peppers, sliced
4 whole onions, chopped
18 oz tomatoes, sliced
4 tbsp olive oil

18 oz eggplant, cubed
4 garlic cloves, minced
18 oz zucchini, sliced
A bunch of thyme sprig

Salt and black pepper to taste
Breadcrumb as needed

Directions

In a bowl, mix eggplant, garlic, oil, and spices and transfer the mix to the greased air fryer basket. Insert the basket into the IP and put the air fryer lid on top. Select Air Fry and set the temperature to 380 F and the cooking time to 10 minutes. Push Start. At the 4-minute mark, add the zucchini, tomatoes, bell pepper, onion cook for the remaining 6 minutes. Serve and enjoy!

Pine Nut & Cheese Balls

Prep + Cook Time: 40 minutes | Serves: 6

Ingredients

28 oz parsnips, chopped	6 ¾ oz crème fraiche	4 tbsp butter
28 oz potato, cubed	1 slice bread, torn	3 tbsp pine nuts
1 ¾ oz Parmesan cheese, shredded	2 tbsp sage	4 tsp mustard

Directions

Add the potatoes and parsnips to your IP and cover with water. Seal the lid, select Manual and cook for 12 minutes on High. Once the cooking process ends, use a quick pressure release. Drain and set in a bowl and mash them with butter using a potato masher. Add in the remaining ingredient and mix to combine.

Shape the mixture into balls and transfer them to the lightly greased air fryer basket. Insert the basket into the IP and put the air fryer lid on top. Select Air Fry and set the temperature to 350 F and the cooking time to 25 minutes. Push Start. Toss halfway through the cooking time. Serve and enjoy!

Greek-Style Feta Zucchini

Prep + Cook Time: 25 minutes | Serves: 4

Ingredients

1 medium zucchini, sliced	12 oz thawed puff pastry	2 tbsp fresh dill, chopped
4 ounces feta cheese, crumbled	4 large eggs	Salt and black pepper to taste

Directions

In a bowl, beat the eggs with salt and pepper. Stir in zucchini, dill, and feta cheese. Roll pastry and arrange them to cover the sides of 8 greased muffin tins. Divide the egg mixture evenly between the holes. Place the prepared tins in the air fryer basket, insert the basket into the IP, and put the air fryer lid on top. Select Bake and set the temperature to 360 F and the cooking time to 12 minutes. Push Start. Serve and enjoy!

Easy Zucchini Fries

Prep + Cook Time: 25 minutes | Serves: 4

Ingredients

2 egg whites	½ cup seasoned breadcrumbs	¼ tsp garlic powder
3 medium zucchini, sliced	2 tbsp grated Parmesan cheese	Salt and black pepper to taste

Directions

Coat cooling rack with cooking spray; place it in the air fryer basket. In a bowl, beat the egg whites and season with salt and pepper. In another bowl, mix garlic powder, cheese, and breadcrumbs. Take zucchini slices and dredge them in eggs, followed by breadcrumbs. Add zucchini to the rack (in the basket) and spray more oil.

Insert the basket into the IP and put the air fryer lid on top. Select Air Fry and set the temperature to 400 F and the cooking time to 20 minutes. Push Start. Flip halfway through the cooking time. Serve and enjoy!

Creole-Style Air Fried Tomatoes

Prep + Cook Time: 15 minutes | Serves: 3

Ingredients

¼ cup flour
1 green tomato, sliced

¼ tbsp creole seasoning
½ cup buttermilk

Breadcrumbs as needed
Salt and black pepper to taste

Directions

Add flour to one bowl and buttermilk to another. Season the tomatoes with salt and pepper. Make a mix of creole seasoning and breadcrumbs. Cover tomato slices with flour, dip in buttermilk, and then into the breadcrumbs. Do the same for all the slices. Arrange the tomato slices on the air fryer basket.

Insert the basket into the IP and put the air fryer lid on top. Select Air Fry and set the temperature to 400 F and the cooking time to 6 minutes. Push Start. Turn over halfway through the cooking time. Serve and enjoy!

Simple Bell Pepper Bites

Prep + Cook Time: 20 minutes | Serves: 4

Ingredients

1 green bell pepper, chopped
1 medium red bell pepper, chopped
1 medium yellow pepper, chopped
3 tbsp balsamic vinegar

2 tbsp olive oil
1 tbsp garlic, minced
½ tsp dried basil
½ tsp dried parsley

½ cup garlic mayo to serve
Salt and black pepper to taste

Directions

In a bowl, mix peppers, oil, garlic, balsamic vinegar, basil, parsley, salt, and pepper. Place the pepper mixture inside the greased air fryer basket. Insert the basket into the IP and put the air fryer lid on top. Select Air Fry and set the temperature to 40 F and the cooking time to 15 minutes. Push Start. Serve with garlic mayo and enjoy.

Cheesy Asparagus & Red Potatoes

Prep + Cook Time: 30 minutes | Serves: 5

Ingredients

1 bunch asparagus, trimmed
4 red potatoes, cubed

¼ cup fresh cream
¼ cup cottage cheese, cubed

1 tbsp wholegrain mustard

Directions

Place the potatoes in the greased air fryer basket and fit in your IP. Place the air fryer lid on top. Select Air Fry and set the temperature to 400 F and the cooking time to 25 minutes. Push Start. At the 15-minute mark, shake the potatoes and add asparagus; cook for the remaining 10 minutes. In a bowl, mix cottage cheese, cream, mustard, salt, and pepper. Spoon the mixture over the cooked potatoes and asparagus and serve.

Air Fried Sushi with Avocado

Prep + Cook Time: 60 minutes | Serves: 4

Ingredients

Soy sauce, wasabi and pickled ginger to serve
1 avocado, sliced
2 cups cooked sushi rice
4 nori sheets

1 carrot, sliced lengthways
1 red bell pepper, sliced
2 tbsp sesame seeds

1 tbsp olive oil mixed with
1 tbsp rice wine vinegar
1 cup panko crumbs

Directions

Prepare a clean working board, a small bowl of lukewarm water, and a sushi mat. Wet hands, and lay a nori sheet onto the sushi mat, and spread ½ cup of sushi rice, leaving ½ inch of nori clear so that you can seal the roll. Place carrot, pepper, and avocado sideways to the rice. Roll sushi tightly and rub warm water along the clean nori strip to seal.

In a bowl, mix olive oil and rice vinegar. In another bowl, mix the crumbs with sesame seeds. Roll each sushi log in the vinegar mixture and then straight to the sesame bowl to coat. Arrange the coated sushi into the air fryer basket and fit in your IP. Place the air fryer lid on top. Select Air Fry and set the temperature to 360 F and the cooking time to 14 minutes. Push Start. Turn once halfway through. When ready, check if the sushi is golden and crispy on the outside. Slice and serve with soy sauce, pickled ginger, and wasabi.

Grana Padano Cauli Balls

Prep + Cook Time: 50 minutes + chilling time | Serves: 4

Ingredients

1 cup breadcrumbs
½ lb mushrooms, diced
1 small red onion, chopped
3 cloves garlic, minced

3 cups cauliflower, chopped
1 cup vegetable stock
1 cup Grana Padano cheese
¼ cup coconut oil

3 tbsp olive oil
2 sprigs chopped fresh thyme
Salt and black pepper to taste

Directions

Heat the olive oil in your IP on Sauté. Sauté the garlic and onion until translucent, 3 minutes. Add the mushrooms and cauliflower and stir-fry for 5-6 minutes. Pour in the stock and thyme. Seal the lid, select Manual, and cook for 5 minutes on High. Once the cooking process ends, use a quick pressure release. Transfer to a food processor and blend until smooth; let cool for a while. Add Grana Padano cheese, pepper, and salt to the cooled mixture and make bite-size balls. Place them on a plate and refrigerate for 30 minutes to harden.

In a bowl, add the breadcrumbs and coconut oil and mix well. Remove the mushroom balls from the refrigerator, stir the breadcrumb mixture again, and roll the balls in the breadcrumb mixture. Place the balls in the air fryer basket without overcrowding and fit in your IP. Place the air fryer lid on top. Select Air Fry and set the temperature to 360 F and the cooking time to 15 minutes. Push Start. Toss halfway through. Serve and enjoy!

Stuffed Peppers with Cauli & Cheese

Prep + Cook Time: 40 minutes | Serves: 4

Ingredients

1 red onion, chopped
1 large tomato, chopped
4 green peppers
½ cup olive oil

½ cup crumbled Goat cheese
3 cups cauliflower, chopped
2 tbsp grated Romano cheese
2 tbsp chopped basil

Salt and black pepper to taste
1 tbsp lemon zest

Directions

Cut the peppers a quarter way from the head down and lengthwise. Remove the membrane and seeds. Season the peppers with pepper, salt, and drizzle olive oil over. Place the pepper bottoms in the air fryer basket and fit in your IP. Place the air fryer lid on top. Select Air Fry and set the temperature to 350 F and the cooking time to 10 minutes. Push Start. The peppers should be softened a little bit.

In a mixing bowl, add the tomatoes, goat cheese, lemon zest, basil, and cauliflower; season with salt and pepper, and mix well. Spoon the cheese mixture into the peppers. Sprinkle Romano cheese on top and cook for 5 minutes in the IP on Bake. Serve warm.

Crispy Tofu

Prep + Cook Time: 25 minutes | Serves: 4

Ingredients

1 green onion, chopped
1 block firm tofu, cubed
1 tbsp potato starch

2 tsp rice vinegar
2 tsp soy sauce
2 tsp sesame oil

2 tbsp basil, chopped
Salt and black pepper to taste

Directions

In a bowl, mix the sesame oil, soy sauce, rice vinegar, salt, and pepper. Add in the tofu and toss to coat. Set aside for 10 minutes to get tasty. Coat the marinated tofu with potato starch. Place into the air fryer basket and fit in your IP. Place the air fryer lid on top. Select Air Fry and set the temperature to 370 F and the cooking time to 20 minutes. Push Start. Shake halfway through the cooking time. Serve with a topping of chopped onion and basil.

Sriracha Potato Wedges

Prep + Cook Time: 30 minutes | Serves: 6

Ingredients

½ cup Greek yogurt
26 oz waxy potatoes, cut into wedges

2 tbsp olive oil
2 tsp smoked paprika

2 tbsp sriracha hot chili sauce

Directions

Coat the potatoes with olive oil and paprika. Arrange them on the air fryer basket. Insert the basket into the IP and put the air fryer lid on top. Select Air Fry and set the temperature to 400 F and the cooking time to 23 minutes. Push Start. Shake once halfway through. Season with salt and pepper. Serve and enjoy!

Vegan-Style Toast

Prep + Cook Time: 15 minutes | Serves: 2

Ingredients

3 white bread slices
1 cup soy chorizo, chopped

1 large spring onion, finely sliced
½ cup sweet corn

1 egg white, whisked
1 tbsp black sesame seeds

Directions

In a bowl, place the soy chorizo, corn, spring onion, and sesame seeds. Add the egg white and mix the ingredients. Spread the mixture over the bread slices. Place in the air fryer basket and fit it in your IP. Place the air fryer lid on top. Select Air Fry and set the temperature to 370 F and the cooking time to 10 minutes. Push Start. Serve.

Homemade Avocado Fries

Prep + Cook Time: 20 minutes | Serves: 2

Ingredients

1 avocado, cubed
¼ cup aquafaba

½ cup breadcrumbs
Salt to taste

Directions

In a bowl, mix crumbs, aquafaba, and salt. Roll the avocado cubes in the crumbs mixture to coat evenly. Place the prepared cubes in the air fryer basket and fit it in your IP. Place the air fryer lid on top. Select Air Fry and set the temperature to 380 F and the cooking time to 10 minutes. Push Start. Serve and enjoy!

Parmesan Broccoli Bowl

Prep + Cook Time: 25 minutes | Serves: 4

Ingredients

1 ounce Parmesan cheese, grated
1 head broccoli, cut into florets

1 tbsp olive oil
1 lemon, juiced

Salt and black pepper to taste

Directions

In a bowl, mix all the ingredients. Add the mixture to the air fryer basket and fit in your IP. Place the air fryer lid on top. Select Air Fry and set the temperature to 370 F and the cooking time to 16 minutes. Push Start. Serve.

Sweet & Spicy Cauliflower Meal

Prep + Cook Time: 20 minutes | Serves: 4

Ingredients

2 cloves garlic, chopped
1 cauliflower head, cut into florets
½ cup soy sauce

1 tsp sesame oil
⅓ cup water
½ chili powder

3 tbsp brown sugar
1 tsp cornstarch

Directions

In a bowl, whisk soy sauce, sugar, sesame oil, water, chili powder, garlic, and cornstarch until smooth. In a bowl, add cauliflower, and pour teriyaki sauce over the top; toss with hands until well-coated. Take the cauliflower to the air fryer basket and fit in your IP. Place the air fryer lid on top. Select Air Fry and set the temperature to 360 F and the cooking time to 14 minutes. Push Start. Turn once halfway through. Serve and enjoy!

Marinara Eggplant Slices

Prep + Cook Time: 20 minutes | Serves: 3

Ingredients

2 tbsp milk
1 whole egg, beaten

1 whole eggplant, sliced
Marinara sauce for dipping

½ cup cheese, grated
2 cups breadcrumbs

Directions

In a bowl, mix beaten egg and milk. In another bowl, mix crumbs and cheese until crumbly. Place eggplant slices in the egg mixture, followed by a dip in the crumb mixture. Place the eggplant slices in the air fryer basket and fit in your IP. Place the air fryer lid on top. Select Air Fry and set the temperature to 400 F and the cooking time to 5 minutes. Push Start. Serve with marinara sauce. Enjoy!

French-Style Vermouth Mushrooms

Prep + Cook Time: 20 minutes | Serves: 3

Ingredients

2 tbsp vermouth
½ tsp garlic powder

2 lb portobello mushrooms, sliced
1 tbsp olive oil

2 tsp herbs
1 tbsp ghee, softened

Directions

Place the mushrooms in the air fryer basket. Mix the ghee, garlic powder, and herbs in a bowl. Pour the mixture over the mushrooms and cover with vermouth. Fit the basket in your IP. Place the air fryer lid on top. Select Air Fry and set the temperature to 350 F and the cooking time to 10 minutes. Push Start. Serve and enjoy!

Golden Cauliflower

Prep + Cook Time: 34 minutes | Serves: 4

Ingredients

1 ½ tbsp curry powder
½ cup olive oil

⅓ cup pine nuts
1 cauliflower head, cut into florets

Salt to taste

Directions

Coat the pine nuts with some olive oil in the air fryer basket and fit it in your IP. Place the air fryer lid on top. Select Air Fry and set the temperature to 380 F and the cooking time to 2 minutes. Push Start. Let them cool.

Place the cauliflower florets in the air fryer basket. Add the curry powder, salt, and the remaining olive oil; mix well. Insert the basket into the IP and put the air fryer lid on top. Select Air Fry and set the temperature to 350 F and the cooking time to 10 minutes. Push Start. Shake halfway through the cooking time. Top with pine nuts.

Cornflake-Crusted Tofu

Prep + Cook Time: 25 minutes | Serves: 4

Ingredients

½ cup flour
14 ounces firm tofu, cut into ½-inch
thick strips

2 tbsp olive oil
½ cup crushed cornflakes
Salt and black pepper to taste

Directions

Sprinkle oil over tofu and massage gently until well-coated. On a plate, mix flour, cornflakes, salt, and black pepper. Dip each strip into the mixture to coat, spray with oil and arrange them on the air fryer basket and fit in your IP. Place the air fryer lid on top. Select Air Fry and set the temperature to 360 F and the cooking time to 14 minutes. Push Start. Turn once halfway through. Serve and enjoy!

Creamy Carrots

Prep + Cook Time: 25 minutes | Serves: 4

Ingredients

3 tbsp parsley, chopped
2 tsp olive oil
2 shallots, chopped

¼ cup yogurt
2 garlic cloves, minced
3 carrots, sliced

Salt to taste

Directions

In a bowl, mix sliced carrots, salt, garlic, shallots, parsley, and yogurt. Sprinkle with oil. Place the veggies in the air fryer basket and fit it in your IP. Place the air fryer lid on top. Select Air Fry and set the temperature to 370 F and the cooking time to 15 minutes. Push Start. Serve with basil and garlic mayo.

Garlicky Veggie Bake

Prep + Cook Time: 30 minutes | Serves: 3

Ingredients

2 cloves garlic, crushed
1 bay leaf, cut into 6 pieces
3 turnips, sliced

1 large red onion, cut into rings
1 tbsp olive oil
1 large zucchini, sliced

Salt and black pepper to taste

Directions

Place the turnips, onion, and zucchini in a bowl. Toss with olive oil and season with salt and pepper. Place the veggies into a baking pan. Slip the bay leaves in the different parts of the slices and tuck the garlic cloves in between the slices. Insert the pan in the air fryer basket and fit it in your IP. Place the air fryer lid on top. Select Air Fry and set the temperature to 380 F and the cooking time to 15 minutes. Push Start. Serve and enjoy!

Coconut Curly Fries

Prep + Cook Time: 20 minutes | Serves: 2

Ingredients

1 tbsp tomato ketchup
2 tbsp olive oil

2 Yukon Gold potatoes
2 tbsp coconut oil

Salt and black pepper to taste

Directions

Use a spiralizer to spiralize the potatoes. In a bowl, mix oil, coconut oil, salt, and pepper. Cover the potatoes with the oil mixture. Place the potatoes in the air fryer basket and fit it in your IP. Place the air fryer lid on top. Select Air Fry and set the temperature to 360 F and the cooking time to 15 minutes. Push Start. Serve and enjoy!

Mom's Vegetable Au Gratin

Prep + Cook Time: 30 minutes | Serves: 3

Ingredients

¼ cup grated mozzarella cheese
1 tbsp breadcrumbs
1 cup cubed eggplant
¼ cup chopped red peppers
¼ cup chopped green peppers

¼ cup chopped onion
⅓ cup chopped tomatoes
1 clove garlic, minced
1 tbsp sliced pimiento-stuffed olives
1 tsp capers

¼ tsp dried basil
¼ tsp dried marjoram
Salt and black pepper to taste

Directions

In a bowl, add the eggplant, green pepper, red pepper, onion, tomatoes, olives, garlic, basil marjoram, capers, salt, and pepper. Lightly grease a baking dish with cooking spray. Spoon the eggplant mixture into the baking dish and level it using the vessel. Sprinkle the mozzarella cheese on top and cover with the breadcrumbs.

Place the dish in the air fryer basket and fit it in your IP. Place the air fryer lid on top. Select Bake and set the temperature to 360 F and the cooking time to 20 minutes. Push Start. Serve and enjoy!

Romanian-Style Polenta Crisps

Prep + Cook Time: 25 minutes + chilling time | Serves: 4

Ingredients

2 cups milk
1 cup instant polenta

Salt and black pepper to taste
Fresh thyme, chopped

Directions

Press the Sauté button to preheat your Instant Pot. Pour in 2 cups of water and milk into and let them simmer. Keep whisking as you pour in the polenta. Continue to whisk until polenta thickens and bubbles; season to taste. Add polenta into a lined baking pan and spread out. Refrigerate for 45 minutes.

Slice the cold, set polenta into batons and spray with oil. Arrange polenta chips on the air fryer basket and fit in your IP. Place the air fryer lid on top. Select Air Fry and set the temperature to 380 F and the cooking time to 16 minutes. Push Start. Turning once halfway through. The fries should be golden and crispy.

Spicy Green Beans

Prep + Cook Time: 20 minutes | Serves: 6

Ingredients

1 ½ pounds green beans
1 cup panko
2 whole eggs, beaten

½ cup Parmesan cheese, grated
½ cup flour
1 tsp cayenne pepper

Salt to taste

Directions

In a bowl, mix breadcrumbs, Parmesan cheese, cayenne pepper, salt, and pepper. Roll the green beans in flour and dip them into the eggs. Dredge beans in the parmesan-panko mix. Place the prepared beans in the air fryer basket and fit it in your IP. Place the air fryer lid on top. Select Air Fry and set the temperature to 400 F and the cooking time to 15 minutes. Push Start. Serve and enjoy!

Classic Beetroot Chips

Prep + Cook Time: 9 minutes | Serves: 2

Ingredients

2 tbsp olive oil
1 tbsp yeast flakes

4 cups golden beetroot, sliced
1 tsp vegan seasoning

Salt to taste

Directions

In a bowl, add the oil, beetroot, vegan seasoning, and yeast and mix well. Dump the coated chips in the air fryer basket. Insert the basket into the IP and put the air fryer lid on top. Select Air Fry and set the temperature to 370 F and the cooking time to 6 minutes. Push Start. Shake once halfway through cooking. Serve and enjoy!

Feta Sandwiches with Homemade Pesto

Prep + Cook Time: 60 minutes | Serves: 2

Ingredients

1 small red onion, thinly sliced
1 clove garlic
1 heirloom tomato
1 (4- oz) block Feta cheese

2 tsp + ¼ cup olive oil
1 ½ tbsp toasted pine nuts
¼ cup chopped parsley
¼ cup grated Parmesan cheese

¼ cup chopped basil
Salt to taste

Directions

Add basil, pine nuts, garlic, and salt to a food processor. Process while adding the ¼ cup of olive oil slowly. Once the oil is finished, pour the basil pesto into a bowl. Place it in the refrigerator for 30 minutes.

Slice the feta cheese and tomato into ½ inch circular slices. Spread the pesto on the tomato slices. Cover with the feta cheese slices. Top with the onion and remaining olive oil. Place the sandwiches in the fryer basket and fit in your IP. Place the air fryer lid on top. Select Bake and set the temperature to 360 F and the cooking time to 20 minutes. Push Start. Sprinkle with salt. Serve with rice if desired. Enjoy!

Blue Cheese Cabbage Wedges

Prep + Cook Time: 25 minutes | Serves: 4

Ingredients

½ head cabbage, cut into wedges
½ cup blue cheese sauce

2 cups Parmesan cheese, chopped
4 tbsp melted butter

Salt and black pepper to taste

Directions

Cover cabbage wedges with melted butter and coat with mozzarella. Place the coated cabbage in the air fryer basket and fit it in your IP. Place the air fryer lid on top. Select Air Fry and set the temperature to 380 F and the cooking time to 20 minutes. Push Start. Serve with blue cheese. Enjoy!

Chickpea and Cashew Balls

Prep + Cook Time: 30 minutes | Serves: 3

Ingredients

1 cup rolled oats	1 tbsp flax meal	Juice of 1 lemon
2 cups cooked chickpeas	½ cup sweet onion, diced	½ tsp turmeric
2 tbsp olive oil	½ cup grated carrots	1 tsp cumin
2 tbsp soy sauce	½ cup roasted cashews	1 tsp garlic powder

Directions

Combine the oil, onions, and carrots into a baking dish and place the baking pan inside the air fryer basket. Insert the basket into the IP and put the air fryer lid on top. Select Bake and set the temperature to 350 F and the cooking time to 6 minutes. Push Start.

Ground the oats and cashews in a food processor. Remove them to a large bowl. Process the chickpeas with lemon juice and soy sauce in the food processor until smooth. Add them to the cashew mixture. Stir in the cooked onions and carrots and add in the remaining ingredients; mix until fully incorporated. Make meatballs out of the mix. Increase the temperature to 370 F and cooking the IP for 12 minutes on Air Fry mode. Flip once.

Mix Veggie Chips

Prep + Cook Time: 45 minutes | Serves: 4

Ingredients

5 potatoes	½ cup cornstarch	Salt to taste
3 zucchinis	½ cup olive oil	
1 large eggplant	½ cup water	

Directions

Cut the eggplant and zucchini into long 3-inch strips. Peel and cut the potatoes into 3-inch strips; set aside. In a bowl, stir in cornstarch, water, salt, pepper, oil, eggplants, zucchini, and potatoes. Place the veggie strips in the air fryer basket and fit it in your IP. Place the air fryer lid on top. Select Air Fry and set the temperature to 390 F and the cooking time to 12 minutes. Push Start. Serve and enjoy!

Fried Veggie Bowl

Prep + Cook Time: 30 minutes | Serves: 2

Ingredients

2 small red onions, cut into wedges	1 cup chopped butternut squash	Salt and black pepper to taste
1 cup chopped celery	2 tsp olive oil	
1 parsnip, sliced	1 tbsp chopped fresh thyme	

Directions

In a bowl, add the turnip, squash, red onions, celery, thyme, pepper, salt, and olive oil; mix well. Pour the vegetables into the air fryer basket. Insert the basket into the IP and put the air fryer lid on top. Select Air Fry and set the temperature to 350 F and the cooking time to 16 minutes. Push Start. Serve and enjoy!

Sweet Air Fried Carrots

Prep + Cook Time: 20 minutes | Serves: 4

Ingredients

1 tbsp olive oil

1 tbsp honey

1 pound baby carrots

1 tsp dried dill

Salt and black pepper to taste

Directions

In a bowl, mix the oil, carrots, and honey; gently stir to coat the carrots. Season with dill, pepper, and salt. Place the prepared carrots in the air fryer basket and fit it in your IP. Place the air fryer lid on top. Select Air Fry and set the temperature to 350 F and the cooking time to 12 minutes. Push Start. Serve and enjoy!

Southern Jacket Potatoes

Prep + Cook Time: 30 minutes | Serves: 4

Ingredients

1 tsp rosemary

1 tsp butter

17 oz potatoes

2 garlic cloves, minced

Salt and black pepper to taste

Directions

Prick the potatoes with a fork. Place them into the air fryer basket and fit in your IP. Place the air fryer lid on top. Select Air Fry and set the temperature to 360 F and the cooking time to 25 minutes. Push Start. Cut the potatoes in half and top with butter and rosemary; season with salt and pepper. Serve immediately.

Cumin Sweet Potato Strips

Prep + Cook Time: 30 minutes | Serves: 4

Ingredients

3 sweet potatoes, cut into thick strips

½ tsp salt

½ tsp garlic powder

½ tsp chili powder

¼ tsp cumin

3 tbsp olive oil

Directions

In a bowl, mix salt, garlic powder, chili powder, and cumin and whisk in oil. Coat the strips well in this mixture and arrange them on the air fryer basket without overcrowding. Fit the basket in your IP. Place the air fryer lid on top. Select Air Fry and set the temperature to 380 F and the cooking time to 20 minutes. Push Start. Serve.

Japanese Tofu with Herbs

Prep + Cook Time: 30 minutes | Serves: 2

Ingredients

1 tbsp vegetable broth

1 tbsp soy sauce

⅓ tsp dried oregano

⅓ tsp garlic powder

⅓ tsp dried basil

⅓ tsp onion powder

6 oz extra firm tofu, cubed

Black pepper to taste

Directions

In a bowl, add the soy sauce, vegetable broth, oregano, basil, garlic powder, onion powder, and black pepper; mix well. Add in the tofu and stir until well coated; set aside to marinate for 10 minutes. Arrange the tofu on the air fryer basket in a single layer. Insert the basket into the IP and put the air fryer lid on top. Select Air Fry and set the temperature to 390 F and the cooking time to 16 minutes. Push Start. Flip at the 6-minute mark.

Mushroom Cheesy Frittata

Prep + Cook Time: 35 minutes | Serves: 2

Ingredients

4 eggs, cracked into a bowl
⅓ cup milk
1 cup baby spinach
⅓ cup sliced mushrooms

1 large zucchini, sliced
1 small red onion, sliced
¼ cup chopped chives
¼ lb asparagus, sliced thinly

2 tsp olive oil
⅓ cup grated Cheddar cheese
⅓ cup crumbled Feta cheese
Salt and black pepper to taste

Directions

In a bowl, place the eggs, milk, salt, and pepper and beat evenly. Add in the asparagus, zucchini, onion, mushrooms, and baby spinach; stir. Pour the mixture into a baking dish and top with feta and cheddar cheeses over and place in the air fryer basket. Insert the basket into the IP and put the air fryer lid on top. Select Bake and set the temperature to 350 F and the cooking time to 15 minutes. Push Start. Garnish with chives.

Quick Mozzarella Eggplant Patties

Prep + Cook Time: 15 minutes | Serves: 2

Ingredients

2 eggplant slices, cut along the round axis
1 pickle, sliced
2 hamburger buns

2 mozzarella slices
1 red onion, cut into rings

2 lettuce leaves
1 tbsp tomato sauce

Directions

Place the eggplant slices in the air fryer basket. Insert the basket into the IP and put the air fryer lid on top. Select Bake and set the temperature to 350 F and the cooking time to 6 minutes. Push Start. Place the mozzarella slices on top of the eggplant and cook for 30 more seconds. Spread the tomato sauce on the bun bottoms.

Place the lettuce leaves on top of the sauce. Place the cheesy eggplant slices on top of the lettuce. Top with onion rings and pickle slices, and then cover with the other bun halves. Serve and enjoy!

Korean Cauliflower Rice with Tofu & Peas

Prep + Cook Time: 30 minutes | Serves: 4

Ingredients

Tofu:
1 cup diced carrot
½ block tofu, crumbled

½ cup diced onion
2 tbsp soy sauce

1 tsp turmeric

Cauliflower:
2 garlic cloves, minced
3 cups cauliflower rice
½ cup frozen peas

2 tbsp soy sauce
½ cup chopped broccoli
1 ½ tsp toasted sesame oil

1 tbsp minced ginger
1 tbsp rice vinegar

Directions

Place all cauliflower ingredients in a large bowl; mix to combine well. Set aside until ready to use. Combine all the tofu ingredients in a baking pan and fit in the air fryer basket. Insert in your IP. Place the air fryer lid on top.

Select Air Fry and set the temperature to 380 F and the cooking time to 20 minutes. Push Start. At the 10-minute mark, Add the cauliflower mixture and stir to combine; cook for the remaining 6 minutes. Serve and enjoy.

Roasted Butternut Squash

Prep + Cook Time: 30 minutes | Serves: 2

Ingredients

1 tbsp dried rosemary	1 butternut squash	Salt to taste

Directions

Place the butternut squash on a cutting board, peel it; cut it in half, and remove the seeds. Cut the pulp into wedges and season with salt. Spray the squash wedges with cooking spray and sprinkle with rosemary. Grease the air fryer basket with cooking spray and place the wedges inside it without overlapping. Place the basket in your IP. Select Air Fry and set the temperature to 380 F and the cooking time to 20 minutes. Push Start. Serve.

Italian Spinach & Pumpkin Bowl

Prep + Cook Time: 30 minutes | Serves: 1

Ingredients

1 spring onion, sliced	½ cup baby spinach, packed	1 tbsp olive oil
1 radish, thinly sliced	2 oz blue cheese, cubed	1 tsp vinegar
½ small pumpkin, cubed	2 tbsp almonds, chopped	

Directions

Place the pumpkin in a baking dish and toss it with olive oil. Place in the air fryer basket. Insert the basket into the IP and put the air fryer lid on top. Select Bake and set the temperature to 390 F and the cooking time to 20 minutes. Push Start. Remove the pumpkin to a serving bowl. Add baby spinach, radish, and spring onion; toss with the vinegar. Stir in the cubed blue cheese and top with almonds. Serve and enjoy!

Simple Black Bean Burritos

Prep + Cook Time: 20 minutes | Serves: 6

Ingredients

1 can (14 oz) black beans	1 cup grated cheddar cheese
6 tortillas	1 tsp taco seasoning

Directions

Mix the beans with the seasoning. Divide the bean mixture between the tortillas and top with cheddar cheese. Roll the burritos and arrange them on the air fryer basket; fit in your IP. Place the air fryer lid on top. Select Air Fry and set the temperature to 350 F and the cooking time to 8 minutes. Push Start. Serve and enjoy!

Veggie Fennel Cabbage Steaks

Prep + Cook Time: 25 minutes | Serves: 3

Ingredients

2 tbsp olive oil	1 tbsp garlic paste	Salt and black pepper to taste
1 cabbage head	2 tsp fennel seeds	

Directions

Slice the cabbage into 1 ½-inch slice. In a small bowl, combine all the other ingredients; brush cabbage with the mixture. Arrange the cabbage steaks on the air fryer basket. Insert the basket into the IP and put the air fryer lid on top. Select Air Fry and set the temperature to 350 F and the cooking time to 15 minutes. Push Start. Serve.

Aunt's Blooming Onions

Prep + Cook Time: 40 minutes | Serves: 4

Ingredients

4 butter dollops

4 onions

1 tbsp olive oil

Directions

Peel the onions and slice off the root bottom so it can sit well. Cut slices into the onion to make it look like a blooming flower. Make sure not to go all the way through; four cuts will do. Place the onions in the air fryer basket. Drizzle with olive oil, place a dollop of butter on top of each onion and fit the basket into the IP. Put the fryer lid on top. Select Air Fry and set the temperature to 350 F and the cooking time to 12 minutes. Push Start.

Creamy Broccoli Florets

Prep + Cook Time: 25 minutes | Serves: 2

Ingredients

½ lb broccoli florets

2 tbsp butter, melted

1 egg white

1 garlic clove, grated

Salt and black pepper to taste

⅓ cup grated Parmesan cheese

Directions

In a bowl, whisk together the butter, egg, garlic, salt, and black pepper. Toss in broccoli to coat well. Arrange broccoli in a single layer in the air fryer basket without overcrowding. Insert the basket into the IP and put the air fryer lid on top. Select Air Fry and set the temperature to 360 F and the cooking time to 10 minutes. Push Start. Remove to a serving plate and sprinkle with Parmesan cheese. Enjoy!

Classic Italian Zucchini

Prep + Cook Time: 40 minutes | Serves: 4

Ingredients

4 garlic cloves, minced

4 small zucchini, cut lengthwise

½ cup grated Parmesan cheese

½ cup breadcrumbs

¼ cup melted butter

Salt and black pepper to taste

Directions

In a bowl, mix breadcrumbs, Parmesan, butter, garlic, salt, and pepper. Arrange the zucchinis with the cut side up on the greased frying basket. Spread the mixture onto the zucchini evenly. Place the basket in your IP. Place the air fryer lid on top. Select Air Fry and set the temperature to 370 F and the time to 14 minutes. Push Start.

Fitness Broccoli & Egg Cups

Prep + Cook Time: 20 minutes | Serves: 4

Ingredients

1 cup cheddar cheese, shredded

1 cup heavy cream

1 lb broccoli, finely chopped

2 eggs

1 pinch of nutmeg

Salt and black pepper to taste

Directions

Steam the broccoli in your IP on Steam for 5 minutes. Remove to a bowl and mix with eggs, heavy cream, nutmeg, salt, and pepper. Spoon the mixture into 4 greased ramekins. Top with the cheese. Place the ramekins in the air fryer basket. Insert the basket into the IP and put the air fryer lid on top. Select Bake and set the temperature to 350 F and the cooking time to 12 minutes. Push Start. Serve and enjoy!

Traditional Russian Veggie Caviar

Prep + Cook Time: 20 minutes | Serves: 3

Ingredients

½ red onion, chopped and blended
3 medium eggplants

2 tbsp balsamic vinegar
1 tbsp olive oil

Salt to taste

Directions

Arrange the eggplants in the air fryer basket and fit it in your IP. Place the air fryer lid on top. Select Bake and set the temperature to 380 F and the cooking time to 16 minutes. Push Start. Remove them and let them cool.

Then cut the eggplants in half, lengthwise, and empty their insides with a spoon. Blend the onion inside of the eggplants in a food processor until smooth. Pour in the vinegar, olive oil, and salt while the blender is running. Serve cool with bread and tomato sauce or ketchup if desired.

Cheesy Green Chilies in Tomato Sauce

Prep + Cook Time: 35 minutes | Serves: 4

Ingredients

1 can tomato sauce
2 cans green chili peppers
1 cup cheddar cheese, shredded

1 cup Monterey Jack cheese.
2 large eggs, beaten
½ cup milk

2 tbsp all-purpose flour

Directions

Arrange half of the green chili peppers on a greased baking dish. Top with cheese and cover with the other half of the chilies. In a medium bowl, combine the eggs, milk, flour and pour mixture over the chilies.

Place the baking dish inside the air fryer basket. Insert the basket into the IP and put the air fryer lid on top. Select Bake and set the temperature to 380 F and the cooking time to 20 minutes. Push Start. At the 15-minute mark, pour the tomato sauce over and cook for the remaining 5 minutes. Serve and enjoy!

Homemade Green Quesadillas

Prep + Cook Time: 20 minutes | Serves: 4

Ingredients

1 lb spinach, torn
1 garlic clove, minced
8 corn tortillas

2 cups mozzarella cheese, shredded
1 cup ricotta cheese
½ cup sliced onions

½ cup sour cream
1 tbsp butter
1 can enchilada sauce

Directions

Heat the olive oil in your IP on Sauté and sauté the garlic and onion until brown, 5 minutes. Stir in the spinach and cook for 5 more minutes. Remove to a bowl and stir in the ricotta cheese, sour cream, and shredded cheese. Spoon the spinach mixture in the middle of the tortillas.

Roll up and place them, seam side down, in the air fryer basket. Pour the enchilada sauce over the tortillas and sprinkle with the remaining cheese. Insert the basket into the IP and put the air fryer lid on top. Select Air Fry and set the temperature to 380 F and the cooking time to 15 minutes. Push Start. Serve and enjoy!

Crunchy Feta Turnovers

Prep + Cook Time: 20 minutes | Serves: 4

Ingredients

1 egg yolk
1 scallion, finely chopped
4 oz feta cheese

2 sheets filo pastry
2 tbsp parsley, finely chopped
2 tbsp olive oil

Salt and black pepper to taste

Directions

In a large bowl, beat the yolk and mix with the cheese, parsley, and scallion. Season with salt and black pepper. Cut each filo sheet into three parts or strips. Put a teaspoon of the feta mixture on the bottom. Roll the strip in a spinning spiral way until the filling of the inside mixture is completely wrapped in a triangle.

Brush the surface of the filo with oil. Place them in the air fryer basket. Insert the basket into the IP and put the air fryer lid on top. Select Bake and set the temperature to 350 F and the cooking time to 12 minutes. Push Start. Serve and enjoy!

Southeast Spicy Sweet Potatoes

Prep + Cook Time: 30minutes | Serves: 4

Ingredients

3 sweet potatoes, cut into ½-inch thick wedges
3 tbsp olive oil
½ tsp salt
½ tsp garlic powder

½ tsp cayenne pepper
¼ tsp cumin
A handful of chopped fresh parsley

Sea salt to taste

Directions

In a bowl, whisk the oil, salt, garlic powder, chili powder, and cumin. Add in the potatoes and toss to coat. Arrange them on the air fryer basket. Insert the basket into the IP and put the air fryer lid on top.

Select Air Fry and set the temperature to 400 F and the cooking time to 20 minutes. Push Start. Toss halfway through the cooking time. Sprinkle with parsley and sea salt. Serve and enjoy!

Greek Spanakopita

Prep + Cook Time: 20 minutes | Serves: 4

Ingredients

1 cup crumbled feta cheese
14 oz store-bought crescent dough

1 cup steamed spinach
¼ tsp garlic powder

¼ tsp Greek oregano
¼ tsp salt

Directions

Roll the dough onto a lightly floured flat surface. Combine the feta, spinach, oregano, salt, and garlic powder in a bowl. Cut the dough into 4 equal pieces. Divide the spinach mixture between the dough pieces. Make sure to place the filling in the center. Fold the dough and seal with a fork. Place onto a lined baking dish.

Fit the dish in the fryer basket. Insert the basket into the IP and put the fryer lid on top. Select Bake and set the temperature to 350 F and the time to 12 minutes. Push Start. The spanakopita should be lightly browned.

SNACKS, APPETIZERS & SIDE DISHES

Party Sweet Ribs

Prep + Cook Time: 30 minutes | Serves: 4

Ingredients

2 lb pork spareribs, individually cut   Garlic salt and black pepper to taste
1 (5-oz) can pineapple juice   7 oz salad dressing

Directions

Sprinkle the ribs with salt and pepper and place them in the air fryer basket. Insert the basket into the IP and put the air fryer lid on top. Select Air Fry and set the temperature to 390 F and the cooking time to 15 minutes. Push Start. Shake halfway through the cooking time. Prepare the sauce by combining the salad dressing and the pineapple juice. Serve the ribs drizzled with the sauce.

Cabbage & Prawn Egg Rolls

Prep + Cook Time: 50 minutes | Serves: 4

Ingredients

1 egg, beaten   1 tbsp minced garlic   1 tbsp sugar
8 cooked prawns, minced   2 tbsp vegetable oil   1 cup shredded Napa cabbage
1 carrot, cut into strips   ¼ cup chicken broth   1 tbsp sesame oil
1-inch piece fresh ginger, grated   2 tbsp reduced-sodium soy sauce 8 egg roll wrappers

Directions

Heat the olive oil in your IP on Sauté and cook ginger and garlic for 40 seconds until fragrant. Stir in carrot and cook for another 2 minutes. Pour in chicken broth, soy sauce, and sugar and bring to a boil. Add cabbage and let simmer until softened, 4 minutes. Remove the mixture and stir in sesame oil. Let cool for 15 minutes.

Strain cabbage mixture and stir in minced prawns. Fill each egg roll wrapper with prawn mixture, arranging the mixture just below the center of the wrapper. Fold the bottom part over the filling and tuck under.

Fold in both sides and tightly roll-up. Seal the roll with the beaten egg. Repeat until all egg rolls are ready. Place the rolls into the greased air fryer basket, spray with oil and cook for 12 minutes at 370 F on Bake, turning once.

Easy Parmesan Chicken Nuggets

Prep + Cook Time: 25 minutes | Serves: 4

Ingredients

1 lb chicken breasts, cubed   ½ tsp ground black pepper   2 tbsp olive oil
¼ tsp kosher salt   5 tbsp plain breadcrumbs   2 tbsp grated Parmesan cheese
¼ tsp seasoned salt   2 tbsp panko breadcrumbs

Directions

Season the chicken with pepper, kosher salt, and seasoned salt; set aside. In a bowl, pour olive oil. In a separate bowl, add crumbs and Parmesan cheese. Place the chicken pieces in the oil to coat, then dip into crumbs.

Transfer to the air fryer basket. Lightly spray chicken with cooking spray. Insert the basket into the IP and put the air fryer lid on top. Select Air Fry and set the temperature to 380 F and the cooking time to 12 minutes. Push Start. The nuggets should be golden brown on the outside and no more pink on the inside.

Sesame Garlic Chicken Wings

Prep + Cook Time: 55 minutes + chilling time | Serves: 4

Ingredients

1 pound chicken wings
½ cup brown sugar
1 cup soy sauce, divided
½ cup apple cider vinegar

2 tbsp fresh garlic, minced
2 tbsp fresh ginger, minced
1 tsp finely ground black pepper
2 tbsp cornstarch

1 tsp sesame seeds
2 tbsp cold water

Directions

Set your IP to Sauté and add the sugar, ½ cup of soy sauce, vinegar, ginger, garlic, and black pepper. Cook until the sauce has reduced slightly, about 6 minutes. Dissolve 2 tbsp of cornstarch in cold water in a bowl and stir in the slurry into the sauce until it thickens, 2 minutes. Set aside until ready to use.

In a bowl, add chicken wings and pour in ½ cup of soy sauce. Refrigerate for 20 minutes; drain and pat dry. Arrange the wings on the air fryer and fit in your IP. Place the air fryer lid on top. Select Air Fry and set the temperature to 380 F and the cooking time to 20 minutes. Push Start. Turn once halfway through. Pour the previously prepared sauce over the wings and sprinkle with sesame seeds. Serve and enjoy!

Veggie Rolls with Noodles

Prep + Cook Time: 30 minutes | Serves: 4

Ingredients

1 cup cooked and cooled vermicelli noodles
4 spring roll wrappers
2 garlic cloves, finely chopped
1 tsp fresh ginger puree

2 tbsp soy sauce
2 tsp sesame oil
1 red bell pepper, chopped

1 cup chopped mushrooms
1 cup chopped carrots
½ cup chopped scallions

Directions

Heat the sesame oil in your IP on Sauté and add garlic, ginger, soy sauce, pepper, mushrooms, carrots, and scallions; stir-fry for 3 minutes until soft. Add in vermicelli noodles; remove. Place the spring roll wrappers onto a working board. Spoon dollops of veggie and noodle mixture at the center of each spring roll wrapper. Roll the spring rolls and tuck the corners and edges in to create neat and secure rolls. Spray with cooking oil.

Transfer them to the air fryer basket. Insert the basket into the IP and put the air fryer lid on top. Select Air Fry and set the temperature to 350 F and the cooking time to 12 minutes. Push Start. Turn once halfway through. The rolls should be golden and crispy. Serve with soy or sweet chili sauce if desired.

Smoky Pear Ham

Prep + Cook Time: 30 minutes | Serves: 2

Ingredients

18 oz smoked ham
1 pear, halved
1 tbsp brown sugar

¾ tbsp allspice
1 tbsp apple cider vinegar
1 tsp black pepper

1 tsp vanilla extract

Directions

In a bowl, mix pear, brown sugar, cider vinegar, vanilla extract, pepper, and allspice. Place the mixture in the air fryer pan and fit in your IP. Place the air fryer lid on top. Select Air Fry and set the temperature to 350 F and the cooking time to 18 minutes. Push Start. At the 5-minute mark, pour the pear mixture over ham and cook for the remaining 6 minutes. Serve ham with hot sauce and enjoy!

Crispy Homemade Squash

Prep + Cook Time: 25 minutes | Serves: 4

Ingredients

2 cups peeled butternut squash, cubed
¼ tsp dried thyme   1 tbsp olive oil
Salt and black pepper to taste   1 tbsp chopped fresh parsley

Directions

In a bowl, add squash, oil, salt, pepper, and thyme, and toss until squash is well-coated. Place squash in the air fryer basket and fit it in your IP. Place the air fryer lid on top. Select Air Fry and set the temperature to 360 F and the cooking time to 14 minutes. Push Start. When ready, sprinkle with freshly chopped parsley and serve.

Golden Chicken Breasts

Prep + Cook Time: 30 minutes | Serves: 4

Ingredients

1 ½ lb chicken breasts, cut into strips   1 egg, lightly beaten   Salt and black pepper to taste
1 cup seasoned breadcrumbs   ½ tsp dried oregano

Directions

Season the chicken with oregano, salt, and black pepper. In a small bowl, whisk in some salt and pepper to the beaten egg. In a separate bowl, add the crumbs. Dip chicken tenders in the egg wash, then in the crumbs.

Roll the strips in the breadcrumbs and press firmly so the breadcrumbs stick well. Spray the chicken tenders with cooking spray and arrange them in the air fryer basket. Insert the basket into the IP and put the air fryer lid on top. Select Air Fry and set the temperature to 390 F and the cooking time to 14 minutes. Push Start. Serve.

Chicken Tacos with Yogurt

Prep + Cook Time: 25 minutes | Serves: 4

Ingredients

1 cup cooked chicken, shredded   1 cup shredded mozzarella cheese   8 flour tortillas
¼ cup salsa   ¼ cup plain yogurt   Salt and black pepper to taste

Directions

In a bowl, mix chicken, cheese, salsa, and yogurt and season with salt and pepper. Spray one side of the tortilla with cooking spray. Lay 2 tbsp of the chicken mixture at the center of the non-oiled side of each tortilla.

Roll tightly around the mixture. Arrange taquitos into the air fryer basket without overcrowding. Insert the basket into the IP and put the air fryer lid on top. Select Air Fry and set the temperature to 380 F and the cooking time to 14 minutes. Push Start. When cooking is complete, the tacos should be crispy. Serve and enjoy!

The Crispiest Kale Chips

Prep + Cook Time: 25 minutes | Serves: 4

Ingredients

4 cups chopped kale leaves, stems removed
1 tsp garlic powder   Salt and black pepper to taste   1 cup tahini sauce
¼ tsp onion powder   2 tbsp olive oil

Directions

In a bowl, mix kale, oil, garlic, salt, onion, and pepper and toss until well-coated. Arrange the kale leaves on the air fryer basket in a single layer. Insert the basket into the IP and put the air fryer lid on top. Select Air Fry and set the temperature to 350 F and the cooking time to 8 minutes. Push Start. Serve with tahini sauce and enjoy!

English Cheesy Balls

Prep + Cook Time: 25 minutes + chilling time| Serves: 6

Ingredients

2 tbsp olive oil
1 ¼ cups cheddar cheese, shredded
1 ½ lb ground sausages
4 eggs

1 ½ cup flour
¾ tsp baking soda
¾ cup sour cream
2 tsp garlic powder

1 tsp dried oregano
1 tsp smoked paprika
½ cup liquid coconut oil

Directions

Heat the olive oil in your IP on Sauté. Brown the sausages for 3-4 minutes; reserve. In a bowl, sift the flour and baking soda. In another bowl, add eggs, sour cream, oregano, paprika, coconut oil, and garlic powder. Whisk to combine. Combine the egg and flour mixtures using a spatula. Add in the cheese and sausages. Let sit for 5 minutes to thicken. Rub your hands with coconut oil and mold out bite-size balls out of the batter.

Place them on a tray and refrigerate for 15 minutes. Then, add them to the air fryer basket without overcrowding. Insert the basket into the IP and put the air fryer lid on top. Select Bake and set the temperature to 400 F and the cooking time to 12 minutes. Push Start. Serve and enjoy!

Easy Fish & Cheese Balls

Prep + Cook Time: 45 minutes | Serves: 6

Ingredients

1 cup smoked fish, flaked
2 eggs, lightly beaten
1 cup panko crumbs

2 cups cooked rice
1 cup grated Grana Padano cheese
¼ cup finely chopped thyme

Salt and black pepper to taste

Directions

In a bowl, add fish, rice, eggs, Parmesan cheese, thyme, salt, and pepper into a bowl; stir to combine. Shape the mixture into 12 even-sized balls. Roll the balls in the crumbs, then spray with oil. Arrange the balls onto the air fryer basket, insert the basket into the IP, and put the air fryer lid on top. Select Air Fry and set the temperature to 400 F and the cooking time to 16 minutes. Push Start. Shake halfway through. Serve and enjoy!

Effortless Pumpkin Seeds

Prep + Cook Time: 20 minutes | Serves: 4

Ingredients

1 cup pumpkin seeds, pulp removed, rinsed
1 tbsp brown sugar
½ tsp salt

1 tbsp butter, melted
1 tsp orange zest

½ tsp cardamom

Directions

Place the seeds in the air fryer basket and Air Fry in your IP for 4 minutes at 320 F to avoid moisture. In a bowl, whisk butter, sugar, zest, cardamom, and salt. Add in the seeds and toss to coat. Transfer the seeds to the air fryer basket and cook for 10 minutes at 300 F, shaking the basket once. The seeds should be lightly browned.

Classic Beef Balls

Prep + Cook Time: 30 minutes | Serves: 4

Ingredients

1 lb ground beef	1 onion, finely chopped	½ cup fresh mixed herbs
2 eggs	3 garlic cloves, finely chopped	Salt and black pepper to taste
1 tbsp mustard	1 cup breadcrumbs	Olive oil

Directions

In a bowl, add beef, onion, garlic, eggs, crumbs, herbs, mustard, salt, and pepper and mix with hands to combine. Shape into balls and arrange them on the air fryer basket. Drizzle with oil and insert the basket into the IP; put the air fryer lid on top. Select Air Fry and set the temperature to 380 F and the cooking time to 16 minutes. Push Start. Shake halfway through the cooking time. Serve and enjoy!

Buffalo Cauli "Wings"

Prep + Cook Time: 25 minutes | Serves: 4

Ingredients

½ head cauliflower, cut into florets	3 tbsp butter, melted	1 egg white
1 cup panko breadcrumbs	3 tbsp buffalo hot sauce	Salt and black pepper to taste

Directions

In a bowl, mix butter, hot sauce, and egg white. Mix breadcrumbs with salt and pepper in a separate bowl. Toss the florets in the hot sauce mixture until well-coated. Roll the coated cauliflower in the crumbs, then transfer the florets to the air fryer basket. Spray with cooking spray. Insert the basket into the IP and put the air fryer lid on top. Select Air Fry and set the temperature to 350 F and the cooking time to 18 minutes. Push Start. Serve.

Hot Sweet Potato Wedges

Prep + Cook Time: 30 minutes | Serves: 2

Ingredients

1 sweet potato, cut into wedges	½ tsp dried thyme	1 tbsp olive oil
¼ tsp salt	½ tsp chili powder	A pinch of cayenne pepper
½ tsp garlic powder	½ tsp smoked paprika	

Directions

In a bowl, mix olive oil, salt, chili powder, garlic powder, smoked paprika, thyme, and cayenne. Toss in the potato wedges until well-coated. Arrange the wedges evenly in the air fryer basket. Insert the basket into the IP and put the air fryer lid on top. Select Air Fry and set the temperature to 380 F and the cooking time to 25 minutes. Push Start. Flip halfway through the cooking time. Serve and enjoy!

Cheesy Jalapeño Chicken Breasts

Prep + Cook Time: 40 minutes | Serves: 4

Ingredients

4 chicken breasts, butterflied and halved
8 Jalapeno peppers, halved lengthwise and seeded

1 cup breadcrumbs	6 oz cream cheese	16 slices bacon
2 eggs	6 oz cheddar cheese	Salt and black pepper to taste

Directions

Season the chicken with pepper and salt on both sides. In a bowl, add cream cheese, cheddar cheese, pepper, and salt. Mix well. Take each jalapeno and spoon in the cheese mixture to the brim.

On a working board, flatten each piece of chicken and lay 2 bacon slices each on them. Place a stuffed jalapeno on each laid-out chicken and bacon set and wrap the jalapenos in them. Add the eggs to a bowl and pour the breadcrumbs into another bowl. Take each wrapped jalapeno and dip it into the eggs and then in the breadcrumbs.

Arrange 4-5 breaded jalapenos on the greased air fryer basket. Insert the basket into the IP and put the air fryer lid on top. Select Air Fry and set the temperature to 350 F and the cooking time to 12 minutes. Push Start. Turn over halfway through the cooking time. Serve with a sweet dip for an enhanced taste.

French-Style Meatballs with Mustard

Prep + Cook Time: 25 minutes | Serves: 3

Ingredients

½ lb ground beef	1 small finger ginger, crushed	2 tbsp sugar
1 tbsp hot sauce	3 tbsp vinegar	¼ tsp dry mustard
½ cup tomato ketchup	1 ½ tsp lemon juice	Salt and black pepper to taste

Directions

In a bowl, add beef, ginger, hot sauce, vinegar, lemon juice, tomato ketchup, sugar, mustard, pepper, and salt and mix well. Shape the mixture into 2-inch sized balls. Add the balls to the air fryer basket without overcrowding. Insert the basket into the IP and put the air fryer lid on top. Select Air Fry and set the temperature to 370 F and the cooking time to 15 minutes. Push Start. Shake halfway through the cooking time. Serve and enjoy!

Classic Vegetarian Croquettes

Prep + Cook Time: 45 minutes | Serves: 4

Ingredients

1 brown onion, chopped	½ cup grated Parmesan cheese	½ cup breadcrumbs
2 garlic cloves, chopped	2 eggs, lightly beaten	1 tsp dried mixed herbs
2 cups cooked rice	Salt and black pepper to taste	

Directions

Combine rice, onion, garlic, eggs, Parmesan cheese, salt, and pepper. Shape into 10 croquettes. Spread the crumbs onto a plate and coat each croquette in the crumbs. Spray each croquette with oil. Arrange the croquettes on the air fryer basket, insert the basket into the IP, and put the air fryer lid on top. Select Air Fry and set the temperature to 380 F and the cooking time to 16 minutes. Push Start. Turn once. Serve and enjoy!

Effortless Chicken Alfredo Wings

Prep + Cook Time: 60 minutes | Serves: 4

Ingredients

1 ½ pounds chicken wings	½ cup Alfredo sauce	Salt to taste

Directions

Season the wings with salt. Arrange them on the air fryer basket without touching. Insert the basket into the IP and put the air fryer lid on top. Select Air Fry and set the temperature to 370 F and the cooking time to 20 minutes. Push Start. Shake halfway through the cooking time. Remove to a bowl and coat with the Alfredo sauce. Serve.

Air Fried Pepperoni Pizza

Prep + Cook Time: 25 minutes | Serves: 2

Ingredients

8 pepperoni slices

⅓ cup tomato sauce

8 ounces fresh pizza dough

⅓ cup mozzarella cheese, shredded

Flour to dust

Directions

On a floured surface, place dough and dust with flour. Stretch with hands into an air-fryer fitting shape. Spray the air fryer basket with cooking spray and place the pizza inside. Brush generously with sauce, leaving some space at the border. Scatter with mozzarella and top with pepperoni. Cook in your IP for 15 minutes on Bake mode at 340 F until crispy. Serve and enjoy!

Effortless Crispy Potatoes

Prep + Cook Time: 45 minutes | Serves: 4

Ingredients

2 tbsp olive oil

4 Yukon gold potatoes

Salt and black pepper to taste

Directions

Rub the potatoes with olive oil. Season generously with salt and pepper and arrange them on the air fryer basket. Insert the basket into the IP and put the air fryer lid on top. Select Air Fry and set the temperature to 400 F and the cooking time to 25 minutes. Push Start. Flip halfway through the cooking time. Let cool slightly, then make a slit on top. Use a fork to fluff the insides of the potatoes. Fill the potato with cheese or garlic mayo.

Homemade BBQ Chicken

Prep + Cook Time: 35 minutes | Serves: 3

Ingredients

1 pound chicken legs

1 cup BBQ sauce

1 tsp garlic powder

1 tsp salt

1 tsp smoked paprika

Directions

Mix salt, paprika, and garlic powder in a bowl and add the chicken legs; toss to coat. Place them in a baking pan and fit in the air fryer basket. Insert the basket into the IP and put the air fryer lid on top. Select Air Fry and set the temperature to 400 F and the cooking time to 25 minutes. Push Start. At the 20-minute mark, turn the chicken legs over and brush them with barbecue sauce; cook for the remaining 5 minutes. Serve and enjoy!

Aunt's Chicken Thighs

Prep + Cook Time: 30 minutes | Serves: 4

Ingredients

1 pound chicken thighs

¼ tsp garlic powder

½ tsp salt

¼ tsp black pepper

Directions

Season the thighs with salt, pepper, and garlic powder. Arrange thighs, skin side down, on the air fryer, insert the basket into the IP, and put the air fryer lid on top. Select Air Fry and set the temperature to 380 F and the cooking time to 20 minutes. Push Start. Serve and enjoy!

Classic Cheesy Dill Pickles

Prep + Cook Time: 25 minutes | Serves: 4

Ingredients

3 cups dill pickles, sliced, drained

2 eggs

1 ½ cups breadcrumbs, smooth

1 cup grated Parmesan cheese

Black pepper to taste

2 tsp water

Directions

Add the breadcrumbs and black pepper to a bowl and mix well. In another bowl, crack the eggs and beat with the water. Add the cheese to a third bowl. Dredge the pickle slices it in the egg mixture, then in breadcrumbs, and then in cheese. Place them in the air fryer basket without overlapping. Insert the basket into the IP and put the air fryer lid on top. Select Air Fry and set the temperature to 380 F and the cooking time to 12 minutes. Push Start. Turn over halfway through the cooking time. The Pickles should be crispy. Serve and enjoy!

Family Chicken Wing Appetizer

Prep + Cook Time: 30 minutes | Serves: 3

Ingredients

15 chicken wings

⅓ cup chili sauce

½ tbsp vinegar

Salt and black pepper to taste

⅓ cup butter

Directions

Melt the butter in your IP on Sauté. Add the vinegar and hot sauce and stir for a minute until well combined. Set aside until ready to use. Season the wings with pepper and salt. Add them to the air fryer basket and fit in your IP. Place the air fryer lid on top. Select Air Fry and set the temperature to 380 F and the cooking time to 20 minutes. Push Start. Shake halfway through the cooking time. Serve the chicken with hot sauce.

Garlic & Lemon Baked Chicken

Prep + Cook Time: 25 minutes | Serves: 4

Ingredients

1 pound chicken breasts

2 garlic cloves

1 lemon, cut into wedges

1 tbsp olive oil

Salt and black pepper to taste

Directions

Rub chicken breasts with olive oil and garlic season with salt and pepper. Arrange them on the air fryer basket. Insert the basket into the IP and put the air fryer lid on top. Select Air Fry and set the temperature to 370 F and the cooking time to 16 minutes. Push Start. Turn over halfway through the cooking time. Serve sliced.

Caeser-Style Crunchy Croutons

Prep + Cook Time: 20 minutes | Serves: 4

Ingredients

2 tbsp butter, melted

2 cups bread, cubed

Garlic salt and black pepper to taste

Directions

In a bowl, toss the bread with butter, garlic salt, and pepper until well-coated. Place the cubes in the air fryer basket and fit it in your IP. Place the air fryer lid on top. Select Air Fry and set the temperature to 380 F and the cooking time to 12 minutes. Push Start. Shake halfway through. The croutons should be golden brown and crispy.

Basic Air Fried Chicken Breasts

Prep + Cook Time: 30 minutes | Serves: 4

Ingredients

4 chicken breasts	1 tsp garlic powder	Salt and black pepper to taste

Directions

Spray the breasts and the air fryer tray with cooking spray. Rub chicken with salt, garlic powder, and black pepper. Arrange the breasts on the air fryer basket. Insert the basket into the IP and put the air fryer lid on top. Select Air Fry and set the temperature to 360 F and the cooking time to 16 minutes. Push Start. Turn over halfway through the cooking time. When cooking is complete, the chicken should be nice and crispy. Serve.

Swiss-Style Stuffed Mushrooms

Prep + Cook Time: 30 minutes | Serves: 4

Ingredients

1 cup cooked brown rice	8 Swiss brown mushrooms	1 tsp dried mixed herbs
1 cup grated Grana Padano cheese	Olive oil to brush the mushrooms	Salt and black pepper to taste

Directions

Brush the mushrooms with oil and lay them onto a board. In a bowl, mix rice, cheese, herbs, salt, and pepper. Stuff the mushrooms with the mixture. Arrange the mushrooms on the air fryer basket and fit in your IP. Place the air fryer lid on top. Select Air Fry and set the temperature to 360 F and the cooking time to 14 minutes. Push Start. The mushrooms should be golden, and the cheese should be melted. Serve and enjoy!

Mediterranean Herby Chickpeas

Prep + Cook Time: 20 minutes | Serves: 4

Ingredients

2 (14.5-ounce) cans chickpeas, rinsed, dried	½ tsp dried thyme	¼ tsp salt
¼ tsp dried sage	2 tbsp olive oil	
	1 tsp dried rosemary	

Directions

In a bowl, mix together chickpeas, oil, rosemary, thyme, sage, and salt. Transfer them to the air fryer basket and fit in your IP. Place the air fryer lid on top. Select Air Fry and set the temperature to 380 F and the cooking time to 14 minutes. Push Start. Shaking once halfway through cooking. Serve and enjoy!

Classic French Fries

Prep + Cook Time: 30 minutes | Serves: 2

Ingredients

2 tbsp olive oil	2 russet potatoes, cut into strips	Salt and black pepper to taste

Directions

Spray the air fryer basket or rack with cooking spray. In a bowl, toss the strips with olive oil until well-coated, and season with salt and pepper. Arrange on the air fryer basket and fit in your IP. Place the air fryer lid on top. Select Air Fry and set the temperature to 400 F and the cooking time to 25 minutes. Push Start. Check for crispiness and serve immediately, with garlic aioli, ketchup, or crumbled cheese if desired.

Thai Shrimp with Coconut

Prep + Cook Time: 30 minutes | Serves: 5

Ingredients

1 lb jumbo shrimp, peeled and deveined

½ cup milk

¾ cup shredded coconut

⅓ cup cornstarch

½ cup breadcrumbs

1 tbsp maple syrup

Directions

Pour the cornstarch in a zipper bag, add shrimp, zip the bag up, and shake vigorously to coat with the cornstarch. Mix the syrup and milk in a bowl and set aside. In a separate bowl, mix the breadcrumbs and shredded coconut. Open the zipper bag and remove each shrimp while shaking off excess starch.

Dip each shrimp in the milk mixture and then in the crumbs mixture while pressing loosely to trap enough crumbs and coconut. Place the coated shrimp in the fryer without overcrowding. Insert the basket into the IP and put the air fryer lid on top. Select Air Fry and set the temperature to 350 F and the cooking time to 12 minutes. Push Start. Flip halfway through the cooking time. Serve with a coconut-based dip.

The Easiest Cheese Crisps

Ready in about: 25 minutes | Serves: 3

Ingredients

4 tbsp grated cheese + extra for rolling

1 cup flour + extra for kneading

¼ tsp chili powder

A pinch of salt

½ tsp baking powder

3 tsp butter

Directions

In a bowl, mix in the cheese, flour, baking powder, chili powder, butter, and salt. The mixture should be crusty. Add some drops of water and mix well to get a dough. Remove the dough on a flat surface.

Rub some extra flour in your palms and on the surface, and knead the dough for a while. Using a rolling pin, roll the dough out into a thin sheet. With a pastry cutter, cut the dough into your desired ling shapes. Add them to the air fryer basket and fit in your IP. Place the air fryer lid on top. Select Air Fry and set the temperature to 350 F and the cooking time to 6 minutes. Push Start. Flip halfway through the time. Serve.

Thai Cheese Fingers

Prep + Cook Time: 2 hrs 20 minutes | Serves: 4

Ingredients

3 eggs

4 tbsp skimmed milk

1 cup sweet Thai sauce

12 mozzarella string cheese

2 cups breadcrumbs

Directions

Pour the crumbs into a medium bowl. Crack the eggs into another bowl and beat with the milk. After the other, dip the cheese sticks in the egg mixture, then in the crumbs, then the egg mixture again, and then in the crumbs again. Place the coated cheese sticks on a cookie sheet and freeze for 1 to 2 hours.

Arrange the sticks on the air fryer basket without overcrowding. Insert the basket into the IP and put the air fryer lid on top. Select Air Fry and set the temperature to 380 F and the cooking time to 6 minutes. Push Start. Flip halfway through the cooking time. Serve with a sweet Thai sauce. Enjoy!

Fatty & Nutty Bombs

Prep + Cook Time: 25 minutes | Serves: 10

Ingredients

15 pancetta slices
15 dried plums, chopped

16 oz soft goat cheese
2 tbsp rosemary, finely chopped

1 cup almonds, chopped
Salt and black pepper to taste

Directions

Line the air fryer basket with baking paper. In a bowl, add cheese, rosemary, almonds, salt, pepper, and plums; stir well. Roll into balls and wrap with a pancetta slice. Arrange the bombs on the air fryer basket and fit in your IP. Place the air fryer lid on top. Select Air Fry and set the temperature to 400 F and the time to 10 minutes. Push Start. Check at the 5-minute mark to avoid overcooking. Let cool for a few minutes. Serve with toothpicks.

Yummy Crispy Fish Fingers

Prep + Cook Time: 20 minutes | Serves: 6

Ingredients

1 egg, beaten
½ cup buttermilk

2 fresh white fish fillets, cut into 4 fingers each

1 cup panko breadcrumbs
Salt and black pepper to taste

Directions

In a bowl, mix egg and buttermilk. On a plate, mix and spread crumbs, salt, and black pepper. Dip each finger into the egg mixture, roll it up in the crumbs, and spray with olive oil. Arrange them on the air fryer basket and fit in your IP. Place the air fryer lid on top. Select Air Fry and set the temperature to 360 F and the cooking time to 10 minutes. Push Start. Turn once halfway through. Serve with garlic mayo and lemon wedges.

Party Nuts with Cinnamon

Prep + Cook Time: 25 minutes | Serves: 5

Ingredients

2 tbsp egg whites
½ cup pecans
½ cup almonds

½ cup walnuts
A pinch of cayenne pepper
2 tbsp sugar

2 tsp cinnamon

Directions

Add the pepper, sugar, and cinnamon to a bowl and mix them well; set aside. In another bowl, mix in the pecans, walnuts, almonds, and egg whites. Add the spice mixture to the nuts and give it a good mix. Lightly grease the fryer basket with cooking spray.

Pour in the nuts, and cook them for 10 minutes at 390 F. Stir the nuts using a wooden vessel and cook for further 10 minutes. Pour the nuts into the bowl. Let cool before crunching on them.

Andalusian-Style Pitas with Chorizo

Prep + Cook Time: 25 minutes | Serves: 5

Ingredients

10 rounds chorizo
10 button mushrooms, sliced
5 tbsp marinara sauce

10 fresh basil leaves
2 cups grated cheddar cheese
1 tsp chili flakes

5 pita bread

Directions

Spray the pitas with oil and scatter the sauce over. Top with chorizo, mushrooms, basil, cheddar, and chili flakes. Place in a baking pan. Place the pan inside the air fryer basket. Insert the basket into the IP and put the air fryer lid on top. Select Bake and set the temperature to 360 F and the cooking time to 10 minutes. Push Start. Serve.

Yummy Avocado Rolls

Prep + Cook Time: 25 minutes | Serves: 6

Ingredients

3 large avocados, sliced
12 thick bacon strips

⅓ tsp chili powder
⅓ tsp cumin powder

⅓ tsp salt

Directions

Stretch the bacon strips to elongate and use a knife to cut in half to make 24 pieces. Wrap each bacon piece around a slice of avocado from one end to the other end. Tuck the end of bacon into the wrap. Arrange on a flat surface and season with salt, chili, and cumin on both sides.

Arrange the wrapped pieces on the air fryer basket and fit in your IP. Place the air fryer lid on top. Select Air Fry and set the temperature to 350 F and the cooking time to 8 minutes. Push Start. Flip halfway through the cooking time. When cooking is complete, the bacon should be crunchy. Serve and enjoy!

Greek Calamari with Olives

Prep + Cook Time: 25 minutes | Serves: 3

Ingredients

1 cup pimiento-stuffed green olives, sliced
1 tbsp olive oil
½ lb calamari rings

½ piece coriander, chopped
2 strips chili pepper, chopped

Salt and black pepper to taste

Directions

In a bowl, add rings, chili pepper, salt, black pepper, oil, and coriander. Mix and let marinate for 10 minutes. Pour the calamari into the air fryer basket. Insert the basket into the IP and put the air fryer lid on top. Select Air Fry and set the temperature to 400 F and the cooking time to 15 minutes. Push Start. Shake halfway through the cooking time. Once ready, transfer to a serving platter. Serve warm with a side of bread slices and mayonnaise.

Spiced Chicken Nuggets

Prep + Cook Time: 20 minutes + chilling time | Serves: 4

Ingredients

2 chicken breasts, bones removed
2 eggs
2 cups milk

2 tbsp paprika
4 tsp onion powder
1 ½ tsp garlic powder

1 cups flour
2 cups breadcrumbs
Salt and black pepper to taste

Directions

Cut the chicken into 1-inch chunks. In a bowl, mix in paprika, onion, garlic, salt, pepper, flour, and breadcrumbs. In another bowl, crack the eggs, add the milk, and beat them together. Prepare a tray. Dip each chicken chunk in the egg mixture, place them on the tray, and refrigerate for 1 hour.

Roll each chunk in the crumb mixture. Place the crusted chicken in the air fryer basket. Spray with cooking spray. Insert the basket into the IP and put the air fryer lid on top. Select Air Fry and set the temperature to 360 F and the cooking time to 8 minutes. Push Start. Flip once halfway through. Serve with ketchup. Yum!

Air Fried Cheesy Mushrooms

Prep + Cook Time: 55 minutes | Serves: 4

Ingredients

2 cups Parmigiano Reggiano cheese, grated
2 eggs, beaten
1 lb small Button mushrooms

2 cups breadcrumbs
Salt and black pepper to taste

Directions

Pour the breadcrumbs into a bowl, add salt and pepper and mix well. Pour the cheese into a separate bowl and set aside. Dip each mushroom in the eggs, then in the crumbs, and then in the cheese. Arrange them on the fryer basket and fit in your IP. Place the air fryer lid on top. Select Air Fry and set the temperature to 360 F and the cooking time to 20 minutes. Push Start. Serve with cheese dip if desired.

Italian Bruschetta with Cheddar

Prep + Cook Time: 25 minutes | Serves: 5

Ingredients

1 cup grated cheddar cheese
10 slices French baguette

3 garlic cloves, minced
1 tsp dried oregano

Olive oil
Salt and black pepper to taste

Directions

Brush the bread with oil and sprinkle with garlic. Scatter the cheese on top, then oregano, salt, and pepper. Arrange the slices on the air fryer basket and fit in your IP. Place the air fryer lid on top. Select Air Fry and set the temperature to 360 F and the cooking time to 14 minutes. Push Start. Serve and enjoy!

Classic Zucchini Crisps with Pecorino

Prep + Cook Time: 20 minutes | Serves: 3

Ingredients

2 eggs, beaten
1 cup grated Pecorino cheese

3 medium zucchinis
1 cup breadcrumbs

1 tsp smoked paprika
Salt and black pepper to taste

Directions

With a mandolin cutter, slice the zucchinis thinly. Use paper towels to press out excess liquid. In a bowl, add crumbs, salt, pepper, cheese, and paprika. Mix well and set aside. Set a wire rack or tray aside.

Dip each zucchini slice in egg and then in the cheese mix while pressing to coat them well. Place them on the wire rack. Spray the coated slices with oil. Put the slices in the air fryer basket in a single layer.

Insert the basket into the IP and put the air fryer lid on top. Select Air Fry and set the temperature to 350 F and the cooking time to 10 minutes. Push Start. Turn halfway through the cooking time. Serve with a spicy dip.

Easy Cheesy Onion Rings

Prep + Cook Time: 20 minutes | Serves: 3

Ingredients

1 onion, peeled and sliced into 1-inch rings
2 medium eggs, beaten
¾ cup Parmesan cheese

1 tsp garlic powder
1 cup flour

1 tsp paprika powder
A pinch of salt

Directions

Add the eggs to a bowl; set aside. In another bowl, add cheese, garlic powder, salt, flour, and paprika. Mix with a spoon. Dip each onion ring in the eggs, then in the cheese mixture, in the eggs again, and finally in the cheese mixture. Add the rings to the air fryer basket and fit in your IP. Place the air fryer lid on top. Select Air Fry and set the temperature to 380 F and the cooking time to 8 minutes. Push Start. Serve with tomato dip.

Cheesy Potatoes Balls

Prep + Cook Time: 50 minutes | Serves: 6

Ingredients

2 red potatoes, peeled and chopped
1 medium onion, finely chopped
2 cups crumbled Cottage cheese
2 cups grated Parmesan cheese

1 ½ tsp red chili flakes
1 green chili, finely chopped
4 tbsp chopped coriander leaves
1 cup flour

1 cup breadcrumbs
Salt to taste

Directions

Place the potatoes in your IP add cover with water. Seal the lid, select Manual, and cook for 25 minutes on High. Do a quick pressure release. Drain the potatoes through a sieve and place them in a bowl. With a potato masher, mash the potatoes and leave to cool. Add the cottage cheese, Parmesan cheese, onion, red chili flakes, green chili, salt, coriander, and flour to the potato mash. Use a wooden spoon to mix the ingredients well, then use your hands to mold out bite-size balls. Pour the crumbs into a bowl and roll each cheese ball lightly in it.

Place them in the fryer basket. Insert the basket into the IP and put the air fryer lid on top. Select Air Fry and set the temperature to 350 F and the cooking time to 15 minutes. Push Start. Turn over halfway through. Serve.

Crispy Brussels Sprouts

Prep + Cook Time: 15 minutes | Serves: 2

Ingredients

1 tbsp olive oil
½ pound Brussels sprouts, halved

½ tsp salt
¼ tsp black pepper

Directions

In a bowl, mix Brussels sprouts, oil, salt, and pepper. Place Brussels sprouts in the air fryer basket. Insert the basket into the IP and put the air fryer lid on top. Select Air Fry and set the temperature to 380 F and the cooking time to 10 minutes. Push Start. Shake halfway through the cooking time. Serve with sautéed onion rings.

Potato Chips with Herbs

Prep + Cook Time: 35 minutes | Serves: 2

Ingredients

2 tbsp olive oil
2 potatoes, sliced
3 garlic cloves, crushed

1 tsp each of fresh rosemary, thyme, oregano, chopped
Salt and black pepper to taste

Directions

In a bowl, add oil, garlic, herbs, salt, and pepper and toss with hands until well-coated. Arrange the slices on the air fryer basket and fit in your IP. Place the air fryer lid on top. Select Air Fry and set the temperature to 380 F and the cooking time to 23 minutes. Push Start. Shake halfway through the cooking time. Enjoy with onion dip.

Cayenne Red Potatoes

Prep + Cook Time: 25 minutes | Serves: 4

Ingredients

2 tsp olive oil

3 red potatoes, sliced, rinsed

1 tsp paprika

2 tsp cayenne pepper

Salt and black pepper to taste

Directions

Place the fries into a bowl and sprinkle with oil, cayenne, paprika, salt, and black pepper. Toss and place them in the air fryer basket. Insert the basket into the IP and put the air fryer lid on top. Select Air Fry and set the temperature to 360 F and the cooking time to 14 minutes. Push Start. The fries should be golden and crispy.

Classic Radish Chips

Prep + Cook Time: 30 minutes | Serves: 4

Ingredients

10 radishes, sliced

Salt to taste

Directions

Salt the radish slices and arrange them on the air fryer basket. Insert the basket into the IP and put the air fryer lid on top. Select Air Fry and set the temperature to 400 F and the time to 8 minutes. Push Start. Flip once.

Nutty Crispy Cauliflower

Prep + Cook Time: 23 minutes | Serves: 4

Ingredients

⅓ cup olive oil

⅓ cup toasted pine nuts

10 oz cauliflower florets

⅓ cup golden raisins, soaked

1 cup hot water

A pinch of salt

Directions

Add the cauliflower florets to the air fryer basket and toss with the olive oil and salt. Insert the basket into the IP and put the air fryer lid on top. Select Air Fry and set the temperature to 360 F and the cooking time to 12 minutes. Push Start. Shake halfway through the cooking time. Top with raisins and pine nuts. Serve and enjoy!

Prosciutto Salad with Brie Croutons

Prep + Cook Time: 20 minutes | Serves: 2

Ingredients

7 oz brie cheese, chopped

2 tbsp olive oil

1 tbsp mixed herbs

2 slices bread, halved

4 thick prosciutto slices

1 cup lettuce, torn into leaves

1 spring onion, sliced

1 tbsp lemon juice

2 tbsp extra virgin olive oil

Salt to taste

¼ tsp crushed red pepper flakes

Directions

In a bowl, mix the olive oil with herbs. Dip the bread slices in the oil mixture to coat. Place the coated slices on a flat surface. Lay the brie cheese on the bread slices. Place the slices into your air fryer basket and fit in your IP. Place the air fryer lid on top. Select Air Fry and set the temperature to 340 F and the cooking time to 7 minutes. Push Start. Shake halfway through the cooking time. Once the bread is ready, cut into cubes. Toss the lettuce, spring onion, lemon juice, olive oil, and salt in a salad bowl. Top the salad with prosciutto and croutons. Serve.

Linguine with Shrimp & Arugula

Prep + Cook Time: 30 minutes | Serves: 4

Ingredients

1 ¼ pounds raw shrimp, deveined
Salt and black pepper to taste
2 tbsp olive oil
2 garlic cloves, minced

¼ cup dry white wine
8 ounces linguine
10 cherry tomatoes
½ tsp red pepper flakes

1 tbsp lemon juice
1 tsp lemon zest
6 cups arugula
¼ cup Parmesan cheese, shredded

Directions

Cover the linguine with salted water in your IP. Seal the lid, select Manual, and cook for 3 minutes on High. When done, use a natural pressure release for 10 minutes. Drain the linguine and set aside. Place the shrimp in a baking pan. Mix with olive oil, garlic, wine, pasta, ½ cup of water, salt, pepper, and red pepper flakes.

Place the pan in the basket and fit in your IP. Put the air fryer lid on top. Select Bake and set the temperature to 400 F and the cooking time to 6 minutes. Push Start. Once the cooking process ends, stir in the lemon juice and zest. Add the arugula and tomatoes and toss them in the sauce to wilt. Top with Parmesan cheese and serve.

Mexican Tortilla Chips

Prep + Cook Time: 30 minutes | Serves: 6

Ingredients

2 cups shredded cheddar cheese
1 cup flour

Salt and black pepper to taste
1 tbsp golden flaxseed meal

Directions

Melt cheddar cheese in the microwave for 1 minute. Once melted, add the flour, salt, flaxseed meal, and pepper. Mix well with a fork. On a board, place the dough, and knead it with your hands while warm until the ingredients are well combined. Divide the dough into 2 and with a rolling pin, roll them out flat into 2 rectangles.

Use a pastry cutter to cut out triangle-shaped pieces and line them in 1 layer on a baking dish. Grease the fryer basket lightly with cooking spray. Arrange some triangle chips in 1 layer in the fryer basket without overlapping.

Spray them with cooking spray. Insert the basket into the IP and put the air fryer lid on top. Select Bake and set the temperature to 350 F and the cooking time to 8 minutes. Push Start. Serve with a cheese dip.

Effortless Cheesy Twists

Prep + Cook Time: 45 minutes | Serves: 6

Ingredients

3 ½ oz oats
1 egg
2 cups cauliflower florets, steamed

1 red onion, diced
1 tsp mustard
5 oz cheddar cheese

Salt and black pepper to taste

Directions

Place the oats in a food processor and pulse until they are the consistency of breadcrumbs. Place the steamed florets in a cheesecloth and squeeze out the excess liquid. Place the florets in a large bowl. Add the rest of the ingredients to the bowl. Mix well with hands to combine the ingredients completely.

Take a little bit of the mixture and twist it into a straw. Place on a lined baking sheet and repeat with the rest of the mixture. Place the sheet inside the air fryer basket. Insert the basket into the IP and put the air fryer lid on top. Select Bake and set the temperature to 350 F and the cooking time to 16 minutes. Push Start. Turn once.

Cheddar & Bacon Fries

Prep + Cook Time: 25 minutes | Serves: 4

Ingredients

5 slices bacon, chopped
2 large russet potatoes, julienned
2 cups cheddar cheese, shredded

2 tbsp vegetable oil
3 oz melted cream cheese
¼ cup scallions, chopped

Salt and black pepper to taste

Directions

In a bowl, mix cheddar and cream cheeses. Set aside until ready to use. Add the potatoes to the air fryer basket and season with salt and pepper. Coat with vegetable oil. Insert the basket into the IP and put the air fryer lid on top. Select Air Fry and set the temperature to 350 F and the cooking time to 25 minutes. Push Start.

At the 20-minute mark, spread the cheese mix over the potatoes and top with the bacon; cook for the remaining 5 minutes. Sprinkle with scallions and serve with your desired dressing. Enjoy!

Fancy Beef Kefta Kebab

Prep + Cook Time: 10 minutes + chilling time | Serves: 3

Ingredients

1 lb ground beef
1 tsp liquid smoke

3 tbsp sugar
A pinch of chili powder

A pinch of garlic powder
Salt to taste

Directions

Place the meat, sugar, garlic powder, chili powder, salt, and liquid smoke in a bowl. Knead until everything is well mixed. Make sausage shapes out of the meat mix, then skewer them onto flat skewers. Refrigerate for 2 hours. Arrange the skewers on the air fryer basket and fit in your IP. Place the air fryer lid on top. Select Air Fry and set the temperature to 350 F and the cooking time to 14 minutes. Push Start. Turn once. Serve immediately.

Party Onion Rings

Prep + Cook Time: 30 minutes | Serves: 4

Ingredients

2 cups buttermilk
2 sweet onions

2 cups pancake mix
1 package cornbread mix

1 tsp salt
2 cups water

Directions

Slice the onions into rings. Combine the pancake mix with the water. Line a baking sheet with parchment paper. Dip the rings in the cornbread mixture first and then in the pancake batter.

Place the onion rings onto the air fryer basket and fit in your IP. Place the air fryer lid on top. Select Air Fry and set the temperature to 370 F and the time to 12 minutes. Push Start. Serve with salsa rosa or garlic mayo.

Air Fried Cod Fingers

Prep + Cook Time: 25 minutes | Serves: 3

Ingredients

1 pound cod fillets, cut into fingers
2 cups flour
1 tsp seafood seasoning

2 whole eggs, beaten
1 cup cornmeal
2 tbsp milk

2 eggs, beaten
1 cup breadcrumbs
Salt and black pepper to taste

Directions

In a bowl, mix beaten eggs with milk. In a separate bowl, mix flour, cornmeal, and seafood seasoning. In another mixing bowl, mix spices with the eggs. In a third bowl, pour the breadcrumbs. Dip cod fingers in the seasoned flour mixture, followed by a dip in the egg mixture, and finally coat with breadcrumb. Place the prepared fingers in the air fryer basket and fit it in your IP. Place the air fryer lid on top. Select Air Fry and set the temperature to 400 F and the cooking time to 10 minutes. Push Start. Serve and enjoy!

Carrot & Salmon Croquettes

Prep + Cook Time: 40 minutes | Serves: 4

Ingredients

1 ½ cups grated carrots
1 cup grated onion
1 (15 oz) tinned salmon, flaked
3 large eggs

1 ½ tbsp chopped chives
4 tbsp mayonnaise
4 tbsp breadcrumbs
2 ½ tsp Italian seasoning

2 ½ tsp lemon juice
Salt and black pepper to taste

Directions

In a bowl, add salmon, onion, carrots, eggs, chives, mayo, crumbs, Italian seasoning, pepper, salt, and lemon juice and mix well. With hands, form 2-inch thick oblong balls from the mixture, resembling croquette shape. Put them on a flat tray and refrigerate for 45 minutes. Grease the air fryer basket with cooking spray.

Remove the croquettes from the fridge and arrange them in a single layer on the air fryer basket without overcrowding. Spray with cooking spray. Insert the basket into the IP and put the air fryer lid on top. Select Air Fry and set the temperature to 400 F and the cooking time to 10 minutes. Push Start. Turn over once. Serve.

Easy Cheese Sticks

Prep + Cook Time: 25 minutes | Serves: 6

Ingredients

2 tbsp butter

6 (6 oz) bread cheese

2 cups panko crumbs

Directions

Put the butter in a bowl and melt in the microwave for 2 minutes; set aside. With a knife, cut the cheese into equal-sized sticks. Brush each stick with butter and dip into panko crumbs. Arrange the cheese sticks in a single layer on the air fryer basket. Fit the basket in your IP. Place the air fryer lid on top. Select Air Fry and set the temperature to 390 F and the cooking time to 10 minutes. Push Start. Flip them halfway through. Serve warm.

Quick Cheddar Mushrooms

Prep + Cook Time: 20 minutes | Serves: 2

Ingredients

2 tbsp olive oil
2 cups mozzarella cheese, chopped
2 cups cheddar cheese, chopped

10 button mushrooms
3 tbsp mixture of Italian herbs
1 tbsp dried dill

Salt and black pepper to taste

Directions

In a bowl, mix oil, salt, pepper, herbs, and dill to form a marinade. Add button mushrooms to the marinade and toss to coat well. In a separate bowl, mix both kinds of cheese. Stuff each mushroom with the cheese mixture. Place the mushrooms in the air fryer basket, fit in the IP, and put the air fryer lid on top. Select Air Fry and set the temperature to 350 F and the cooking time to 12 minutes. Push Start. Serve and enjoy!

Homemade Chicken Croquettes

Prep + Cook Time: 20 minutes | Serves: 4

Ingredients

4 chicken breasts
1 cup oats, crumbled
1 whole egg

1 tbsp parsley
1 tbsp thyme
½ tsp garlic powder

Salt and black pepper to taste

Directions

Pulse chicken breast in a processor food until well blended. Add seasoning to the chicken alongside garlic, parsley, thyme, and mix well. In a bowl, add beaten egg and beat until the yolk is mixed. In a separate bowl, add crumbled oats. Form croquettes using the chicken mixture and dip in beaten egg and oats until coated.

Place the croquettes in the air fryer basket. Insert the basket into the IP and put the air fryer lid on top. Select Air Fry and set the temperature to 360 F and the cooking time to 16 minutes. Push Start. Shake once. Serve.

Turkish Minty Meatballs

Prep + Cook Time: 22 minutes | Serves: 4

Ingredients

Meatballs:

4 oz ground turkey
1 lb ground lamb
1 ½ tbsp chopped parsley
1 tbsp chopped mint

1 egg white
2 garlic cloves, chopped
2 tsp harissa
¼ cup olive oil

1 tsp cumin
1 tsp coriander
Salt and black pepper to taste

Yogurt:

½ cup yogurt
¼ cup sour cream

¼ cup chopped mint
2 tbsp buttermilk

1 garlic clove, minced
¼ tsp salt

Directions

Combine all the meatball ingredients in a large bowl. Make meatballs out of the mixture and arrange them on the greased air fryer basket. Insert the basket into the IP and put the air fryer lid on top. Select Air Fry and set the temperature to 390 F and the cooking time to 8 minutes. Push Start. Combine all yogurt ingredients in another bowl. Serve the meatballs topped with yogurt sauce and enjoy!

Easy Mushroom Pilaf

Prep + Cook Time: 40 minutes | Serves: 4

Ingredients

1 cup long-grain rice
3 tbsp olive oil
1 onion, chopped
2 cups vegetable stock

2 garlic cloves, minced
2 cups cremini mushrooms, chopped
Salt and black pepper to taste

1 tbsp fresh chopped parsley

Directions

Heat the olive oil in your IP on Sauté. Add the onion, garlic, and mushrooms and cook for 3 minutes. Pour in the stock and whisk well. Season with salt and pepper. Cook for 2-3 minutes and transfer to a baking pan. Fit in the air fryer basket and put the air fryer lid on top. Select Bake and set the temperature to 350 F and the cooking time to 20 minutes. Push Start. Serve sprinkled with fresh chopped parsley.

Yummy Eggplant Cakes

Prep + Cook Time: 20 minutes | Serves: 4

Ingredients

½ cup shredded eggplants
2 tbsp cream cheese
1 tbsp yogurt
1 ½ cups flour

2 tsp baking powder
1 tsp cinnamon
3 eggs
2 tbsp sugar

1 cup milk
2 tbsp butter, melted
Pinch of salt

Directions

In a bowl, whisk the eggs and sugar, salt, cinnamon, cream cheese, flour, and baking powder. In another bowl, combine all of the liquid ingredients. Gently combine the dry and liquid mixtures; stir in eggplant. Line the muffin tins and pour the batter inside. Place the tins into the air fryer basket.

Insert the basket into the IP and put the air fryer lid on top. Select Bake and set the temperature to 350 F and the cooking time to 12 minutes. Push Start. Check with a toothpick; when the toothpick comes out clean, your muffins are done. Place on a rack to cool slightly before removing from the muffin tins. Serve and enjoy!

Homemade Macaroni Quiche with Yogurt

Prep + Cook Time: 30 minutes | Serves: 4

Ingredients

8 tbsp leftover macaroni with cheese
2 tbsp cheddar cheese
12 ounces refrigerated puff pastry
1 tsp garlic puree

2 tbsp Greek yogurt
2 whole eggs
11¾ oz milk

Salt and black pepper to taste

Directions

Roll the pastry to form 4 shells. Place them in the air fryer basket. In a bowl, mix leftover macaroni with cheese, yogurt, eggs, milk, and garlic puree. Pour this mixture over the pastry shells.

Top with the cheddar cheese evenly. Place the basket into your IP. Put the air fryer lid on top. Select Bake and set the temperature to 360 F and the cooking time to 20 minutes. Push Start. Serve and enjoy!

Spiced Crab Cakes

Prep + Cook Time: 20 minutes | Serves: 6

Ingredients

2 eggs, beaten
½ cup breadcrumbs
1 lb crab meat, shredded
1 tsp sweet chili sauce

⅓ cup finely chopped green onion
¼ cup parsley, chopped
1 tbsp mayonnaise
½ tsp paprika

Olive oil to spray
Salt and black pepper to taste

Directions

In a bowl, add meat, eggs, crumbs, green onion, parsley, mayo, chili sauce, paprika, salt, and black pepper; mix well with hands. Shape into 6 cakes and grease them lightly with oil.

Arrange them on the air fryer basket without overcrowding. Insert the basket into the IP and put the air fryer lid on top. Select Air Fry and set the temperature to 400 F and the cooking time to 8 minutes. Push Start. Turn once halfway through. Serve and enjoy!

Fancy Mozzarella Sticks

Prep + Cook Time: 20 minutes + chilling time | Serves: 2

Ingredients

1 cup breadcrumbs	8 oz mozzarella cheese	½ tsp salt
1 egg	1 tsp garlic powder	Olive oil

Directions

Cut the mozzarella into 6 strips. Whisk the egg along with the salt and garlic powder in a bowl. Dip the mozzarella into the egg mixture first and then into the breadcrumbs. Place in the freezer for about 30 minutes.

Arrange the mozzarella sticks inside the greased air fryer basket. Insert the basket into the IP and put the air fryer lid on top. Select Air Fry and set the temperature to 370 F and the cooking time to 12 minutes. Push Start. Make sure to turn them over at least 2 times to ensure even cooking until golden on all sides. Serve and enjoy!

Cheese Watermelon

Prep + Cook Time: 15 minutes | Serves: 4

Ingredients

8 oz halloumi cheese	2 tbsp chopped parsley	Olive oil
12 kalamata olives	2 tbsp chopped mint	Salt and black pepper to taste
8 thick watermelon slices	Juice and zest of 1 lemon	

Directions

Season the watermelon with salt and pepper, and gently brush them with olive oil. Place in the Air fryer and cook for about 4 minutes. Brush the cheese with olive oil and add it to the air fryer basket.

Insert the basket into the IP and put the air fryer lid on top. Select Air Fry and set the temperature to 350 F and the cooking time to 4 minutes. Push Start. Serve with olives and sprinkle with herbs, lemon zest, and juice.

Homemade Pickle Chips

Prep + Cook Time: 20 minutes | Serves: 2

Ingredients

18 sweet pickle chips	¼ cup cornmeal	3 tbsp smoked paprika
1 ½ cups flour	1 cup buttermilk	Salt and black pepper to taste

Directions

In a bowl, mix flour, paprika, pepper, salt, cornmeal, and powder. Place pickles in buttermilk and set aside for 5 minutes. Dip the pickles in the spice mixture and place them in the air fryer basket. Insert the basket into the IP and put the air fryer lid on top. Select Air Fry and set the temperature to 400 F and the cooking time to 10 minutes. Push Start. Shake halfway through the cooking time. Serve and enjoy!

Air Fried Baby Carrots

Prep + Cook Time: 25 minutes | Serves: 4

Ingredients

2 tbsp olive oil	1 tsp cumin seeds	Salt and black pepper to taste
1 ¼ lb baby carrots	½ tsp cumin powder	
½ tsp garlic powder	1 handful cilantro, chopped	

Directions

Place the baby carrots in a large bowl. Add cumin seeds, cumin, olive oil, salt, garlic powder, and pepper, and stir to coat them well. Place the baby carrots in the greased air fryer basket. Insert the basket into the IP.

Put the air fryer lid on top. Select Air Fry and set the temperature to 370 F and the cooking time to 20 minutes. Push Start. Place on a platter and sprinkle with chopped cilantro. Serve and enjoy!

Stuffed Eggplant Boats

Prep + Cook Time: 20 minutes | Serves: 2

Ingredients

4 ham slices, chopped

1 eggplant

1 cup shredded mozzarella cheese

1 tsp dried parsley

Salt and black pepper to taste

Directions

Peel the eggplant and scoop some of the flesh out. Season with salt and pepper. Divide half of the mozzarella cheese between the eggplant halves and top with ham. Sprinkle with the remaining mozzarella cheese and parsley. Place in a greased baking pan. Place the baking pan inside the air fryer basket.

Insert the basket into the IP and put the air fryer lid on top. Select Bake and set the temperature to 350 F and the cooking time to 12 minutes. Push Start. When cooking is complete, the top should be golden brown. Serve.

Homemade Ham Rolls with Veggies

Prep + Cook Time: 20 minutes | Serves: 4

Ingredients

4 slices ham

4 carrots

1 zucchini

2 oz walnuts, finely chopped

1 clove garlic

1 tbsp olive oil

1 tbsp ginger powder

¼ cup basil leaves, finely chopped

Salt and black pepper to taste

Directions

Heat the olive oil in your IP on Sauté and add the zucchini, carrots, garlic, ginger, and salt; cook for 5 minutes. Add the basil and walnuts and keep stirring; remove. Divide the filling among the ham slices and roll-up.

Arrange them on the air fryer basket. Insert the basket into the IP and put the air fryer lid on top. Select Air Fry and set the temperature to 350 F and the cooking time to 4 minutes. Push Start. Serve and enjoy!

Effortless Sausage Bowl

Prep + Cook Time: 20 minutes | Serves: 4

Ingredients

1 lb Italian sausage, sliced

1 cup artichoke hearts, chopped

1 sweet onion, diced

2 cups Monterrey Jack, shredded

4 eggs

Fresh cilantro to garnish

Salt and black pepper to taste

Directions

Arrange the sausage on a greased baking pan. Top with onion and serrano pepper; spread the cheese on top. In a bowl, beat the eggs, and season with salt and black pepper. Pour the mixture over the cheese.

Place the pan in the fryer basket and fit in your IP. Place the air fryer lid on top. Select Air Fry and set the temperature to 350 F and the cooking time to 15 minutes. Push Start. Serve with fresh cilantro.

Classic Apple-Cinnamon Chips

Prep + Cook Time: 25 minutes | Serves: 2

Ingredients

1 whole apple, sliced

½ tsp cinnamon

1 tsp sugar

1 tsp salt

Confectioners' sugar for serving

Directions

In a bowl, mix cinnamon, salt, and sugar; add the apple slices. Place the prepared apple slices in the fryer basket and fit in your IP. Place the air fryer lid on top. Select Air Fry and set the temperature to 400 F and the cooking time to 8 minutes. Push Start. Shake halfway through the cooking time. Dust with confectioners' sugar to serve.

Easy Rutabaga Chips

Prep + Cook Time: 20 minutes | Serves: 6

Ingredients

1 tsp olive oil

1 rutabaga, sliced

1 tsp soy sauce

Salt to taste

Directions

In a bowl, mix oil, soy sauce, and salt to form a marinade. Add rutabaga pieces and allow to stand for 5 minutes. Place in the greased air fryer basket and fit in your IP. Place the air fryer lid on top. Select Air Fry and set the temperature to 400 F and the cooking time to 5 minutes. Push Start. Turn halfway through the cooking time.

Tasty Parsnip Fries

Prep + Cook Time: 15 minutes | Serves: 3

Ingredients

⅓ cup olive oil

6 large parsnips

⅓ cup cornstarch

1 pinch of salt

⅓ cup water

Directions

Peel and cut the parsnips to ½ inch by 3 inches. Mix the cornstarch, olive oil, water, and parsnips in a large bowl. Combine the ingredients and coat the parsnips. Arrange them on the greased air fryer basket. Insert the basket into the IP and put the air fryer lid on top. Select Air Fry and set the temperature to 390 F and the cooking time to 12 minutes. Push Start. Shake halfway through the cooking time. Serve and enjoy!

Greek-Style Eggplant Chips with Yogurt Sauce

Prep + Cook Time: 20 minutes | Serves: 2

Ingredients

⅓ cup olive oil

1 cup yogurt

2 eggplants

⅓ cup cornstarch

Salt to taste

½ cup water

Directions

Cut the eggplants in slices of ½-inch each. In a bowl, mix the cornstarch, water, half of the olive oil, and the eggplants; carefully coat the eggplants. Arrange them on the greased air fryer basket. Insert the basket into the IP and put the air fryer lid on top. Select Air Fry and set the temperature to 370 F and the cooking time to 15 minutes. Push Start. Mix the yogurt with the remaining olive oil and salt. Serve on the side of the eggplants.

Air Fryer Ham Wraps

Prep + Cook Time: 20 minutes | Serves: 3

Ingredients

1 tbsp softened butter
3 packages Pepperidge farm rolls

1 lb chopped ham
1 tsp mustard seeds

1 tsp poppy seeds
1 small chopped onion

Directions

Mix butter, mustard, onion, and poppy seeds in a bowl. Spread the mixture on top of the rolls. Cover the bottom halves with the chopped ham. Arrange the rolls on the air fryer basket and fit in your IP. Place the air fryer lid on top. Select Air Fry and set the temperature to 350 F and the cooking time to 15 minutes. Push Start.

Delicious Cheese Sticks

Prep + Cook Time: 15 minutes + chilling time | Serves: 6

Ingredients

12 sticks mozzarella cheese
¼ cup Parmesan cheese, grated

Marinara sauce for serving
¼ cup flour

2 cups breadcrumbs
2 whole eggs

Directions

Pour breadcrumbs into a bowl. Beat the eggs in a separate bowl. In a third bowl, mix Parmesan and flour. Dip each cheese stick in the flour mixture, then in eggs, and finally in breadcrumbs. Place the sticks in the fridge for 2 hours. Put the sticks in the greased air fryer basket, fit in the IP, and put the air fryer lid on top. Select Air Fry and set the temperature to 350 F and the time to 8 minutes. Push Start. Turn once. Serve with marinara sauce.

Veggie Salmon Balls

Prep + Cook Time: 15 minutes | Serves: 2

Ingredients

1 large egg
6 oz tinned salmon
3 tbsp olive oil

5 tbsp breadcrumbs
4 tbsp chopped celery
4 tbsp spring onion, sliced

1 tbsp dill, chopped
½ tbsp garlic powder

Directions

In a large bowl, mix salmon, egg, celery, onion, dill, and garlic powder. Shape the mixture into golf-ball-sized balls and roll them in the crumbs. Transfer them to the air fryer basket, fit in the IP, and put the air fryer lid on top. Select Air Fry and set the temperature to 370 F and the cooking time to 10 minutes. Push Start. Serve.

Crunchy Bok Choy Chips

Prep + Cook Time: 10 minutes | Serves: 2

Ingredients

4 cups packed bok choy
2 tbsp olive oil

1 tsp vegan seasoning
1 tbsp yeast flakes

Sea salt to taste

Directions

In a bowl, mix oil, bok choy, yeast, and vegan seasoning. Dump the coated kale in the greased air fryer basket. Insert the basket into the IP and put the air fryer lid on top. Select Air Fry and set the temperature to 360 F and the cooking time to 5 minutes. Push Start. Shake after 3 minutes. Serve sprinkled with sea salt.

Homemade Eggplant Fries

Prep + Cook Time: 20 minutes Serves: 2

Ingredients

1 tsp olive oil
1 eggplant, sliced

1 tsp soy sauce
Salt to taste

Directions

Make a marinade of 1 tsp oil, soy sauce, and salt. Mix well. Add in the eggplant slices and let stand for 5 minutes. Place the prepared eggplant slices in your air fryer basket and fit in your IP. Place the air fryer lid on top. Select Air Fry and set the temperature to 400 F and the cooking time to 16 minutes. Push Start. Serve with maple syrup.

Canapes a la Amul

Prep + Cook Time: 15 minutes | Serves: 2

Ingredients

1 cube Amul cheese
1 whole cabbage, cut into rounds

½ carrot, cubed
¼ onion, cubed

¼ bell pepper, cubed
Fresh basil to garnish

Directions

In a bowl, mix the onion, carrot, bell pepper, and cheese. Toss to coat everything evenly. Add cabbage rounds to the greased air fryer basket. Insert the basket into the IP and put the air fryer lid on top. Select Air Fry and set the temperature to 360 F and the cooking time to 12 minutes. Push Start. Serve with a garnish of fresh basil.

Butterbeans, Bacon & Feta Bowl

Prep + Cook Time: 10 minutes | Serves: 2

Ingredients

3 ½ oz feta
3 ½ oz bacon, sliced

1 (14 oz) can butter beans
1 tbsp chives

1 tsp olive oil
Black pepper to taste

Directions

Blend beans, oil, and pepper in a blender. Arrange bacon slices on the air fryer basket. Sprinkle chives on top and fit in your IP. Place the air fryer lid on top. Select Air Fry and set the temperature to 350 F and the cooking time to 10 minutes. Push Start. Add feta cheese to the butter bean blend and stir. Serve bacon with the dip.

French Beans with Almonds

Prep + Cook Time: 25 minutes | Serves: 5

Ingredients

1 ½ lb French beans
½ pound shallots, chopped

3 tbsp olive oil
½ cup almonds, toasted

Salt and black pepper to taste

Directions

Put a pan over medium heat, mix beans in hot water and boil until tender, about 5-6 minutes. Mix the cooked beans with oil, shallots, salt, and pepper. Add the mixture to the air fryer basket and fit in your IP. Place the air fryer lid on top. Select Air Fry and set the temperature to 400 F and the cooking time to 20 minutes. Push Start. Serve with almonds and enjoy!

Cajun-Spiced Shrimp

Prep + Cook Time: 15 minutes | Serves: 3

Ingredients

1 tbsp olive oil
½ pound shrimp, deveined

½ tsp Cajun seasoning
¼ tsp paprika

Salt and black pepper to taste

Directions

In a bowl, mix the paprika, salt, pepper, oil, and seasoning. Cut shrimp and cover with the mixture. Place the prepared shrimp in the air fryer basket and fit it in your IP. Place the air fryer lid on top. Select Air Fry and set the temperature to 390 F and the cooking time to 8 minutes. Push Start. Flip halfway through the cooking time.

Air Fried Brussels Sprouts with Garlic

Prep + Cook Time: 25 minutes | Serves: 4

Ingredients

2 tbsp olive oil
1 block brussels sprouts

½ tsp garlic, chopped
Salt and black pepper to taste

Directions

Wash the Brussels thoroughly under cold water and trim off the outer leaves, keeping only the head of the sprouts. In a bowl, mix oil and garlic. Season with salt and pepper. Add prepared sprouts to this mixture and let rest for 5 minutes. Place the coated sprouts in the air fryer basket and fit it in your IP. Place the air fryer lid on top. Select Air Fry and set the temperature to 390 F and the cooking time to 15 minutes. Push Start. Serve.

Luscious Curly Potatoes

Prep + Cook Time: 20 minutes | Serves: 2

Ingredients

1 tbsp extra-virgin olive oil
2 whole potatoes, spiralized

1 tsp paprika
Salt and black pepper to taste

Directions

Place the potatoes in a bowl and coat with oil. Transfer them to the air fryer basket and fit in your IP. Place the air fryer lid on top. Select Air Fry and set the temperature to 390 F and the cooking time to 15 minutes. Push Start. Sprinkle a bit of salt and paprika and serve.

Chili Flaked French Fries

Prep + Cook Time: 35 minutes | Serves: 6

Ingredients

2 tbsp olive oil
6 medium russet potatoes, sauce

Salt to taste
1 tsp red chili flakes

Directions

Cut potatoes into ¼ by 3-inch pieces and place in a bowl with cold water; let soak for 30 minutes. Strain and allow to dry. Drizzle oil on the dried potatoes and toss to coat. Place the potatoes in the air fryer basket and fit it in your IP. Place the air fryer lid on top. Select Air Fry and set the temperature to 390 F and the cooking time to 25 minutes. Push Start. Season with salt and chili flakes and serve.

Carrot & Oat Cookies

Prep + Cook Time: 30 minutes | Serves: 6

Ingredients

1 whole egg, beaten	1 tbsp parsley	1 tbsp thyme
6 carrots, shredded	1 ¼ oz oats	Salt and black pepper to taste

Directions

In a bowl, add the beaten egg, carrots, oats, parsley, salt, pepper, and thyme and stir well to combine. Form the batter into cookie shapes. Place in a greased baking pan and fit in the air fryer basket. Insert in your IP and put the air fryer lid on top. Select Bake and set the temperature to 350 F and the cooking time to 12 minutes. Push Start. When cooking is complete, the edges of the cookies should be browned. Serve chilled.

Delicious Cabbage with Parmesan

Prep + Cook Time: 30 minutes | Serves: 4

Ingredients

4 tbsp butter, melted	2 cup Parmesan cheese, grated	Salt and black pepper to taste
½ head cabbage, cut into 4 wedges	1 tsp smoked paprika	

Directions

Brush the butter over the cabbage wedges. Season with salt and pepper. Coat the cabbage with the Parmesan cheese and arrange on the air fryer basket; sprinkle with paprika. Insert the basket into the IP and put the air fryer lid on top. Select Air Fry and set the temperature to 350 F and the cooking time to 15 minutes. Push Start. Flip the wedges over halfway through the cooking time. Serve and enjoy!

Feta Corn Ears

Prep + Cook Time: 20 minutes | Serves: 2

Ingredients

4 oz feta cheese	Juice of 2 small limes
2 ears of corn	2 tsp paprika

Directions

Peel the corn and remove the silk. Place the feta cheese in the freezer. Place the corn into the greased air fryer basket. Squeeze the juice of 1 lime on top of each ear of corn. Take the cheese out of the freezer and grate it onto corn. Insert the basket into the IP and put the air fryer lid on top. Select Air Fry and set the temperature to 350 F and the cooking time to 12 minutes. Push Start. Serve and enjoy!

Potato Chips with Lemon Dip

Prep + Cook Time: 25 minutes | Serves: 3

Ingredients

3 tbsp olive oil	½ tsp lemon juice	2 scallions, white part minced
3 large potatoes	1 cup sour cream	Salt and black pepper to taste

Directions

Slice the potatoes into thin slices; do not peel them. Soak them in water for 10 minutes, then dry them and spray with oil. Arrange the slices onto the greased air fryer basket and fit in your IP. Place the air fryer lid on top.

Select Air Fry and set the temperature to 380 F and the cooking time to 18 minutes. Push Start. Flip halfway through the cooking time. Season with salt and pepper. Mix the sour cream, olive oil, scallions, lemon juice, salt, and pepper. Serve on the side of potato chips. Enjoy!

Chili Ham & Pumpkin Fritters

Prep + Cook Time: 10 minutes | Serves: 4

Ingredients

1 egg

2 tbsp canned puree pumpkin

1 oz ham, chopped

1 cup dry pancake mix

1 oz cheddar, shredded

½ tsp chili powder

3 tbsp of flour

1 oz beer

2 tbsp scallions, chopped

Directions

In a bowl, mix the pancake mix and chili powder. Add the egg, puree pumpkin, beer, shredded cheddar, ham, and scallions. Roll the mixture in 3 tbsp of flour. Arrange the balls on the greased fryer basket and fit in your IP.

Place the air fryer lid on top. Select Air Fry and set the temperature to 380 F and the cooking time to 16 minutes. Push Start. Flip halfway through the cooking time. Serve and enjoy!

Fancy Pumpkin Wedges

Prep + Cook Time: 30 minutes | Serves: 3

Ingredients

1 tbsp paprika

½ pumpkin, cut into wedges

1 whole lime, squeezed

1 cup paleo dressing

1 tbsp balsamic vinegar

1 tsp turmeric

Salt and black pepper to taste

Directions

Add the pumpkin wedges in the air fryer basket; fit in your IP. Place the air fryer lid on top. Select Air Fry and set the temperature to 360 F and the cooking time to 20 minutes. Push Start. Flip halfway through cooking.

In a mixing bowl, mix lime juice, vinegar, turmeric, salt, pepper, and paprika to form a marinade. Five minutes before the end, pour the marinade over the pumpkin and cook for the remaining 5 minutes. Serve and enjoy!

Mouthwatering Wrapped Asparagus

Serves: 4 | Prep + Cook Time: 25 minutes | Serves: 4

Ingredients

4 bacon slices

20 spears asparagus

1 tbsp sesame oil

1 tbsp olive oil

1 tbsp brown sugar

1 garlic clove, crushed

Directions

In a bowl, mix the oils, sugar, and crushed garlic. Separate the asparagus into 4 bunches (5 spears in 1 bunch) and wrap each bunch with a bacon slice. Coat the bunches with the sugar and oil mix.

Place the bunches in the greased air fryer basket and fit in your IP. Place the air fryer lid on top. Select Air Fry and set the temperature to 380 F and the cooking time to 8 minutes. Push Start. Turn over halfway through the cooking time. Serve and enjoy!

Garlic Potato Chips

Prep + Cook Time: 30 minutes | Serves: 3

Ingredients

¼ cup olive oil

1 tbsp garlic

3 whole potatoes, cut into thin slices

2 tbsp rosemary

Directions

In a bowl, combine the olive oil, garlic, and salt and add the potato slices. Lay them into the air fryer basket and fit in your IP. Place the air fryer lid on top. Select Air Fry and set the temperature to 400 F and the cooking time to 20 minutes. Push Start. Turn halfway through the cooking time. Top with rosemary to serve.

Simple Cheese Sandwich

Prep + Cook Time: 20 minutes | Serves: 1

Ingredients

2 tbsp butter

2 slices bread

2 scallions

¾ cup cheddar cheese

2 tbsp Parmesan cheese, shredded

Directions

Lay the bread slices on a flat surface. On one slice, spread the exposed side with butter, followed by cheddar and scallions. On the other slice, spread butter and then sprinkle cheese. Bring the buttered sides together to form sand. Place the sandwich in the air fryer basket and fit it in your IP. Put the air fryer lid on top. Select Air Fry and set the temperature to 360 F and the cooking time to 10 minutes. Push Start. Serve with berry sauce.

Effortless Cheddar Biscuits

Prep + Cook Time: 35 minutes | Serves: 6

Ingredients

½ cup Cheddar cheese, grated

2 tbsp sugar

1 ⅓ cups buttermilk

½ cup + 1 tbsp butter

3 cups flour

Directions

Lay parchment paper on a baking plate. In a bowl, mix sugar, flour, ½ cup butter, cheese, and buttermilk to form a batter. Make 8 balls from the batter and roll in flour. Place the balls in the air fryer basket and flatten into biscuit shapes. Sprinkle cheese and the remaining butter on top. Fit the basket in your IP. Place the air fryer lid on top. Select Bake and set the temperature to 380 F and the cooking time to 30 minutes. Push Start. Serve.

Fried Cashews

Prep + Cook Time: 20 minutes | Serves: 6

Ingredients

3 cups cashews

3 tbsp liquid smoke

2 tbsp molasses

2 tsp salt

Directions

In a bowl, add salt, liquid, molasses, and cashews; toss to coat well. Place the coated cashews in the air fryer basket. Insert the basket into the IP and put the air fryer lid on top. Select Air Fry and set the temperature to 360 F and the cooking time to 6 minutes. Push Start. Shake halfway through the cooking time. Serve and enjoy!

Classic French Ham & Cheese Sandwich

Prep + Cook Time: 15 minutes | Serves: 2

Ingredients

¼ cup butter

2 mozzarella cheese slices

2 ham slices

4 bread slices

Directions

Place 2 bread slices on a flat surface. Spread butter on the exposed surfaces. Lay cheese and ham on two of the slices. Cover with the other 2 slices to form sandwiches. Place the sandwiches in the air fryer basket and fit it in your IP. Place the air fryer lid on top. Select Air Fry and set the temperature to 360 F and the cooking time to 5 minutes. Push Start. Serve and enjoy!

Cajun-Spiced Shrimp

Prep + Cook Time: 15 minutes | Serves: 3

Ingredients

1 tbsp olive oil

½ pound shrimp, deveined

½ tsp Cajun seasoning

¼ tsp paprika

Salt and black pepper to taste

Directions

In a bowl, mix the paprika, salt, pepper, oil, and seasoning. Cut shrimp and cover with the mixture. Place the prepared shrimp in the air fryer basket and fit it in your IP. Place the air fryer lid on top. Select Air Fry and set the temperature to 390 F and the cooking time to 8 minutes. Push Start. Flip halfway through the cooking time.

Chicken Sausage Wrappers

Prep + Cook Time: 20 minutes | Serves: 4

Ingredients

2 tbsp scallions, chopped

½ pound chicken sausage

1 garlic clove, minced

½ tbsp oyster sauce

1 tbsp hot sauce

16 wonton wrappers

1 egg, beaten

Salt and black pepper to taste

Directions

In a bowl, mix the scallions, chicken sausage, garlic, oyster sauce, hot sauce, salt, and pepper. Spoon the mixture onto the center of the wonton wrappers and fold them in half. Press the edges, and coat the wrappers with beaten egg. Arrange them on the lightly greased fryer basket and fit it in your IP. Put the air fryer lid on top. Select Air Fry and set the temperature to 360 F and the cooking time to 10 minutes. Push Start. Serve.

Tasty Little Smokies

Prep + Cook Time: 20 minutes | Serves: 5

Ingredients

14 oz beef Little Smokies

1 cup BBQ sauce

1 tsp Worcestershire sauce

Directions

Prick the smokies with a fork and place them in the greased air fryer basket; fit it in your IP. Place the air fryer lid on top. Select Air Fry and set the temperature to 390 F and the cooking time to 10 minutes. Push Start. Turn once. Mix the BBQ and Worcestershire sauces with a fork and pour them over the smokies. Serve and enjoy!

DESSERTS

Chocolate Brownies with Nuts

Ready in about: 35 minutes | Serves: 10

Ingredients

6 oz dark chocolate	6 oz butter	2 tsp vanilla extract
1 cup chopped walnuts	¾ cup white sugar	¾ cup flour
1 cup white chocolate chips	3 eggs	¼ cup cocoa powder

Directions

In a saucepan, melt chocolate and butter over low heat. Do not stop stirring until you obtain a smooth mixture. Let cool slightly, whisk in eggs and vanilla. Sift flour and cocoa and stir to mix well. Sprinkle the walnuts over and add the white chocolate into the batter. Pour the batter into a parchment-lined pan.

Place the baking pan in the fryer basket. Insert the basket into the IP and put the air fryer lid on top. Select Bake and set the temperature to 350 F and the cooking time to 20 minutes. Push Start. Serve with raspberry syrup.

Raspberry Chocolate Cake

Ready in about: 40 minutes | Serves: 8

Ingredients

2 eggs	⅓ cup cocoa powder	⅔ cup butter
1 cup freeze-dried raspberries	2 tsp baking powder	2 tsp vanilla extract
1 cup chocolate chips	¾ cup white sugar	1 cup milk
1 ½ cups flour	¼ cup brown sugar	1 tsp baking soda

Directions

Line a cake tin with baking paper. In a bowl, sift the flour, cocoa and baking powders. Place the sugars, butter, vanilla, milk, and baking soda into a microwave-safe bowl and heat for 60 seconds until the butter melts, and the ingredients incorporate; let cool slightly. Whisk the eggs into the mixture.

Pour the wet ingredients into the dry ones, and fold to combine. Add the raspberries and chocolate chips into the batter. Pour the batter into the cake tin. Place the tin inside the air fryer basket. Insert the basket into the IP and put the air fryer lid on top. Select Bake and set the temperature to 350 F and the cooking time to 30 minutes. Push Start. Serve well chilled. Enjoy!

Kids' Favorite Marshmallows Pie

Ready in about: 10 minutes | Serves: 4

Ingredients

8 squares each of dark, milk, and white chocolate
4 graham cracker sheets, snapped in half
8 large marshmallows

Directions

Arrange the cracker halves on a board. Put 2 marshmallows onto half of the graham cracker halves. Place 2 squares of chocolate onto the cracker with the marshmallows. Put the remaining crackers on top to create 4 sandwiches. Wrap each one in the baking paper so it resembles a parcel. Transfer the packets to a baking pan.

Place the baking pan inside the air fryer basket. Insert the basket into the IP and put the air fryer lid on top. Select Bake and set the temperature to 350 F and the cooking time to 5 minutes. Push Start. Serve and enjoy!

Fall Apple & Cinnamon Cake

Ready in about: 40 minutes | Serves: 4

Ingredients

2 apples, peeled, sliced
3 oz butter, melted
1 vanilla box cake

½ cup brown sugar
1 tsp cinnamon
½ cup flour

1 cup caramel sauce

Directions

In a bowl, mix butter, sugar, cinnamon, and flour until you obtain a crumbly texture. Prepare the cake mix according to the instructions (no baking). Pour the batter into a parchment-lined tin and arrange the apple slices on top. Spoon the caramel over the apples and add the crumble over the sauce.

Place the baking tin inside the air fryer basket. Insert the basket into the IP and put the air fryer lid on top. Select Bake and set the temperature to 360 F and the cooking time to 35 minutes. Push Start. Make sure to check it halfway through so it's not overcooked. Serve and enjoy!

Traditional Crème Caramel

Ready in about: 60 minutes | Serves: 3

Ingredients

10 egg yolks
1 cup whipped cream

1 cup milk
2 vanilla pods

4 tbsp sugar + extra for topping

Directions

Set your IP to Sauté and add the milk and cream. Cut the vanilla pods open and scrape the seeds into the pot with the vanilla pods also. Bring to a boil while stirring regularly. Remove. Beat the egg yolks in a bowl. Add the sugar and mix well but not too frothy. Remove the vanilla pods from the milk mixture; pour the mixture onto the eggs mixture while stirring constantly. Let it sit for 25 minutes. Fill 3 ramekins with the mixture.

Place the ramekins in the fryer basket and fit in your IP. Place the air fryer lid on top. Select Bake and set the temperature to 190 F and the cooking time to 50 minutes. Push Start. Once ready, remove the ramekins and let sit to cool. Sprinkle the remaining sugar over and use a torch to melt the sugar, so it browns at the top.

Aunt's Blueberry & Yogurt Cups

Ready in about: 30 minutes | Serves: 10

Ingredients

1 cup blueberries
1 egg
1 ½ cup flour

½ tsp salt
½ cup sugar
¼ cup vegetable oil

2 tsp vanilla extract
2 tsp baking powder
Yogurt, as needed

Directions

Combine the flour, salt, and baking powder in a bowl. In another bowl, add the oil, vanilla extract, and egg. Fill the rest of the bowl with yogurt, and whisk the mixture until fully incorporated. Combine the wet and dry ingredients; gently fold in the blueberries. Divide the mixture between 10 muffin cups. Arrange them on the air fryer basket. Insert the basket into the IP and put the air fryer lid on top. Select Bake and set the temperature to 350 F and the cooking time to 10 minutes. Push Start. Serve and enjoy!

Luscious Figs with Mascarpone

Ready in about: 10 minutes | Serves: 4

Ingredients

1 oz butter	6 oz mascarpone cheese	3 tbsp honey
8 figs	1 tsp rose water	2 tbsp toasted almond slices

Directions

Open the figs by cutting a cross on top and gently squeezing them. Divide the honey between the figs. Place them on a lined baking sheet and fit in the air fryer basket. Insert the basket into the IP and put the air fryer lid on top. Select Bake and set the temperature to 350 F and the cooking time to 5 minutes. Push Start. Combine the mascarpone with rose water. Place a dollop of mascarpone onto the figs, top with almonds and serve.

Quick Chocolate & PB Fondant

Ready in about: 25 minutes | Serves: 4

Ingredients

4 eggs, room temperature	½ cup peanut butter, crunchy	¼ tsp salt
⅛ cup flour, sieved	2 tbsp butter, diced	¼ cup water
¾ cup dark chocolate	¼ cup + ¼ cup sugar	

Directions

Make a salted praline to top the chocolate fondant. Add ¼ cup of sugar, salt, and water into a saucepan. Stir and bring it to a boil over low heat. Simmer until the desired color is achieved and reduced.

Pour it into a baking tray and leave to cool and harden. Place a pot of water over medium heat and place a heatproof bowl over it. Add the chocolate, butter, and peanut butter to the bowl.

Stir continuously until fully melted, combined, and smooth. Remove the bowl from the heat and allow to cool slightly. Add the eggs to the chocolate and whisk. Add the flour and remaining sugar; mix well.

Grease 4 small loaf pans with cooking spray and divide the chocolate mixture between them. Place 2 pans at a time in the air fryer basket and fit it in your IP. Put the air fryer lid on top. Select Bake and set the temperature to 350 F and the cooking time to 7 minutes. Push Start. Serve the fondants with a piece of salted praline.

Yummy White Chocolate Bake

Ready in about: 40 minutes | Serves: 2

Ingredients

4 large egg whites	¼ cup sugar + more for garnishing	¼ tsp vanilla extract
2 egg yolks, at room temperature	1 tbsp melted butter	1 ½ tbsp flour
3 oz white chocolate	1 tbsp unmelted butter	

Directions

Coat two 6-oz ramekins with melted butter. Add the sugar and swirl it in the ramekins to coat the butter. Pour out the remaining sugar and keep it. Melt the unmelted butter with the chocolate in a microwave; set aside. In another bowl, beat the egg yolks vigorously. Add the vanilla and kept sugar; beat to incorporate fully. Add the chocolate mixture and mix well. Add the flour and mix it with no lumps.

Whisk the egg whites in another bowl till it holds stiff peaks. Add ⅓ of the egg whites into the chocolate mixture; fold in gently and evenly. Share the mixture into the ramekins with ½ inch space left at the top. Place the ramekins in the fryer basket and fit in your IP. Place the air fryer lid on top. Select Bake and set the temperature to 330 F and the cooking time to 14 minutes. Push Start. Dust with the remaining sugar and serve.

Classic Orange Curd

Ready in about: 30 minutes | Serves: 2

Ingredients

1 egg
1 egg yolk

¾ orange, juiced
3 tbsp butter

3 tbsp sugar

Directions

Add sugar and butter in a medium ramekin and beat evenly. Add egg and yolk slowly while still whisking. The fresh yellow color will be attained. Add the orange juice and mix. Place the bowl in the fryer basket and fit in your IP. Put the air fryer lid and cook on Bake for 6 minutes at 250 F.

Increase the temperature again to 320 F and cook for 15 minutes. Remove the bowl onto a flat surface; use a spoon to check for any lumps and remove. Refrigerate overnight or serve immediately.

Quick White Cookies

Ready in about: 30 minutes | Serves: 4

Ingredients

Cookies:
3 oz sugar
5 ½ oz flour

1 tsp vanilla extract
½ cup oats

1 small egg, beaten
¼ cup coconut flakes

Filling:
2 oz butter
1 oz white chocolate, melted

4 oz powdered sugar
1 tsp vanilla extract

Directions

Beat all the cookie ingredients with an electric mixer, except the flour. When smooth, fold in the flour. Drop spoonfuls of the batter onto a greased cookie sheet. Place the sheet inside the air fryer basket. Insert the basket into the IP and put the air fryer lid on top. Select Bake and set the temperature to 350 F and the cooking time to 18 minutes. Push Start. Remove and then let cool.

Meanwhile, prepare the filling by beating all ingredients together; spread the filling on half of the cookies. Top with the other halves to make cookie sandwiches.

Choco Vanilla Chip Cookies

Ready in about: 15 minutes | Serves: 5

Ingredients

1 egg yolk
½ cup chocolate chips
¾ cup flour

¼ tsp baking soda
¾ tsp salt
⅓ cup brown sugar

¼ cup unsalted butter, softened
2 tbsp white sugar
½ tbsp vanilla extract

Directions

Line the basket or rack with foil. Whisk the flour, baking soda, and salt together in a small bowl. Combine brown sugar, butter, and white sugar in a separate bowl. Add egg yolk and vanilla extract and whisk until well-combined. Stir flour mixture into butter mixture until dough is just combined; gently fold in chocolate chips. Scoop dough by the spoonfuls and roll into balls; place onto the foil-lined air fryer basket, 2 inches apart.

Place in your IP and put the air fryer lid on top. Select Bake and set the temperature to 350 F and the cooking time to 6 minutes. Push Start. Transfer foil and cookies to wire racks or a plate, and let cool completely. Serve.

Mom's Buttermilk Biscuits

Ready in about: 25 minutes | Serves: 4

Ingredients

½ cup cake flour	¾ tsp salt	1 tsp sugar
1 ¼ cups flour, plus some for dusting	½ tsp baking powder	¾ cup buttermilk
½ tsp baking soda	4 tbsp butter, chopped	

Directions

Combine all dry ingredients, except for the butter, in a bowl. Place the chopped butter in the bowl and rub it into the flour mixture until crumbed. Stir in the buttermilk. Flour a flat and dry surface and roll out until half-inch thick. Cut out 10 rounds with a small cookie cutter. Arrange the biscuits on a lined baking sheet.

Place the baking sheet inside the air fryer basket. Insert the basket into the IP and put the air fryer lid on top. Select Bake and set the temperature to 350 F and the cooking time to 15 minutes. Push Start. Serve and enjoy!

Air Fried White Chocolate Cake

Ready in about: 30 minutes | Serves: 8

Ingredients

4 oz butter	6 oz self-rising flour	1 tbsp honey
2 oz white chocolate chips	3 oz brown sugar	1 ½ tbsp milk

Directions

Beat the butter and sugar until fluffy. Beat in honey, milk, and flour. Gently fold in the chocolate chips. Drop spoonfuls of the mixture onto a greased cookie sheet. Place the sheet inside the air fryer basket. Insert the basket into the IP and put the air fryer lid on top. Select Bake and set the temperature to 350 F and the cooking time to 18 minutes. Push Start. Serve well chilled.

Yogurt & Lime Muffins

Ready in about: 30 minutes | Serves: 6

Ingredients

8 oz cream cheese	Juice and zest of 2 limes	¼ cup superfine sugar
2 eggs plus 1 yolk	1 cup yogurt	1 tsp vanilla extract

Directions

In a bowl, combine the yogurt and cheese. In another bowl, beat together the rest of the ingredients. Gently fold the lime with the cheese mixture. Divide the batter between 6 lined muffin tins. Transfer them to the air fryer basket. Insert the basket into the IP and put the air fryer lid on top. Select Bake and set the temperature to 330 F and the cooking time to 10 minutes. Push Start. Serve and enjoy!

Californian Pineapple Chocolate Cake

Ready in about: 45 minutes | Serves: 4

Ingredients

7 oz pineapple chunks	4 oz butter	2 tbsp milk
2 oz dark chocolate, grated	½ cup pineapple juice	½ cup sugar
8 oz self-rising flour	1 egg	

Directions

Place the butter and flour into a bowl and rub the mixture with your fingers until crumbed. Stir in pineapple chunks, sugar, chocolate, and juice. Beat eggs and milk separately, and then add to the batter.

Transfer the batter to a greased cake pan. Place the baking pan inside the air fryer basket. Insert the basket into the IP and put the air fryer lid on top. Select Bake and set the temperature to 350 F and the cooking time to 30 minutes. Push Start. Let cool for at least 10 minutes before serving.

Air Fried Snickerdoodle Cookies

Ready in about: 30 minutes | Serves: 6

Ingredients

1 can of Pillsbury Grands Flaky Layers Biscuits

1 box instant vanilla Jell-O   1 ½ cups cinnamon sugar   2 tbsp melted butter

Directions

Unroll the flaky biscuits; cut them into fourths. Roll each ¼ into a ball. Arrange the balls on a lined baking sheet and place the sheet inside the air fryer basket. Insert the basket into the IP and put the air fryer lid on top. Select Bake and set the temperature to 350 F and the cooking time to 7 minutes. Push Start. The balls should be golden.

Meanwhile, prepare the Jell-O following the package's instructions. Using an injector, inject some of the vanilla pudding into each ball. Brush the balls with melted butter and then coat them with cinnamon sugar.

North Eastern Cherry Pie

Ready in about: 30 minutes | Serves: 8

Ingredients

21 oz cherry pie filling   1 egg yolk

2 store-bought pie crusts   1 tbsp milk

Directions

Place one pie crust in a pie pan; poke holes into the crust. Place the baking pan inside the air fryer basket. Insert the basket into the IP and put the air fryer lid on top. Select Bake and set the temperature to 310 F and the cooking time to 5 minutes. Push Start. Remove and spread the pie filling over. Cut the other pie crust into strips.

Arrange the pie-style over the baked crust. Whisk milk and egg yolk, and brush the mixture over the pie. Return the pie to the IP and bake for 15 more minutes.

Parisian Apple Cake

Ready in about: 25 minutes | Serves: 9

Ingredients

2 whole apple, sliced   5 tbsp sugar   3 tbsp cinnamon

2 ¾ oz flour   1 ¼ oz butter

Directions

In a bowl, mix 3 tbsp sugar, butter, and flour until you form a pastry batter. Roll out the pastry on a floured surface and transfer it to the air fryer basket. Arrange the apple slices atop. Cover apples with sugar and cinnamon. Insert the basket into the IP and put the air fryer lid on top. Select Bake and set the temperature to 360 F and the cooking time to 20 minutes. Push Start. Sprinkle with powdered sugar and mint to serve.

Effortless Lemon Cupcakes

Ready in about: 30 minutes | Serves: 6

Ingredients

½ cup milk
1 small egg
1 cup flour
½ cup sugar

1 tsp lemon zest
¾ tsp baking powder
¼ tsp baking soda
½ tsp salt

2 tbsp vegetable oil
½ tsp vanilla extract

Glaze:

½ cup powdered sugar

2 tsp lemon juice

Directions

In a bowl, combine all dry muffin ingredients. In another bowl, whisk together the wet ingredients. Gently combine the two mixtures. Divide the batter between 6 greased muffin tins. Place the tins in the fryer basket.

Insert the basket into the IP and put the air fryer lid on top. Select Bake and set the temperature to 350 F and the cooking time to 15 minutes. Push Start. Whisk the powdered sugar with lemon juice. Spread the glaze over the muffins. Serve and enjoy!

Sunshine Sponge Cake

Ready in about: 50 minutes | Serves: 6

Ingredients

9 oz butter
3 eggs
9 oz sugar

9 oz self-rising flour
1 tsp baking powder
1 tsp vanilla extract

zest of 1 orange

Frosting:

7 oz superfine sugar
4 egg whites

Juice of 1 orange
1 tsp orange food coloring

zest of 1 orange

Directions

Place all cake ingredients in a bowl and beat with an electric mixer. Transfer the batter to a greased cake pan and place the pan inside the air fryer basket. Insert the basket into the IP and put the air fryer lid on top. Select Bake and set the temperature to 350 F and the cooking time to 15 minutes. Push Start.

Meanwhile, prepare the frosting by beating all frosting ingredients together. Spread the frosting mixture on top of one cake. Top with the other cake. Serve and enjoy!

Quick Banana Fritters

Ready in about: 25 minutes | Serves: 6

Ingredients

4 large eggs, beaten
6 bananas

1 cup breadcrumbs
1 cup flour

1 cup oil

Directions

Peel the bananas and cut them into pieces of less than 1-inch each. In a bowl, mix the beaten eggs with flour and oil. Dredge the banana first into the flour, then dip in the beaten eggs, and finally in the crumbs. Line the banana pieces in the air fryer basket and fit in your IP. Place the air fryer lid on top. Select Air Fry and set the temperature to 350 F and the cooking time to 10 minutes. Push Start. Shake once halfway through. Serve.

Classic Apple Pie

Ready in about: 30 minutes | Serves: 9

Ingredients

3 large puff pastry sheets
4 apples, diced
1 egg, beaten

2 oz butter, melted
2 oz sugar
1 oz brown sugar

2 tsp cinnamon
¼ tsp salt

Directions

Whisk white sugar, brown sugar, cinnamon, salt, and butter. Place the apples in a baking dish and coat them with the mixture. Place the baking dish in the air fryer basket and insert the basket into the IP. Put the air fryer lid on top. Select Bake and set the temperature to 350 F and the cooking time to 10 minutes. Push Start.

Meanwhile, roll out the pastry on a floured flat surface, and cut each sheet into 6 equal pieces. Divide the apple filling between the pieces. Brush the edges of the pastry squares with the egg. Fold them and seal the edges with a fork. Place on a lined baking sheet and cook in the IP at 350 F for 8 minutes. Flip over, increase the temperature to 390 F, and cook for 2 more minutes.

Foresty Lemon Crumble

Ready in about: 30 minutes | Serves: 6

Ingredients

5 oz fresh blueberries
12 oz fresh strawberries
7 oz fresh raspberries

½ cup sugar
5 tbsp cold butter
2 tbsp lemon juice

1 cup flour
1 tbsp water
A pinch of salt

Directions

Gently mass the berries, but make sure there are chunks left. Mix with lemon juice and 2 tbsp of sugar. Place the berry mixture at the bottom of a greased round cake. Combine the flour with the salt and sugar in a bowl. Add the water and rub the butter with your fingers until the mixture becomes crumbled.

Arrange the crisp batter over the berries. Place the baking pan inside the air fryer basket. Insert the basket into the IP and put the air fryer lid on top. Select Bake and set the temperature to 390 F and the cooking time to 20 minutes. Push Start. Serve chilled.

Quick Almond Cookies

Ready in about: 45 minutes | Serves: 4

Ingredients

1 ⅓ cups sugar
8 egg whites
½ tsp almond extract

¼ tsp salt
2 tsp lemon juice
1 ½ tsp vanilla extract

Melted dark chocolate to drizzle

Directions

In a mixing bowl, add egg whites, salt, and lemon juice. Beat using an electric mixer until foamy. Slowly add the sugar and continue beating until completely combined; add the almond and vanilla extracts. Beat until stiff peaks form and glossy. Line a round baking sheet with parchment paper. Fill a piping bag with the meringue mixture and pipe as many mounds on the baking sheet as you can, leaving 2-inch spaces between each mound.

Place the baking sheet in the fryer basket and bake at 250 F for 5 minutes. Reduce the temperature to 220 F and bake for 15 more minutes. Then, reduce the temperature once more to 190 F and cook for 15 minutes. Remove the baking sheet and let the meringues cool for 2 hours. Drizzle with the dark chocolate before serving.

Authentic Pecan Pie

Ready in about: 40 minutes | Serves: 4

Ingredients

½ cup chopped pecans
¾ cup maple syrup
2 eggs
½ tsp salt

¼ tsp nutmeg
½ tsp cinnamon
2 tbsp almond butter
2 tbsp brown sugar

1 tbsp butter, melted
1 8-inch pie dough
¾ tsp vanilla extract

Directions

Coat the pecans with the melted butter. Place the pecans in the air fryer basket and place in your IP. Put the air fryer lid on top. Select Air Fry and set the temperature to 370 F and the cooking time to 5 minutes. Push Start.

Place the pie crust into an 8-inch round pie pan, and place the pecans over. Whisk together all remaining ingredients in a bowl. Pour the maple mixture over the pecans. Place the pan in the IP. Set the air fryer lid to 320 F and the cooking time to 25 minutes. Push Start.

Perfect Banana Dessert

Ready in about: 15 minutes | Serves: 5

Ingredients

5 bananas, sliced
2 eggs, beaten
1 ½ cups flour

1 tsp salt
3 tbsp sesame seeds
1 cup water

1 tsp baking powder
½ tbsp sugar

Directions

In a bowl, mix salt, sesame seeds, flour, baking powder, eggs, sugar, and water. Coat sliced bananas with the flour mixture. Place the prepared slices in the air fryer basket and fit it in your IP. Place the air fryer lid on top. Select Air Fry and set the temperature to 340 F and the cooking time to 8 minutes. Push Start. Serve and enjoy!

Sweet & Nutty Apples

Ready in about: 20 minutes | Serves: 2

Ingredients

2 oz mixed seeds
4 apples
1 oz butter

2 oz breadcrumbs
Zest of 1 orange
2 tbsp chopped hazelnuts

1 tsp cinnamon
2 tbsp honey

Directions

Core the apples. Make sure also to score their skin to prevent from splitting. Combine the remaining ingredients in a bowl; stuff the apples with the mixture, and arrange them on a baking pan. Place the baking dish in the air fryer basket and insert the basket into the IP. Put the air fryer lid on top. Select Bake and set the temperature to 350 F and the cooking time to 10 minutes. Push Start. Serve topped with chopped hazelnuts.

Air Fryer Doughnuts

Ready in about: 25 minutes | Serves: 4

Ingredients

1 egg
2 oz brown sugar

8 oz self-rising flour
1 tsp baking powder

½ cup milk
2 ½ tbsp butter

Directions

Beat the butter with the sugar until smooth. Add in the eggs and milk and whisk well. In a bowl, combine the flour with the baking powder. Gently fold the flour into the butter mixture. Form donut shapes and cut off the center with cookie cutters. Arrange on a lined baking sheet. Place the baking sheet inside the air fryer basket.

Insert the basket into the IP and put the air fryer lid on top. Select Bake and set the temperature to 350 F and the cooking time to 15 minutes. Push Start. Serve with whipped cream or icing.

Dark Lava Cake

Ready in about: 20 minutes | Serves: 4

Ingredients

3 ½ oz dark chocolate, melted | 3 ½ tbsp sugar | 2 eggs
3 ½ oz butter, melted | 1 ½ tbsp self-rising flour

Directions

Grease 4 ramekins with butter. Beat the eggs and sugar until frothy. Stir in the butter and chocolate; gently fold in the flour. Divide the mixture between the ramekins and place them in the air fryer basket. Insert the basket into the IP and put the air fryer lid on top. Select Bake and set the temperature to 350 F and the cooking time to 15 minutes. Push Start. Let cool for 2 minutes before turning the lava cakes upside down onto serving plates.

Yummy Chocolate Soufflé

Ready in about: 25 minutes | Serves: 2

Ingredients

3 oz chocolate, melted | ¼ cup butter, melted | 3 tbsp sugar
2 eggs, whites and yolks separated | 2 tbsp flour | ½ tsp vanilla extract

Directions

Beat the yolks along with the sugar and vanilla extract; stir in butter, chocolate, and flour. Whisk the whites until a stiff peak forms. Working in batches, gently combine the egg whites with the chocolate mixture. Divide the batter between two greased ramekins. Place the baking pan inside the air fryer basket.

Insert the basket into the IP and put the air fryer lid on top. Select Bake and set the temperature to 320 F and the cooking time to 14 minutes. Push Start. Serve and enjoy!

Blackberries & Apricots Crumble

Ready in about: 30 minutes | Serves: 4

Ingredients

2 ½ cups fresh apricots, de-stoned and cubed
5 tbsp butter | ½ cup sugar | 1 cup flour
1 cup fresh blackberries | 2 tbsp lemon Juice | Salt to taste

Directions

Add the apricot cubes to a bowl and mix with lemon juice, 2 tbsp sugar, and blackberries. Scoop the mixture into a greased dish and spread it evenly. In another bowl, mix flour and remaining sugar.

Add 1 tbsp of cold water and butter and keep mixing until you have a crumbly mixture. Place the fruit mixture in a greased baking pan and fit in the cooking basket. Top with crumb mixture and fit in your IP. Put the air fryer lid on top. Select Bake and set the temperature to 350 F and the cooking time to 20 minutes. Push Start. Serve.

Fried Brownie Squares

Ready in about: 25 minutes | Serves: 2

Ingredients

¼ cup cocoa powder

⅓ cup flour

1 whole egg, beaten

¼ cup chocolate chips

2 tbsp white sugar

2 tbsp safflower oil

1 tsp vanilla

Directions

In a bowl, mix the beaten egg, sugar, oil, and vanilla. In another bowl, mix cocoa powder and flour. Add the flour mixture to the vanilla mixture and stir until fully incorporated. Pour the mixture into a greased baking pan and fit in the air fryer basket. Sprinkle the chocolate chips on top. Place the baking pan in your IP.

Put the air fryer lid on top. Select Bake and set the temperature to 350 F and the cooking time to 12 minutes. Push Start. Chill and cut into squares to serve.

Traditional Raisin Apple Treat

Ready in about: 15 minutes | Serves: 4

Ingredients

¾ oz raisins

4 apples, cored

1 ½ oz almonds

2 tbsp sugar

Directions

In a bowl, mix the sugar, almonds, raisins. Blend the mixture using a hand mixer. Fill cored apples with the almond mixture. Place the prepared apples in the air fryer basket and fit it in your IP. Place the air fryer lid on top. Select Air Fry and set the temperature to 360 F and the cooking time to 10 minutes. Push Start. Serve.

Made in the USA
Coppell, TX
02 May 2021

54772246R00087